WOLVES
AGAINST THE WORLD

To Dan & Doug

with every good wish

WOLVES

AGAINST THE WORLD
EUROPEAN NIGHTS
1953-1980

John Shipley

TEMPUS

This book is dedicated to my family and to every Wolves fan that has ever lived, but principally to my father and mother, Harry and Edna Shipley, who first took me to Molineux and made me what I am – a true supporter of Wolverhampton Wanderers.

First published 2003

Tempus Publishing Limited
The Mill, Brimscombe Port,
Stroud, Gloucestershire, GL5 2QG

© John Shipley, 2003

The right of John Shipley to be identified as the Author
of this work has been asserted in accordance with the
Copyrights, Designs and Patents Act 1988.

British Library Cataloguing in Publication Data.
A catalogue record for this book is available from the British Library.

ISBN 0 7524 2947 7

Typesetting and origination by Tempus Publishing Limited.
Printed in Great Britain by Midway Colour Print, Wiltshire.

CONTENTS

ACKNOWLEDGEMENTS

I would like to say a big thank you to the following people for the assistance they have given to me during the production of this book. In particular to James Howarth and everyone at Tempus Publishing, without whom this book may never have been finished.

My eternal gratitude to Mel Eves for his help and for taking the time to read my draft, plus of course a big thank you for writing the foreword. A huge extra-special thank you to Wolverhampton Wanderers Football Club for putting up with my questions, and allowing me look at, photograph and reproduce artefacts and memorabilia in this homage to Wolves: in particular my thanks go to Wolves' archivist Graham Hughes and Wolves' historian John Hendley for their kindness and assistance with this project; also to Rachael Heyhoe Flint MBE, Lorraine Hennessy, the directors, management, players and staff at Wolverhampton Wanderers. Plus ex-Wolves players Mel Eves and Geoff Palmer.

Thanks also to:

Peter Harrington of Ivanhoe Photography, Stourbridge.

Everyone and anyone who has ever written about the Wolves, in particular those whose contributions graced the Wolves programme over the decades: Ivan Sharpe, WANDERER, Jack Ramsey, Phil Morgan and Geoff Allman, together with every journalist and author that has ever put pen to paper about Wolves.

Peter Evans, Wolverhampton City Archivist, and the staff at Wolverhampton Archives and Local Studies services.

Everyone who has helped me with proof-reading, or have loaned Wolves memorabilia: my long-suffering wife Kate, my sons John and Peter, Ray Whitehouse, Mike and Jill Dunn, and Ron Hollingworth.

Ben Smallman of the *Bridgnorth Journal*. Charles Ross at ALOB. The *Shropshire Star* and its sister newspaper the *Express & Star*. The *Birmingham Post & Mail* Ltd.

Truls Mansson of the Swedish Wolves Supporters Association for his generous help.

Rick Mayston at Getty Images.

The staff at the Birmingham City Library, Archives and Local Studies service.

British Association of Picture Libraries and Agencies (BAPLA).

Photographic acknowledgements

While every effort has been made to trace and acknowledge all copyright holders, we apologise for any errors or omissions. The author wishes to thank and acknowledge the following people for providing photographs and for permission to reproduce copyright material:

Peter Evans and all the staff at Wolverhampton Archives and Local Studies services.

Geoff Allman, Ron Hollingworth and the Hollingworth family.

Graham Hughes plus the directors, management, players and staff at Wolverhampton Wanderers for allowing me to take and reproduce photographs of Wolves memorabilia, and for supplying a few photographs.

Mel Eves.

Dave Ash at Mirrorpix and Patricia O'Gorman at the Birmingham Post & Mail, for providing the bulk of the action shots.

Michael Willis at Simmons Aerofilms Ltd., e-mail: library@aerofilms.com

J. S. Roper.

Jennie Lee Centre.

Maureen A. Hunt

John K. Shipley, spring 2003

FOREWORD
by Mel Eves

Like the majority of lads growing up near Wolverhampton in the 1950s, I was steeped in the history of the Black Country's most famous club – Wolverhampton Wanderers; I wanted to play for the mighty Wolves from the time that I first kicked a football. When it actually happened, I had to pinch myself to make sure that I wasn't dreaming.

I was filled with trepidation as I walked into the hallowed halls of Molineux for the first time as a footballer. Here I was, a 16-year-old Black Country lad; one of the faithful, raised on the North Bank from the age of seven, now about to play for his team.

I officially signed for Wolves in July 1975, when I was 18, after I had left Wolverhampton Grammar School, having been lucky enough to play for the youth team and the reserves. Actually my first visit to Molineux's inner sanctum had been eight years earlier when as a 10-year-old schoolboy I and my schoolmates were fortunate to have been taken on a guided tour.

By the time I arrived, the famous players of the 1950s had left the club, however I was fortunate enough to meet many of my heroes when they visited our dressing room on match days; just to be able to chat to them was fantastic. I was thrilled to see how humble and welcoming they were to me and the other players. After I had finished playing I was invited to join the Wolves' Former Players Association; a real honour and a privilege, allowing me to again rub shoulders with those great Wolves' players that I so much admired.

Being selected for the first team was brilliant, and making my debut alongside a Wolves' legend like John Richards, well, words can't really describe it. I'd watched John's career develop and blossom as he became one of the country's top goalscorers, so I'm sure you can understand my feelings now that I was actually playing in the same team; this is just one of so many wonderful Wolves' memories. Of course, one of the best was running out for the first time at Wembley on that thrilling League Cup-winning day. Our fans were at the changing-room end and so when we emerged from the tunnel we were almost deafened by the noise. Seeing the sea of old-gold and black banners and scarves was a very emotional moment. And of course, the day we brought the trophy back to Wolverhampton was incredible; crowds lined the streets, everyone smiling and cheering as we rode round the town.

I often get asked what it feels like to be the last Wolves' player to score a goal in a European competition; the answer is simple: at the time, neither I, nor anyone else that I know of, could have imagined that this would be Wolves' last European goal; I'd never have believed it if someone had told me that. I suppose my best answer is that it was great

10-year-old Mel Eves and Steve Walton looking at Wolves' trophy cabinet at Molineux, 1966.

to score any goal for Wolves. Now I can't wait to lose the tag because for someone to score a European goal would mean we'd have regained our rightful place in the top echelon of English football, back where Wolves belong.

I had nine pretty wonderful years at Molineux and certainly never wanted to leave Wolves, the club I've supported all my life. Happily, as an FA Licensed Football Agent I'm still involved with the sport I love, and being player-manager of the Wolves All Stars football team helps keep me fit and able to help raise tens of thousands of pounds each year for various charities and good causes. It's still a thrill for me to be on the same pitch as stars like England full-back Bobby Thompson, as well as many of my former teammates. Now we regularly field players from more recent Wolves' teams such as Steve Bull, Robbie Dennison and Jon Purdie, all of whom give their time freely.

Some say that nostalgia is not what it used to be! And whilst obviously this must be true, it is my view that it's vital to record our memories; after all, the past has an enormous influence on the shape of the present and the future. I never tire of reading about Wolves' history; I love it, and so can heartily recommend this book to you. John takes the reader on a detailed and entertaining walk through more than 25 years of memories, from the time when Wolves were amongst the pioneers of floodlit football, right up to that last European goal. He has also included information about Molineux's origins, its subsequent demise, and its dramatic re-emergence from the ashes of despair to become a fantastic stadium once again, capturing the true spirit of the time.

In nostalgically chronicling the glorious history of Wolverhampton Wanderers, John evokes so many wonderful memories which must never be forgotten. *Wolves Against The World* is a timely souvenir as we celebrate the 50th anniversary of the first floodlight game at Molineux on September 30th 2003. A true member of the faithful, John's passion for Wolves shines through onto every page,

Here's to the next 50 years.

I hope you will enjoy John's book as much as I have.
Best wishes
Mel Eves

INTRODUCTION

The great Bill Shankly reputedly proclaimed, 'Football's not a matter of life and death, it's much more important than that!' A passionate footballing giant telling it like it was for him. Surely, there can be no doubt that the game of football provokes levels of passion seldom seen outside the bedroom. I guess that most football fanatics agree with Shankly's sentiment, because football *is* a passionate game, and as such, has also provoked the coining of a wide variety of words and descriptive phrases over the years. The legendary Pele referred to football as, 'the beautiful game,' a phrase that looks like it has now entered the dictionary of 'football speak' right up there alongside 'over the moon' and 'sick as a parrot,' but slightly more gentile. In company with the majority of fans, I agree that football has a certain grace and beauty about it. However, I submit that there are many other adjectives that can describe the game of football: exciting, thrilling, rousing, electrifying, exhilarating. For some it's even sexy – the best thing you can do with your clothes on! While I'm not sure if the latter is true, I am certain that watching your team makes your pulse race, your skin tingle, and sometimes your blood boil, little wonder that Pele's alternative description has become so popular. The list of emotional descriptions about football would be longer than most arms, so, leaving out the negative and as the song says, accentuating the positive, I'll submit a couple more for your consideration. Starting with the buzz of excitement as you make your way to the match, then the electrifying atmosphere inside the football ground, the banter and the chanting, the seemingly spontaneous humour, the anticipation of what is to come as you await the kick-off – it's just – well – wonderful! To football fans, there is nothing as mouth-watering as going to a live match, especially when that match involves the team you love and support. You can have a shout, a moan about your least favourite player, and yell encouragement to your favourites. Heck! You can even swear if you want to. Then there are the names of the some of the Stadia. Names designed to conjure-up evocative messages; maybe sometimes to entice the uncommitted punter inside, such as 'The Theatre of Dreams', or 'The Stadium of Light', not forgetting the unofficial ones of course, like 'The Golden Palace', and 'The Golden Temple'. We all know where they are, don't we? Everything about the game promotes excitement and passion in the hearts of those who love this 'beautiful game'!

As I am sure you will gather from reading this book, I love football, but most of all I love the Wolves; in terms of importance it's up there with oxygen. I love to go to the 'Golden Palace', Molineux, and if you are reading this then there's every chance that you do too. So, dear fellow Wolf, may I welcome you to this unashamed celebration of the history of Wolverhampton Wanderers FC against teams from Europe and the rest of the world. The book is about Molineux and the fabulous Wolves teams of the past, our heroes, the great players that have graced our famous stadium. I have started with the floodlit friendlies at Molineux, followed by the games from Wolves forays into Europe, and I just couldn't let pass the opportunity to include a few important matches that were played in daylight. The pages are packed with match highlights, results, teams, scorers, player pen-pictures, anecdotes, general information and photographs. The games refered to include friendlies, the European Champions Cup, the European Cup Winners Cup, the UEFA Cup, the Anglo-Italian Cup and the Texaco Cup – A veritable feast of Wolves memories.

Let me begin by telling you a little about my own Wolves pedigree. Both my parents were ardent Wolves fans, so naturally when I was a baby they took me to my very first football game, mum carrying me to Molineux in her arms. No, I don't remember the occasion at all, but what I do know is that the football team playing was Wolverhampton Wanderers – WOLVES – my team. For as long as I can remember I have watched the Wolves. First with mum and dad, then just dad, and now with my two sons, both of whom have old-gold and black eyes in true family tradition. They are adults now, and like me, season ticket holders, but that doesn't stop me from regularly regaling them with stories of the mighty Wolves – the most successful team of the 1950s. One of my most treasured memories is of 16 March 1957, when as a 14-year-old schoolboy, I was fortunate to have entered the hallowed Molineux stadium by the front door. The thrill of it all will always remain with me. I'm sure that I drooled over every sight, as the smartly uniformed commissionaire guided me through a Wolves treasure-trove. A fantastic experience and one I'll never forget. The match that day was Wolves versus Manchester United, in front of an almost sell-out crowd of over 53,000, the atmosphere was electric. When I had sufficiently recovered my composure from my bedazzlement in Wolves Wonderland, I was led down the player's tunnel. It was just like in my recurring dream – I was captaining Wolves and leading the team out – well, in reality, not quite! I was being allowed to stand in a prestigious spot in the corner of the Waterloo Road enclosure, that bit where the fence at the side of the player's tunnel met the wall surrounding the pitch. The commissionaire ushered me to my place, and I settled down to wait for the teams to run out for the kick-off – it was heaven. I could touch the players as they passed and was convinced that several of them actually smiled and waved to me personally. My view of the game was fantastic (if a bit kind of worms-eye-like, but I didn't care) – it was a privilege to be there. Unfortunately the match ended one-all, but never mind, what stories I told my mates.

Two seasons earlier, Wolves had triumphed over the great Moscow Spartak, and then beaten Honved of Hungary – surely the second-best team in the world after Wolves. They followed this winning streak a year later with a victory over the mighty Moscow Dynamo in another of those memorable games in the series of floodlit matches that Wolves and Molineux had become famous for.

I adored those magical night games – I still do; the lights, the satin shirts, the excitement, the fantastic attacking football, the ball swinging wing to wing from the boots of Johnny Hancocks and Jimmy Mullen – what a place to be. What a privilege it was to be a supporter of the finest team in the land; I reckoned that all my Albion mates were pig-sick with jealousy. They had good reason in spite of their own, not insignificant, success because throughout the 1950s Wolverhampton Wanderers went from strength to strength, competing against, and beating, the best teams in Europe, plus giants from other parts of the world; pioneering in every sense. Wolves spearheaded English football's

FOOTBALL LEAGUE — FIRST DIVISION

MOLINEUX GROUNDS, WOLVERHAMPTON
(Covered Accommodation for 30,000)

SATURDAY, MARCH 16th, 1957

Match No. 32.   Kick-off 3 p.m.

Shirts :
Gold

Knickers :
Black

WOLVES

RIGHT   LEFT

WILLIAMS

TETHER   HARRIS
2   3

CLAMP   WRIGHT   FLOWERS
4   5   6

HOOPER   MURRAY   BONSON   BROADBENT   DEELEY
7   8   9   10   11

Linesman—Yellow Flag   Referee—   Linesman—Red Flag
C. B. BROOME   J. POWELL   K. R. B. HALE
(London)   (Rotherham)   (Bristol)

PEGG   CHARLTON   EDWARDS   WHELAN   BERRY
11   10   9   8   7

McGUINNESS   BLANCHFLOWER   GOODWIN
6   5   4

BYRNE   FOULKES
3   2

WOOD

LEFT   RIGHT

Shirts :
Red

Knickers :
White

MANCHESTER UNITED

THE TEAMS ARE SUBJECT TO ALTERATION

The teams for the 1957 game between Wolves and Manchester United, when I first entered Molineux by the front door.

European onslaught in those heady days. The team in the distinctive old-gold and black won a fearsome reputation, and in the process salvaged the English pride that had been so severely dented by the great Hungarian team of the 1950s. It was fantastic to be a supporter of the best team in the Midlands, England, the British Isles, the United Kingdom, the world! So many wonderful Molineux memories. Actually, that's what I wanted to capture when I set out to put this book together – to share my memories of those magical nights with Wolves fans everywhere, so that they too could experience some of the thrills and excitement that bathed the Molineux faithful of the day. Hopefully I have managed to catch and convey the feeling of the time and of the spirit of true Wolves fans, as well as all the other boys from the Black Country. This is the story of those never to be forgotten Molineux days and nights, when the name of Wolves, preceded by a fearsome reputation, was amongst the best in the world, putting the town, now city, of Wolverhampton on the world map. In the words of a loyal Molineux legend from Tipton, 'Like as I say', just for fun I have included details of a few away matches, specifically the two-legged European encounters, plus one or two other important games in Wolves history, together with a fair amount of Wolves trivia.

I watched the majority of those Molineux adventures from a strategic vantage point in the South Bank, but some I observed from a wide variety of viewing places. Against Honved, for instance, I sat on the wall on the left of the South Bank, not too far from the refreshment kiosk, trying, unsuccessfully, to avoid sitting on the pieces of glass that were embedded on top of the brickwork. At other times, I stood on the North Bank, and sometimes when I was younger, in the kids' enclosure in the North Bank, and occasionally in the Waterloo Road enclosure. These days I sit in the Steve Bull (formerly John Ireland) Stand. Incidentally, the glass hurt, but we won 3-2 against the mighty Honved, so the pain didn't really matter, and miraculously I didn't rip my trousers, so I didn't get a clout round the back of my ear when I got home. These are just a couple of my wonderful Molineux memories that I'd like to share with other Wolves fans, those who were at the games, as well as those who weren't.

Happy reading.

Come on you Wolves!

John Shipley, lifelong Wolves fan,
Bridgnorth

MOLINEUX: 1744–1889

In the simplest terms, Molineux takes its name from the family that owned and lived on the site in the eighteenth century. So let's start this historical journey in the 1740s with the story of how our beloved Molineux stadium got its famous name, and how it became the home of the Wolverhampton Wanderers.

The dawning of the Industrial Revolution created much wealth for those who had the vision and wherewithal to capitalise on the technological innovation that followed Abraham Darby's successful introduction of coke smelting in 1709. Most of these rich forerunners of today's industrialists built large houses as a means of showing their worth to the rest of society. Wolverhampton had its share of such men, among them a prominent local ironmaster and merchant by the name of Benjamin Molineux Esquire.

In 1744, he purchased a tract of land on the north side of Wolverhampton near Wadham's Hill from John Rotton and Richard Wilkes for the sum of £700. It's not absolutely clear whether there was an existing building already on the site, but by 1750, Molineux House stood proudly on a hill overlooking extensive gardens. Although not the most pleasing from an architectural viewpoint, this nonetheless impressive house was one of the largest in the town. Isaac Taylor's 1750 'Plan of Wolverhampton' shows 'Mr Molineuxe's close' in some detail.

Benjamin Molineux died in 1772, but the family, now very much part of the local gentry, continued to reside in Molineux House until 1856, the last family occupant of the house being Charles Edward Molineux. On 6 April 1859, Molineux House was advertised for sale by private treaty, described as a 'handsome and spacious mansion, with extensive outoffices, buildings, coach-houses, stabling, and beautiful grounds, plus gardens, pool, elegant conservatory and greenhouses, $4\frac{1}{2}$ acres within the walls'. From the house's elevated position, delightful views of the Clee Hills and the Wrekin were promised, along with panoramic views of Chillington and the woods. Three-and-a-half acres of land extending from the grounds of Molineux House to, and fronting, the Waterloo road could be purchased separately.

Of course, one cannot say if it was this mouth-watering description that did the trick, but subsequently the estate was bought in 1860 by Mr O.E. McGregor (no relation to William McGregor, the founding father of the Football League). McGregor was obviously a man with vision. He retained the name Molineux Grounds, spending £7,000 in returning the house to its former glory and converting the estate into a pleasure park, which he then opened to the public for a small admission fee. The grounds, the first park of its kind in Wolverhampton, boasted a number of attractions, such as a skating rink,

Part of Isaac Taylor's 1750 map of Wolverhampton with Mr Molineuxe's Close clearly marked on it. (Reproduced with the permission of Wolverhampton Archives and Local Studies)

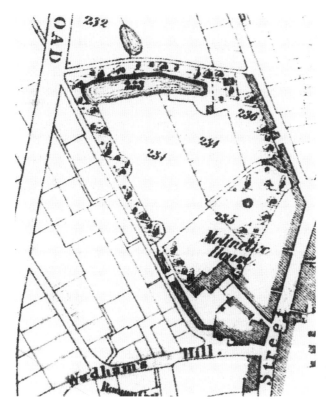

Part of the Wolverhampton Tithe Map of 1842. (Reproduced with the permission of Wolverhampton Archives and Local Studies)

Bicycle race at the Molineux Grounds.

boating lake with fountain, croquet lawns, flower-beds, walkways and lawns, plus amenities for football and cricket, and soon became established as a popular place of recreation, with many fêtes and galas being held there. The venue proved to be extremely popular with the locals, and staged the prestigious 1869 South Staffordshire Industrial and Fine Arts Exhibition.

At the end of August 1870, Mr McGregor was granted a spirits licence, enabling him to sell alcohol on the premises. By 1872, the grounds had been further developed to include a number of additional facilities, and were subsequently used to stage a wide variety of sporting events, including cycle racing, football and cricket matches, and athletics meetings. When the Northampton Brewery acquired the entire site they converted Molineux House into a hotel, and in 1889, rented the grounds to Wolverhampton Wanderers at the very low annual rent of £50, recognising that they could make a lot of money from the thousands of thirsty football fans attending each match.

By 1901, the building had been purchased by W. Butler & Co. the Wolverhampton brewers. Sadly, the Molineux Hotel closed in 1979 upon the expiry of the lease, and has been allowed to rot away ever since.

The Molineux Hotel in 1960.

The sad state of the Molineux Hotel in 2002, view from the south-east. This once-proud mansion is now sadly dilapidated.

MOLINEUX AND WOLVES:
1877–1939

Our beloved Wolves came into being in 1877 when St Luke's school in Blakenhall formed a football team, which became Wolverhampton Wanderers a couple of years later when St Luke's joined forces with Blakenhall Wanderers cricket club. Wolves, as they had become popularly known, first played a game on the Molineux Grounds in 1886, losing 2-1 to Walsall Town in the final of the Walsall Cup and, despite losing, must have liked the place. The status of Wolverhampton Wanderers Football Club was enhanced when they entered the FA Cup for the first time in 1883/84, reaching the second round. Then on 2 March 1888, Wolves joined the Football League as one of the founder members for the 1888/89 season, playing their first ever league fixture on their sloping pitch at Dudley Road on 8 September 1888, in a 1-1 draw with Aston Villa. Wolves' team for that game was Baynton; Mason, Baugh; Fletcher, Allen, Lowder; Hunter, Cooper, Anderson, Cannon and White. The scorers were Green for Villa, and Cox with an own-goal for Wolves. The foundations for greatness had been established, but still something was missing: the club needed a more permanent and prestigious home to match their footballing aspirations. After the club had reached its first FA Cup Final in 1888, unfortunately losing 1-0 to Preston North End, the Wolves committee members decided to accept the offer to move to the Molineux Leisure Grounds site, and thus the Molineux legend had begun. Prior to this, Wolves had played their home games on four different sites, starting off at Windmill Field, Goldthorn Hill from 1877 to 1879, followed by John Harper's field, Lower Villiers Street from 1879 to 1881, Dudley Road from 1881 to 1889, and occasionally the ground of Blakenhall Wanderers Cricket Club, near the old Fighting Cocks pub. However, the quality of those pitches left a lot to be desired; now Wolves had a much better playing surface on which to entertain the best teams in the league.

Before Wolves could move into their new Molineux Grounds home, the land between the track and the house had to be cleared of trees. The development also involved removing fencing and the bandstand. The lake was drained and filled in, and the iron bridge that spanned its narrowest point was dismantled. The brewery paid for the construction of players' changing rooms, refurbished the existing 300-seat grandstand, and alongside this built a shelter to house a further 4,000 spectators on a raised embankment, with a further narrow cinder bank on the north side of the pitch. Thus, Wolves had their new home – MOLINEUX.

The first football match played by Wolves on their new home ground was a friendly against Aston Villa, when on Monday 2 September 1889 at 5.30 p.m. a crowd of around 3,900 spectators watched Wolves win 1-0, centre-forward Wykes scoring the winning goal

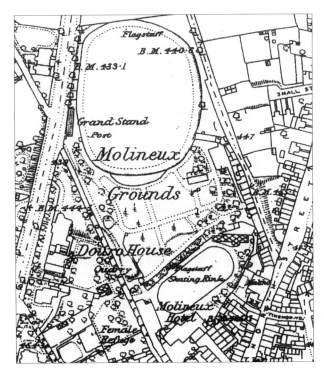

Part of the Ordnance Survey map of 1889, showing the layout of the leisure grounds just prior to being taken over by Wolves. Note the grandstand, running track, winning post and skating rink. (Reproduced with the permission of Wolverhampton Archives and Local Studies)

with a low shot. This seems an odd choice of day and kick-off time, as the majority of potential punters would probably have been at work. Apparently, spectators familiar with the old Molineux Grounds would have been hard-pressed to recognise the place. The freshly laid 115x75-yard pitch looked as level as a billiard table. Chairman of the Wanderers committee, Councillor Hollingsworth, kicked-off for the Wolves, and history was made. Wolves' team that day was Rose; Mason, Baugh; Allen, Fletcher, Knight; Worrall, Perry, Wykes, Wood and Booth (umpire: Mr Dallard). Aston Villa's team was Warner; Coulton, Aldridge; Devey, Cowan, Burton; Brown, Allen, Hunter, Dickson and Garvey (umpire: Mr Allbat). The match referee was Mr Charles Crump. After the game, 70 people, players, friends and officials, were entertained to a well-served dinner.

Five days later, on a beautiful Saturday, 7 September 1889, Wolves staged the very first league game, the first of the season, at their new Molineux home. This time it was Notts County's turn to provide the opposition, or victims, as Wolves won 2-0. The game eventually kicked-off at 4.20 p.m. having been delayed by the late arrival of the visitors. Wolves' team on this historic day was Rose; Baugh, Mason; Fletcher, Allen, Knight; Worrall, Perry, Wykes, Wood and Booth.

Once again, there was only a low turnout, with around 4,000 watching the game. The spectacle of Association Football hadn't yet captured the imagination of the populace of Wolverhampton, with gates for league games seldom reaching 5,000. However, the committee members felt that larger crowds could be attracted, and this notion was borne out by the fact that later that year 19,000 watched Wolves home game on Boxing Day against Blackburn Rovers. Subsequent games played over the Christmas period always swelled the size of the gate considerably, attesting to the popularity of matches at that time of year, particularly the Boxing Day fixtures. During these pioneering years, the Molineux

Above: A football match at the Molineux Grounds in the 1890s.

Right: Part of the Ordnance Survey map of 1902. Now we see Wolves' new Molineux home after the removal of the leisure grounds. Note the extended terraces on the Waterloo Road side and the North end, the small stand on the Molineux Street side and the layers of banking on the Molineux Hotel end of the ground. (Reproduced with the permission of Wolverhampton Archives and Local Studies)

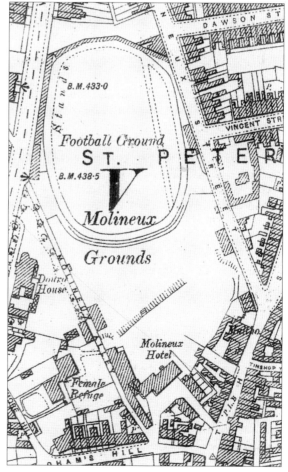

Above: Wolverhampton Wanderers Football Club, 1904/05. From left to right, back row: Whitehouse, Jones, Betterley, Walker, Badderley, Annis. Front row: Baynam, Haywood, Wooldridge, Smith, Miller.

Left: Wolverhampton Wanderers, winners of the English (FA) Cup, 1908.

Hotel hosted a number of meetings of the Football League management committee, and in March 1891 Molineux was the venue for England's international with Ireland, which incidentally England won 6-1.

In February 1892 a crowd of 21,000 watched Molineux host its first FA Cup semi-final, when West Bromwich Albion met Nottingham Forest. Three more semi-finals and one international followed, but by 1905 Molineux was out of favour as a suitable stage for these high-profile matches, its basic facilities having fallen behind those of its near neighbours, Birmingham, Aston Villa and West Bromwich Albion. Molineux stayed pretty much that way until 1911 when a curved roof was built over half the north end of the ground, its nickname 'Cowshed' coming from the iron fencing that fronted it.

Meanwhile, since their founding, Wolves had experienced a reasonable measure of success in the FA Cup, winning the trophy in 1892/93, then again in 1907/08, reaching the final on three other occasions, in 1888/89, 1895/96 and 1920/21, also losing a semi-final in 1889/90.

In 1923, Wolves bought the Molineux freehold from the brewery for £5,607, and Wolverhampton Wanderers Limited came into being. Two years later, the Scottish engineer Archibald Leitch was commissioned to construct the first major grandstand on the Waterloo Road side of the ground. This stand had a capacity in excess of 2,600 seating, plus a paddock to house 4,000 standing. Leitch also carried out a number of other modifications. The old roof cover of the Waterloo Road Stand was moved to the Molineux Street side of the ground as shelter for the spectators. The 'Cowshed' was demolished, but that part of the ground retained its nickname. It was replaced with wooden terracing at the rear, its full width being covered by a pitched roof, and following this, the South Bank was terraced. In 1932 a brand new Molineux Street Stand was built to replace the old roof structure, which, by the way, had been blown down by severe gale force winds eight years after being moved. The new Molineux Street Grandstand had a distinctive multi-span roof design with seven gold-painted gable-ends. The centre gable

Wolverhampton Wanderers c. 1905/06. From left to right, back row: Raybould, J. Jones, Baddeley, Lunn, Lloyd, Juggins, Ward, J.H. Jones. Front row: Williams, Wooldridge, Hedley, Hawkins, Roberts, Breakwell, Pedley. Front, sitting on ground: Bishop.

Wolverhampton Wanderers' losing FA Cup Final team, 1921. From left to right, back row: Woodward, Hodnett, George, Gregory, Riley, Marshall. Front row: Lea, Burill, Edmunds, Potts, Brooks. They lost 1-0 to Tottenham Hotspur.

Newspaper cutting showing Santander v. Wolves in an international tournament. Wolves goalkeeper Toothill and centre-half Reg Hollingworth can only look on as Spaniard Larringa gets in a shot.

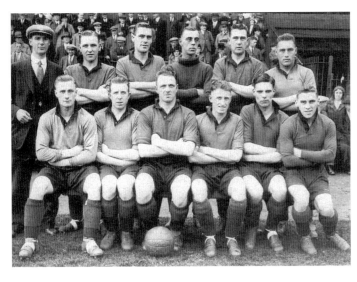

Wolves team 1932/33.

Wolves 1933/34 squad, players and officials, pose for a photograph in an off-duty moment.

Wolves first-team squad, 1934/35.

The terracing on the South Bank at Molineux.

housed a clock. Instantly recognisable and accommodating a total of 8,000 spectators – 3,400 seated, plus 4,600 standing – the new stand was unique, its design not only having to take account of the Molineux Street gradient, but its orientation also; it tapered from around 75 feet wide at the South Bank end to a third of that at its northernmost end. A covering for the rear of the South Bank was added in 1935, in the form of a pitched roof, which was subsequently extended to provide shelter for the spectators that used it. I speak from experience when I tell you that the views from the rear terracing were magnificent. When it was completed it could hold an estimated 30,000 spectators. Along with Villa's Holte End and Liverpool's Spion Kop, it was one of the largest in the country. Now the ground had four stands for the first time in its history – Molineux was truly a stadium, a home to be proud of, having been transformed from a basic ground to one of the finest in Britain.

In keeping with the successful development of Molineux, the then manager, legendary Major Frank Buckley, produced a match-winning team that cemented Wolves reputation for fast, attacking football, finishing second in Division One in seasons 1937/38 and 1938/39. Major Buckley had such a strong impact on the establishment of Wolverhampton Wanderers as a powerful force in English football that it would be wrong of me not to include a word or two about the great man, therefore, I have done so later in the book. Match attendances also rose with Buckley's and Wolves' success, culminating in the record Molineux gate of 61,315 for the Cup-tie with Liverpool on 11 February 1939, which Wolves won 4–1. Unfortunately, that was the season Wolves lost the Cup Final 4–1 to lowly Portsmouth, when according to almost every knowledgeable pundit, all they had to do was turn up. As well as halting Wolves run of success, the outbreak of the Second World War put paid to plans to relocate from Molineux to a new stadium, that is, assuming that the project could have been funded. Wolves had advertised for a central 10-acre site with good road access. Would the new stadium have been called Molineux? Who knows? I for one am glad we stayed at our Molineux home; surely nothing else would have been quite the same?

Fortunately, the Molineux name has continued to live despite all of the close encounters with tragedy suffered by the club in the 1980s. We'll take a look at this later, but now a new chapter in the development of Wolverhampton Wanderers was about to be written.

Aerial view of Molineux, 1924.

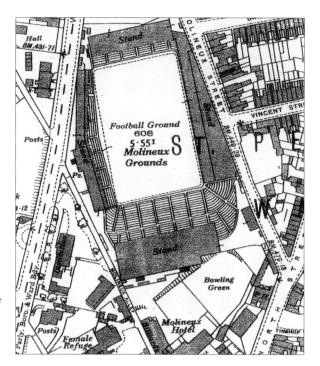

Part of Ordnance Survey map LXII 6 from 1938. Now Molineux stadium has taken shape, with grandstands on all four sides. Note the bowling green at the rear of the Molineux Hotel. (Reproduced with the permission of Wolverhampton Archives and Local Studies)

Wolves' new signing Reg Hollingworth is greeted at Molineux by Major Frank Buckley.

Left: Wolves' centre-half Reg Hollingworth.

Below: Hollingworth flanked by teammates Tom Smalley (left) and Dai Richards.

Wolves' team being presented to the King before the 1939 FA Cup Final.

Wolves' 1939 FA Cup Final-losing team.

1946–53 AND BEYOND

Season 1946/47 heralded the resumption of top-flight football after the end of the Second World War. That year, Wolves were disappointed to finish 3rd in Division 1, having won the same number of points as second-placed Manchester United and only one less than champions Liverpool. Wolves manager at that time was Ted Vizard, who had succeeded the legendary Major Frank Buckley in April 1944. Ted had had a distinguished playing career, being capped 22 times for Wales and being an FA Cup winner on two occasions with Bolton Wanderers. His Wolves team included many stars, and one of the brightest was the great Stanley Cullis, who surprised a lot of fans in May 1947, when at the relatively young age of 31, he retired from playing to become assistant manager to Ted Vizard, taking over the manager's reins in June 1948.

Cullis was a tough, uncompromising and inspirational manager who steered Wolves to the most successful period in their history. In 1947/48 Wolves ended the season in fifth spot, and a year later in 1948/49 achieved sixth position, also winning the FA Cup that season. In 1949/50 Wolves were runners-up in both League and Cup, their second spot in the League equalling the highest finish that they had thus far achieved in their history, matching as it did the two runners-up finishes in the two seasons before the outbreak of the War. Not winning the title that season was a bitter pill to swallow, as Portsmouth only won the Championship on goal difference, both teams having 53 points. Over the course of the next two seasons Wolves form dipped considerably, falling to fourteenth position in 1950/51, and in 1951/52 ending the season in sixteenth spot. The following season, 1952/53, saw a resurgence of Wolves fortunes as they once again claimed third place. In ten seasons, excluding the war break, Wolves had finished second three times, third twice, had two fifth and one sixth placing, and won the FA Cup once, to earn the recognition as being among the top clubs in the country.

Towards the end of this successful period, the forward-thinking Molineux board took the monumental decision to be among the first football league clubs to install floodlights, thus heralding a series of memorable night games. Wolves fans everywhere owe the board of directors of that time a huge debt of gratitude, because without their courage and vision we would have been deprived of the magnificent spectacles that were to follow. In 1953 the Wolves board comprised Chairman J.S. Baker, Esq., Vice-Chairman A.H. Oakley, Esq., J.P., J. Evans, Esq., C.H. Hunter, Esq., and J.H. Marshall, Esq. Club Secretary was John T. Howley, and the manager Stanley Cullis, Esq.

In those days, Wolves' programme proudly proclaimed that the Molineux Grounds boasted covered accommodation for 30,000, plus uncovered space for more than an

Right: The front cover of the programme for the 1949 FA Cup Final between Leicester City and Wolves.

Below: Billy Wright, in the coach doorway, proudly holds up the FA Cup. Many of Wolves' 1949 Cup-winning squad are in the foreground.

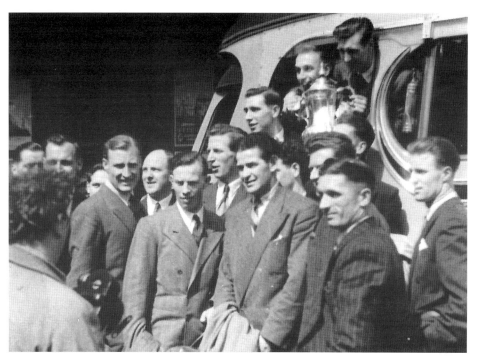

additional 30,000. A system of floodlights would be a great addition to the stadium; however, the Football League and the FA put a bit of a dampener on the proposal when they pronounced that floodlights were not allowed to be used for League and Cup games, but could be used for friendly matches and Charity Shield games.

Before moving on, a word about a loyal Wolves servant, club Secretary Jack Howley. Jack started working for Wolves as office boy in 1923, and was appointed Secretary in June 1948, carrying out his duties through all the great Wolves years until he retired in June 1968 after 45 years service. For his last 5 years with Wolves he also acted as General Manager. He sadly died on 23 March 1971, a Wolves man through and through.

In order for this book to tell the fullest story of those fabulous floodlit Molineux nights, I believe it right to provide a little information about the first floodlighting system itself. The board decided that they wanted to see Molineux equipped with the brightest, most up-to-date floodlighting system that money could buy; after all, the club was among the most successful in the country, and therefore could afford the best, so why not have the best? The contract was awarded to France's Electric Ltd, of Darlaston, who were tasked with providing the best floodlights in England. The firm's Managing Director Mr W.G. France applied his mind to solving the not-insignificant problems involved. His quest for knowledge of this infant technology took in valuable information from the Continent and America. The story goes that he built a scale model of the Molineux pitch, complete with model floodlight towers, on the dining table of his Bilston home. Mr France calculated that the towers holding the floodlights would have to be high enough to ensure that glare would be almost negligible for both players and spectators. His meticulous research included such diverse things as checking the probable maximum height that a ball could be kicked, and the effect of reflection from blades of grass made shiny by rain or dew. We waited nearly two years to see the dreams of our directors come true, the work eventually being completed in 1953. When it was finished, the system was reported to have cost around £10,000. It involved 270 tons of concrete, nearly 20 tons of steelwork and 6,000 yards of electrical wiring, all controlled from a nine-inch by three-inch push-button

Wolves legend Johnny Hancocks kicking a ball.

switch panel. The four towers were erected by Wilfred Robbins Ltd of Great Bridge, each comprising four sets of fifteen lights: twelve 1,500 watt lamps, plus three 1,000 watt projectors, which illuminated the goalmouth at the far ends of the field, each tower having provision for additional lights. Back-up was provided via a diesel generator, which also supplied emergency lighting for stands, passageways, bars and offices. The system was a fantastic feat of electrical and structural engineering, and reportedly cost a mere seven shillings and sixpence an hour to run!

The honour of playing the very first floodlit game at Molineux introduced a measure of controversy, because this privilege had been originally promised to Glasgow Celtic, the fixture scheduled for 14 October 1953. However, the system was ready for use before that date, and a prestigious match against the South African tourists was about to take place on 30 September; a game originally arranged to be played in the afternoon. Wolves' board weighed all of the factors: they wanted to make the inaugural floodlit match as grand an affair as was possible, and had the idea to switch the game against South Africa from what might have been a dull Wednesday afternoon fixture into something that would live in the memory of all who witnessed it. Probably only a gate of between 5,000 and 6,000 would have been at the afternoon match, as most people would be working, additionally the spell of bad weather that had been around at that time might also adversely affect the size of an afternoon gate. Allying the first use of the new floodlights to an international match would be something to see. This new thinking on the staging of this truly semi-social occasion was now made possible by the generosity of the Celtic board, whose directors readily agreed to withdraw when the situation was explained to them – and so the stage was set.

So great an occasion was Wolves first floodlit match at Molineux on Wednesday 30 September, that it even dimmed the crushing 8-1 defeat handed out to Chelsea four days earlier, Johnny Hancocks getting a memorable hat-trick in that game.

Let me now take you back to 30 September 1953, the start of our nostalgic journey back in time to relive the night when, out of darkness, came floodlights.

Johnny Hancocks' size 4 boots and the ball used in the 1949 FA Cup Final.

1953/54

Wolves 3 South Africa 1
Floodlit Friendly at Molineux

The inaugural match under the brand new Molineux floodlights proved to be a quite magical occasion. Dubbed variously by the press as 'Football in Wonderland', 'Football in Fairyland', 'Football in Technicolor', and a 'Footballing Spectacular', it was Wolves versus South Africa. The game played on that Wednesday night, 30 September 1953, kicked-off at 7.45 p.m. Over 33,000 curious supporters turned out to witness the fun, pleased that the wet weather had cleared up in time for the match. The directors were probably a little disappointed that the gate wasn't larger considering that this was such a monumental occasion. I deemed it a privilege to be amongst the crowd that night. A four-page programme for the game would have set you back 3d in old money (remember this was pre-decimalisation). The programme incorporated a commemorative front cover to mark the special occasion, a springbok emblem being chosen to honour the visitors from South Africa.

For many years, the centre two pages of the programme had featured 'Today's Topical Talk', written by Ivan Sharpe of the *Sunday Chronicle*, a distinguished journalist who penned his programme notes for many years, regaling the reader with memories of games past against the visitors on that particular day. In his article for this match, he referred to 'the first night of the Molineux Illuminations', which I think was a gorgeous way to describe the occasion. Unfortunately, Ivan Sharpe was unable to continue writing his feature article after being taken ill in early November 1967; despite fighting a terrific battle against his illness, he sadly died in April of the following year. Also, for as long as I could remember, page 3 of the normal 8-page programme included 'Notes By 'WANDERER'', who welcomed the visiting team and provided a little information about them.

During Ivan Sharpe's illness, Jack Ramsey, to use his own words, 'wore the substitute's jersey' in November 1967, taking over the role officially for the remainder of that season. His final contribution, and that of 'WANDERER', was printed in the programme of 11 May 1968 when Wolves played Tottenham Hotspur in their last match of the 1967/68 season. The following season saw Wolves launch a new-style match programme: *MOLINEWS*. Volume 1, No. 1 introduced the game against Q.P.R. on Saturday 7 August 1968. Issue No. 2, saw the start of 'BACKTRACK', Phil Morgan taking up the task of reminding the reader of previous encounters against that days opponents. Phil's name disappeared from the byline after a couple of months then reappeared in issue 15. In 1968,

Front cover of the programme from the
first floodlit match at Molineux.

a 'Did you miss this?' page was also introduced, initially presenting headlines about Wolves. This feature, written by Alan Williams of the *Daily Express* looked at current hot topics from the world of football. Dennis Shaw of the *Evening Mail* took over for a while when Alan was in hospital. The following season Dennis wrote his article under the title of 'Press Talk', which itself became 'Paper Talk' when Alan Williams returned. In September 1969 Geoffrey Allman also began to contribute a 'Memory Lane' feature to the match-day programme. 'BACKTRACK' mysteriously ended in January 1970, and restarted the following season, now written by Geoff Allman. But I'm skipping forward too fast; let's get back to the fabulous '50s and those South Africans.

Wolves had successfully toured South Africa in May and June 1951, playing and winning all 12 matches, scoring 60 goals, conceding only 5, and in the process winning many admirers. Now in 1953, it was Wolves turn to play host. The South Africans were no strangers to floodlit football, having drawn 2-2 with Arsenal under the Highbury lights a week earlier to cap the other fine performances on their English tour. They had beaten an England amateur side, including Wolves Bill Slater, 4-0 at Selhurst park, Charlton Athletic 3-1 at The Valley, British Universities 3-1, and Norfolk FA 4-2, also earning a 2-2 draw against Birmingham County FA; the visitors were obviously no pushovers.

Captain for the night, Eddie Stuart, led out the Wolves team, his opposite number, Ross Dow at the head of the South Africans, to the cheers of the expectant spectators. Wolves' team captain Bill Shorthouse had stepped down to allow South African-born Stuart the honour of captaining Wolves against his native country; Shorthouse watched the game from the stand. There was a sharp contrast between the teams as they ran onto the pitch, Wolves in their new luminous gold strip against the bright green shirts of the South Africans. The match kicked off to a crescendo of applause and developed into a showcase for Wolves power play, when good football matched with excellent sportsmanship was displayed in abundance. The visitors played well, but couldn't match Wolves' quicker thinking and movement, although their individual speed surprised a lot of people, as did their outstanding ball control, particularly that of their two inside forwards Warren and Gibson. Goalkeeper Rudham, who had played against Wolves on their 1951 South African tour, had a magnificent game, having already been besieged by offers from several English Football League clubs, but like the rest of his colleagues he was under a two-year non-professional embargo. Twenty-year-old centre-forward Salton was also attracting lots of interest after scoring five goals in the tourists' first two games. That night, Wolves dynamic wingers Johnny Hancocks and Jimmy Mullen were in tremendous form. Together with wing-halves Bill Slater and Billy Wright, they gave a fabulous exhibition of long cross-field passing. Wolves ran out comfortable 3-1 winners and with a little more luck, might have scored more than three. Jimmy Mullen got Wolves' first on 32 minutes, then 2 minutes later Peter Broadbent lashed in terrific narrow-angle cross-shot to put Wolves two up. Three-minutes after the restart, Gibson headed a goal for South Africa to bring the visitors a measure of hope, but it was not to be their day. Four minutes from time, Roy Swinbourne deflected a Hancocks cross past the impressive Rudham to wrap it up for Wolves at 3-1. The two teams had provided the crowd with an enjoyable evening of first-class football, an experience that the South Africans said they'd never forget. To the Wolverhampton's credit, the biggest crowd to watch the tourists on their tour had turned out to see them, despite the fact that the weather was a bit dodgy. There weren't many people who saw this one that would want to miss the next floodlit match at Molineux, against Celtic.

Wolves' team at Molineux: Williams; Short, Pritchard; W.J. Slater, Stuart, Wright; Hancocks, Broadbent, Swinbourne, Stockin, Mullen. (At that time Bill Slater held amateur status)
South Africa: Rudham; Machanik, Jacobson; Dow, Naish, Jacques; Claassens, Warren, Salton, Gibson, Le Roux.
Referee: Mr F. Read (Willenhall)
Score: Wolves 3, South Africa 1
Wolves' scorers: Jimmy Mullen, Peter Broadbent, Roy Swinbourne
Scorer for South Africa: Gibson
Attendance: 33,681

As a memento of their visit, the South African players and officials were presented with a Walsall-made leather wallet and a Brierley Hill-made cut-glass bowl, all of the players being amateurs and therefore not eligible to be paid. The President of the South African FA said that Wolves had made a big impression in his country in 1951, and had reaffirmed this on this visit to Wolverhampton. It had been a great night for Wolves fans, a taster for the wonderful floodlit football matches that were to follow; football at Molineux would never be the same again.

To keep the night games as something special, the Wolves board planned only four or five floodlit games per year. Despite that announcement, the next match was already planned for one month's time, when Glasgow Celtic would be Wolves' opponents:

Wolves 2 Glasgow Celtic 0
Floodlit Friendly at Molineux

A lot of people I've spoken to believe that this was Wolves' first ever match under floodlights, but as you know, it wasn't; it was the second, the confusion is for the reasons stated earlier. This game was played on Wednesday night, 14 October 1953, kick-off 7.30 p.m., and once again Wolves didn't disappoint their fans, comfortably beating Celtic 2-0. It's interesting to note the admission prices in those days compared to today: Waterloo Road Stand (centre) 7s 6d, (wings) 5s 6d. Molineux Street Stand (centre) 6s 0d, (wings) 5s 6d. Enclosures 3s 6d, North Bank 2s 0d, South Bank 1s 9d. All prices included tax and are in old money – e.g. 7s 6d (7 shillings and 6 pence) equates to about $37\frac{1}{2}$ new pence.

For this match Wolves made a number of changes. A 17-year-old Tipton lad named Bobby Mason was given the chance to make his debut for the first team. Peter Broadbent, who was on the point of finishing his National Service, had been released to play for a Service XI at White Hart Lane on the same night, and Bobby got the vote to take his place. Returning from successful England duty for this game were Billy Wright, Jimmy Mullen and Dennis Wilshaw, the latter the scorer of 2 goals on his England debut in the win against Wales in Cardiff. Roy Pritchard and Bill Slater were absent through injury, Bill Guttridge and Bill Baxter replacing them. In goal, Nigel Sims deputised for Bert Williams. Over 40,000 turned out on a fine night to witness even better football than we saw from the South Africans, it was some of the most exhilarating seen at Molineux since the match against Chelsea. The game was billed as a friendly, but both teams gave a committed performance as if fighting for League points or Cup survival; exactly how football should be played. Celtic, without their Scottish international centre-half Jock Stein, thrilled the bumper crowd in the first half with a display of almost incredible speed of thought and movement. They were obviously much better than we had expected. No goals at half-time was not a true reflection of the exciting football we had witnessed in the first 45 minutes. In the second half, it seemed that the Scots fierce attacking impetus had finally worn itself out. However, we still had to wait a long time before Wolves scored. Dennis Wilshaw was the man who did it, topping a fine team performance with two excellent goals. His first, four minutes from the end brought a strong protest from the Scots, who believed that he had used his hand to control the ball, however their objections were waved away and the goal stood. The Celtic players were still bemoaning the referee's decision when they unnecessarily gave away a free kick, from which Wilshaw scored his second with a cleanly executed hook-shot that flew past the Celtic goalkeeper. The Scots had their share of chances, and in fact earlier in the game twice had the ball in Wolves net only to see both disallowed by referee Leafe. The knowledgeable crowd showed their appreciation of Celtic's international wing-half Bobby Evans. It was he that prompted the majority of Scottish raids in all-round display brimful with quality. In the final analysis, Wolves lasted the pace better than Celtic, and over the 90 minutes proved to be that bit more effective. Wolves' left-back, the hard-as-nails Bill 'Chopper' Guttridge, surprisingly curbed his sometimes overly aggressive style of play, resulting in one of his most effective games, and prompting a number of dangerous moves in the process. He was a real crowd favourite, the 'Psycho' of his day – the fans gave him his nickname 'Chopper'. I'll bet you can guess how he earned it! Wing-half Bill Baxter also had a good game. His best effort was a flashing long-range shot that was well saved by Hunter. It crowned a good performance from him, along with the rest of his teammates. Young Bobby Mason did well in his first trial with the senior side, his enthusiasm fully deserving a goal. He almost got one, but goalkeeper Hunter made the save of the game. So in the end Wolves won. Although to be fair, no one would have complained if the match had finished as a draw.

> Wolves' team at Molineux: Sims; Short, Guttridge; Baxter, Shorthouse, Wright; Hancocks, Mason, Swinbourne, Wilshaw, Mullen.
> Celtic: Hunter; Haughney, Fallon; Evans, McIlroy, Peacock; Collins, Fernie, McPhail, Walsh, Mochan.
> Referee: Mr R.J. Leafe (Nottingham)
> Score: Wolves 2, Glasgow Celtic 0
> Wolves' scorer: Dennis Wilshaw (2)
> Attendance: 41,820

In February 1954, Bill Slater decided to change his playing status from amateur to semi-professional. Bill had played in Blackpool's losing team against Newcastle United in the 1951 FA Cup final, and had subsequently played several times for Brentford before signing for Wolves in August 1952, joining another former Brentford player at the club, Peter Broadbent. This was around the time that Bill had accepted a post as lecturer at Birmingham University, and he was keen to retain his amateur status, sometimes finding it difficult to train with the Wolves first-team squad. A footballer of real quality, Bill Slater played 12 times for the full England team, and 21 times for England amateur XI, turning out 339 times for Wolves, in the process scoring 25 goals. A member of Wolves' 1953/54 Championship-winning side, he also played in the successive League Championship-winning teams of 1957/58 and 1958/59, and captained the FA Cup-winning side of 1959/60. Also in that year he was voted footballer of the year and gained his BSc. He was awarded the OBE in 1982 and the CBE in 1998 for his services to sport. Like teammate Billy Wright, Bill Slater was never cautioned in a long and distinguished career.

Early in 1954, Wolves played an away friendly against Aberdeen at Pittodrie Park, their directors eager for a return game under the Molineux floodlights; they would have to wait. It snowed an hour before kick-off and must have been freezing cold; Wolves lost 5-3, our goals coming from Taylor, Flowers and Broadbent.

We supporters had to wait almost six months for the third floodlit game at Molineux. This one would also prove to be memorable as we got a taste of a completely different style of football, with the right-back acting as a deep centre-half, the right-half at right-back, the centre-half roving and the centre forward playing deep to draw the opposing defence – confused? Actually in these days of almost innumerable playing systems where we are used to 4-4-2, 4-3-3, 3-5-1, the Christmas tree, the diamond etc., this one seems pretty simple; this was Argentinian football, and it was coming to Molineux.

Wolves 3 Racing Club of Buenos Aires 1
Floodlit Friendly at Molineux

On Wednesday, 10 March 1954, Wolves took on the pride of Argentina, Racing Club of Buenos Aires, a team noted for their delightful brand of football, and for their singing of the club anthem, 'Cancione de America' (Song of America) on the way to a match. By the time they reached Molineux, the Argentinians had already played matches in Rome, Zagreb, Belgrade, Valencia, Bilbao, Madrid and Brussels. Following their game with Wolves, Racing were scheduled to round off the British leg of their tour against Chelsea and West Ham, before playing the final game of their European tour in Paris. Interestingly, in a preview of the game, one newspaper described the visitors as 'those gay caballeros from Racing Club'. I guess that nowadays this might not be politically correct, especially as in what today would be called the 'warm-up', the boys from Buenos Aires were reported to have performed a series of dainty balletic twirls and contortions. The lads from the Black Country couldn't quite figure it out. Me? I was much too young to understand such things! Another thing I remember was that their trainer reputedly carried large red-meat vitamin pills in his bag, which were apparently used at half-time to supplement or top-up the energy levels of his players. My mate told me this – I don't know if it was true or if he was taking the Mickey. Anyway, these 'guys' from Argentina used the formation mentioned previously – which incidentally failed to confuse the mighty Wolves – who that night played powerful and purposeful quick-fire-football that didn't disappoint any of the crowd at all, running out easy 3-1 winners. The Argentinians themselves weren't completely without merit, they played an immaculate short-passing game, involving constant positional interchanges, and were obviously specialists in ball-control, coupled with great heading ability. Their football was impressive, and surprisingly their sportsmanship was first-class. Mind you, if the 'pill story' was true, they certainly weren't very effective because the South Americans didn't seem to have much beef! Leading the Wolves attack that night and deputising for the injured Roy Swinbourne was debutant Doug Taylor. It was Doug who scored Wolves' opening goal after 16 minutes when he tapped in a downward header from Dennis Wilshaw; we all went crackers with joy, but were quickly silenced when less than a minute later the Argentinians drew level, turning our cheers to tears. Veteran international Mendez slipped the ball through the middle for Pizzuti to flash it into the net, a fine goal of speed and precision. On the hour, Norman Deeley, playing at left-half (incidently, I sat in his old desk at Holyhead Road School, Wednesbury; he'd carved his name into the underside of the lid) hit a screaming 25-yarder to make it 2-1. Eleven minutes later, Jimmy Mullen sealed it for Wolves with a smart cross-shot; now it was cheers of joy as the referee blew for full-time. All too frequently the Racing Club forwards ran into offside positions, consequently causing the referee to have to keep stopping the game. Perhaps it was the skill of Wolves defenders that confused them – who knows? Wolves won so who cared?

> Wolves' team at Molineux: Williams; Stuart, Shorthouse; Slater, Wright, Deeley; Hancocks, Broadbent, Taylor, Wilshaw, Mullen.
> Racing: Dominguez; Dellachia, Fernandez; Gimenez, Balay, Alvarez; Cupo, Mendez, Pizzuti, Simes, Sued.
> Referee: J. H. Clough (Bolton)
> Score: Wolves 3, Racing Club of Buenos Aires 1
> Wolves' scorers: Doug Taylor, Norman Deeley, Jimmy Mullen
> Scorer for Racing: Pizzuti
> Attendance: 37,122

What a great season 1953/54 turned out to be. Wolves improved on the previous season's league position by winning the First Division Championship for the first time in

Left: Billy Wright holding the 1953/54 First Division Championship trophy. *Right*: Front cover of the souvenir booklet issued to mark Wolves winning the League.

their history. The Wolverhampton-supporting portion of the Black Country was ecstatic; the other half had to put up with second place as Wolves topped the league, four clear points ahead of the Baggies, which of course made it all the more satisfying. Oh, and the Albion won the FA Cup to make it a full house for the Black Country! Wolves' first championship success increased the club's growing reputation as a fast attacking and well-disciplined outfit. 1954 was also a milestone year in middle-distance running; on 6 May Roger Bannister became the first man to break the four-minute-mile barrier, setting a new world record of 3 min 59.4 sec. There is no doubt that Bannister was fit, but Cullis's Wolves were super-fit; he had them running up and down the steep Spion-Kop banking of the South Bank. Wolves' players had to be tremendous athletes, and they were.

In the summer of 1954, Switzerland staged the World Cup Finals, and fittingly, champions Wolves provided a number of players for the England squad. Billy Wright captained England in both their group matches: against Belgium, which England won 4-3 after extra time – Billy being the only Wolves player in that match; and against Switzerland – England winning 2-0, with Dennis Wilshaw and Jimmy Mullen joining their captain and scoring a goal apiece, Mullen standing in for Nat Lofthouse at centre-forward. In the quarter-finals, England unfortunately lost 4-2 to Uruguay, Wright and Wilshaw making the starting line-up for that match.

1954/55

Early in the 1954/55 season, Wolves played the return match against Celtic in Glasgow on Wednesday night, 20 September 1954, managing to force a 3-3 draw in what was once again a tight game. Roy Swinbourne (2) and Peter Broadbent scored for Wolves. In August of that year, Wolves had travelled to Austria to play a friendly against First Vienna FC. The rain poured down on a very wet Sunday afternoon as Wolves beat the Austrians to win a gold-plated trophy. Our triumphant lads returned to Wolverhampton, and on the evening of 29 September 1954, Molineux staged League Champions Wolves' FA Charity Shield clash with their FA Cup-winning neighbours West Bromwich Albion, who you'll remember Wolves had pipped for the 1953/54 First Division Championship, preventing Albion from winning the double. The game was a floodlit epic 4-4 draw, with Roy Swinbourne grabbing two goals and Norman Deeley and Johnny Hancocks getting the other two. A crowd of over 40,000 witnessed a fabulous game, Wolves racing into a 4-1 lead before being pegged back by the Baggies, Ronnie Allen, later to manage Wolves, getting a hat-trick in the process.

This was the year that a pleased Billy Wright was presented with his second Wolves benefit cheque, this one for £750; this doesn't seem much for the captain of Wolves and England, but these were the days of the maximum wage. Ironbridge born, Billy Wright CBE was a marvellous man, a true ambassador for the sport and a great footballer. He made a total of 541 appearances for Wolves, scoring 16 goals, having joined the groundstaff in 1938 after initially being turned down by Major Buckley for being too small, making his debut in 1939 before turning professional in 1941. Billy won 105 full England caps, his first in 1946, captaining England on 90 occasions, and playing in the finals of three World Cups. In his exemplary 20-year top-level career Billy was never booked or sent off. A great man, and a great Wolves captain. Sadly, Billy died on 3 September 1994; he was 70 years of age.

First Vienna of Austria were the next team to come to Molineux for a mid-week floodlit friendly.

Wolves o First Vienna FC o
Floodlit Friendly at Molineux

This was Wolves first floodlit match against European opposition at Molineux. The crack Austrian team arrived at Molineux with a reputation for being difficult to beat, although

Wolves had beaten them in Vienna. The match was played on Wednesday night, 13 October 1954, kick-off 7.30 p.m. Again, Wolves had to make a number of enforced changes, the most noticeable being Bill Slater playing at centre forward. Somehow Bill failed to score, but on any other day his excellent play might have seen him bag three at least. First he headed Hancocks's corner over, before hitting the bar with another, somehow contriving to put the rebound a foot wide. Chance after chance went begging and some hurried passing and shooting did nothing to calm the growing anxiety in the crowd. Near the end, Menasse had a great chance to put the Austrians ahead. Cutting in from the right, he beat three defenders before fortunately being blocked out. Surprisingly, Wolves didn't win. Even more amazing was the fact that they didn't score. They really should have, in a game that was a close-shave for the Austrians; their defence withstood a terrific second-half barrage from Wolves. Kurt Smied, Austria's goalkeeper, played a hero's role in holding hungry Wolves at bay, blunting attack after attack to earn his side a 0-0 draw, thus becoming the first team to avoid defeat in the series of floodlit friendlies at Molineux. Billy Wright gave his customary immaculate performance, to be described as 'man of the match', which was so often the case.

> Wolves' team at Molineux: Williams; Stuart, Shorthouse; Flowers, Wright, Clamp; Hancocks, Broadbent, Slater, Deeley, Mullen.
> Vienna: Schmied; Roeckl, Nickerl; Ungehler, Koller, Schweiger; Menasse, Watzhofer, Jerica, Suchs (Medweth), Peyer.
> Referee: Mr B.M. Griffiths (Newport, Monmouthshire)
> Score: Wolves 0, First Vienna FC 0
> Attendance: 39,969

We didn't have to wait long for the next one.

Wolves 10 Maccabi Tel-Aviv 0
Floodlit Friendly at Molineux

Wolves' next victims were Israel's top outfit, Maccabi of Tel-Aviv, a team with seven full internationals in their line-up. Sadly for them, they found Wolves in rampant mood, and were gobbled up eagerly on the night of Thursday 28 October 1954. Wolves played as if they had something to prove following their failure to score against the Austrians two weeks earlier, and no, it isn't a misprint, Wolves scored ten! Roy Swinbourne notched up a hat-trick, the pick of them his 16th-minute effort; it was a cracker of a goal, as Wolves whipped the Israeli champions by the amazing scoreline of 10-0. Wolves' other goalscorers were Johnny Hancocks and Peter Broadbent, who grabbed a brace each, Tommy McDonald, netting the eighth on his debut, Ron Flowers with a terrific shot and Dennis Wilshaw. The Israelis had no answer to Wolves' power-play style of all-out attacking, as the home side demonstrated the huge gulf that existed in the abilities of the players. It was a night when our boys certainly had their shooting boots on, and well and truly polished.

Wolves' team at Molineux: Sims; Stuart, Shorthouse; Slater, Wright, Flowers; Hancocks, Broadbent, Swinbourne, Wilshaw, McDonald.
Maccabi: Ben-Dori (Buch); Reznik, Glazer (Ben-Dror); Chilvner, Schneur, Turika; Israeli, Goldstein, Spigel (Glazer), Studinski, Merinovitz.
Referee: Mr A. Murdoch (Sheffield)
Score: Wolves 10, Maccabi Tel-Aviv 0
Wolves' scorers: Roy Swinbourne (3), Johnny Hancocks (2), Peter Broadbent (2), Ron Flowers, Tommy McDonald, Dennis Wilshaw
Attendance: 26,901

Wolves had embarked on a goal-scoring spree on 23 October 1954, starting with a marvellous 4-0 win over Albion. They scored 19 in five matches, making it 29 in six, including the Maccabi game – what we wouldn't give today for an average like that!

The previous floodlit matches had all been great occasions, but now Wolves were to embark upon a series of games against the very best teams in Europe. The first of these was the team of the Soviet Producers' Co-operative Movement, Moscow Spartak. The 'tongue-in-cheek' newspapers informed us that the lead-up to this match had produced an epidemic of an infectious and previously unheard-of local disease known as Spartakitis! Apparently the Wolves board had inadvertently caused the outbreak when they decided to make this game an all-ticket affair, thus creating a clamour for the almost priceless pieces of card. Actually, a ticket for the South Bank cost 2s 6d. Extra floodlights were installed to aid the television pictures after the BBC had decided to televise this 'mepic' event.

Wolves 4 Spartak Moscow 0
Floodlit Friendly at Molineux

Russian aces Moscow Spartak came to Molineux with an awesome reputation, having recently crushed two of Belgium's finest, Liege and Anderlecht. A week earlier they had beaten Arsenal 2-1 at Highbury, so Wolves knew they were in for a tough night. This match was played on a foggy Wolverhampton evening on Tuesday 16 November 1954, the BBC simultaneously televising and broadcasting the game. A memorable spectacle that had almost everything, ending with a finale that included a 6-minute goal-rush. As Billy Wright led out the Wolves team clad in their fluorescent gold shirts and black shorts the crowd roared in anticipation; we had waited eagerly for this match. Manager Stan Cullis had asked his team for their best efforts, and they didn't let him down. Wolves started confidently, using their typical storming tactics designed to grind down the opposition and in the process crush their resistance. However, in a goalless first half they were gradually eased out of it by the superbly fit Russians. The visitors moved the ball around the pitch with great skill, playing with unbounded enthusiasm and panache. Twice the ball had to be cleared from Wolves goal line with Bert Williams beaten. Bert then saved several more good attempts on his goal. Wolves countered with a display of fierce but fair tackling, moving the ball around with purpose, and finally went ahead in the 62nd minute through the outstanding Dennis Wilshaw. The roar that greeted his goal was deafening. He somehow managed to scramble the ball home after the Spartak keeper, Piraev, had tried unsuccessfully to punch the ball clear. That's the way it stayed until

7 minutes from time when, seeing the Russians noticeably begin to tire, Johnny Hancocks got Wolves' second. It began to look good for the home team. Sighs of relief echoed around the terraces, as Wolves' superior stamina now began to tell. In the 88th minute Roy Swinbourne added a third, followed a minute later by Hancocks, who made it four. Wolves had dominated the latter stages of the game, scoring three in a little over five minutes against one of the tightest defences in Europe. Maybe the 4-0 scoreline was a little flattering, maybe not. Bill Shorthouse was a tower of strength; his perfectly timed tackles broke up many a threatening Russian attack. Billy Wright too was at his magnificent best.

> Wolves' team at Molineux: Williams; Stuart, Shorthouse; Slater, Wright, Flowers; Hancocks, Broadbent, Swinbourne, Wilshaw, Smith.
> Spartak: Piraev; Ogonkov, Sedov; Parchine, Bachachkine, Netto; Tatushin, Paramanov (Isayev), Simonyan, Morochilov, Ilyin.
> Referee: B.M. Griffiths (Newport)
> Score: Wolves 4, Spartak Moscow 0
> Wolves' scorers: Johnny Hancocks (2), Roy Swinbourne, Dennis Wilshaw
> Attendance: 55,184

Next came the big one, the amazing Magyar soccer machine was coming to town, the team of the Hungarian Army – Honved. The Mighty Magyars had burst onto the international scene in the early 1950s, when the Hungarian national side had been proclaimed as the first great Eastern European team, a claim confirmed during the 1954 World Cup Final, when Hungary were unlucky to lose 3-2 to West Germany. They were widely acknowledged to be the best football team in the tournament. At the same time, the growing reputation of Wolverhampton Wanderers meant that the top foreign teams of Europe wanted the privilege of matching their skills against Wolves. Now the exciting Honved came to Molineux to play them. With their emphatic 6-3 win over England at Wembley in 1953, Hungary had become the first non-British Isles team to beat England on home soil. If this wasn't bad enough, it was followed in the summer of 1954 by a 7-1 mauling in Budapest, two humiliating results that were still fresh in the minds of English fans. Honved were Hungary's top team with many famous internationals in their side. Including the legendary Lieutenant-Colonel Ferenc Puskas and his other famous well-drilled stars: Bozsik, Kocsis, Grosics, Lorant, Czibor and Budai; Kocsis having won the leading scorer prize in the 1954 World Cup in Switzerland. The prospect of entertaining the tormentors of England at Molineux was mouth-watering, especially following Wolves sensational win over Moscow Spartak a month earlier, no wonder the fans were salivating.

Wolves 3 Honved 2
Floodlit Friendly at Molineux

Wolves' game against Honved was played under the Molineux floodlights on Monday night, 13 December 1954. Almost 55,000 cheering fans watched intently as the game kicked off, Wolves' players again resplendent in their specially-made gold satin shirts. A programme that night would have set you back 6d in old money, double the usual 3d, but it was worth every penny. As with the game against Spartak, the BBC again deemed the occasion so important to English football that they televised it, fine for those that couldn't attend that had a television set, but nothing like being there; for those without a TV the BBC broadcast the game on the radio. This caused pandemonium when in the dying seconds of the game, the radio commentary was actually faded out. The BBC switchboard was alive with complaints and the Corporation issued on-air apologies later in the evening. Billy Wright led out Wolves, side by side with Ferenc Puskas leading his team of soccer sorcerers. The Hungarians wore rugby-style tracksuits, marching onto the pitch like the soldiers they were. One piece of good news for Wolves was that ace goalkeeper Grosics was unavailable for selection. Wolves knew they were in for a tough game against the best team to come to Molineux yet, and when the visitors started to play with fantastic ball control and speed of passing, we all feared the worst. Despite being a bit on the chunky side, Puskas was surprisingly very quick. But it was his mesmerising skill with the ball that was so wonderful to see. Even the predicted problems of the heavy pitch were easily overcome by the tormentors of England. As it turned out, we were right to be worried. By half-time, the Hungarians, playing their unique brand of evolved soccer science were 2-0 up, their precision passing and speed of attack drawing gasps of appreciation from all sections of the crowd. The visitors' first came after Ron Flowers had handled the ball. Puskas' whipped in a perfect free kick and sharpshooter Sandor Kocsis scored with a marvellous header. Little wonder he was acclaimed as the best header of the ball in Europe; it flew past Bert Williams like a bullet. Honved followed this up with a second. Kocsis put speedy winger Machos through to score with a low shot to put the Hungarians 2-0 up inside the first 14 minutes. The crowd rose to salute the artistry of the visitors. Bert Williams had played a blinder in the first half to keep the score down to two, rekindling memories of the Wembley and Budapest humiliations. Something had to be done; this was a matter of national pride. In the second half, Wolves called upon all their reserves of energy and spirit. They took the game to Honved and were awarded a hotly disputed penalty 4 minutes after the restart. It seemed a harsh decision by match referee Mr Leafe, but we didn't care. Our penalty king Johnny Hancocks stepped forward and walloped the ball past Farago's left hand into the Honved net; the home crowd went berzerk – myself included. But we were still losing, and there seemed no way that the Honved defence would crumble as had that of Spartak. Wolves' marking was now much more effective, the tackling crisper, and with the visitors being put under pressure all around the pitch, the fans hoped for the best. Our nerves were jangling until around fifteen minutes from time when Dennis Wilshaw floated over an inch-perfect cross and Roy Swinbourne rose majestically to head the equaliser; two apiece, could we do it? A minute or so later, Bill Shorthouse won the ball and got it to Wilshaw, again his pass found Swinbourne, who scored his second of the night, this time with a fine hook-shot, to win the game 3-2 for Wolves, and send the crowd wild with joy. Everyone was cock-a-hoop, it was a truly memorable night, one on which it felt good to be English; we were singing all the way home on the bus. 'Delirious' was how one national newspaper described the scene, whilst another proudly proclaimed on its front page that 'Wolves are champions of the world'. Hungary's Vice-Minister for Sport said that the game had been a clean-spirited fight, and went on to praise Wolves fighting qualities. Kocsis claimed that the penalty knocked the Magyars out of their stride, from which they never recovered. Other Hungarian complaints were about the pitch, which was wet not dry. It's a pity that the European Champions Cup had not yet been launched at this time, when Wolves were so dominant; I'm certain that this Wolves team would have won it. The club's prestige had been taken to a higher level than ever before as Wolves gave English football a much-needed boost. The morale of a group of National Servicemen was also boosted by this victory. Wolves' archivist Graham Hughes explains:

'In 1954, I was serving with the Royal Corps of Signals, stationed at Sherford Camp near Taunton. On the day of Wolves' game with Honved our orders were to move chairs into the NAAFI so the servicemen could watch the BBC broadcast of the game. Myself and my two mates, Taffy Townsend and Les Cockin, being from Wolverhampton, were guests of honour and given front-row seats; it was great. When Wolves scored the winner everybody jumped up, shouting and cheering: Scousers, Cockneys, Geordies, the lot; even the officers. In fact, the officers were so pleased, they ordered the NAAFI to stay open so we could celebrate Wolves win properly. Fantastic!'

Wolves' team at Molineux: Williams; Stuart, Shorthouse; Slater, Wright, Flowers; Hancocks, Broadbent, Swinbourne, Wilshaw, Smith.
Honved: Farago; Rakoczi, Kovaks; Bozsik, Lorant, Banyai; Budai, Kocsis, Machos (Tichy), Puskas, Czibor.
Referee: Mr R. J. Leafe (Nottingham)
Score: Wolves 3, Honved 2
Wolves' scorers: Johnny Hancocks (penalty), Roy Swinbourne (2)
Scorers for Honved: Kocsis 1, Machos 1
Attendance: 54,998

The Hungarian uprising in 1956 proved to be the end of this great Magyar side, which incidentally was touring at the time of the conflict. Understandably many of the players decided against returning to their homeland, preferring instead to ply their skills in the free world; we would never see their like again.

Wolves ended the 1954/55 season as runners-up to Chelsea by 4 points, including that great game when Wolves beat Albion 4-0 at home. The biggest disappointment was that Wolves didn't win the League Championship that season, as they deserved to. A near-disastrous run-in, that saw Wolves take only 8 points out of a possible 22 from the final 11 games, put paid to our hopes of retaining the title. Centre-forward Roy Swinbourne missed the final six games of the campaign through injury, which didn't help. Another factor was Jimmy Mullen's absence from eight of the last ten games. It was a season when, strangely, Wolves sometimes laboured to score, although to be fair, they still managed to total 89 from their 42 games. Those final 11 games saw them score just 13, whilst defensively holding the opposition to a mere 18 against. The problem was that Wolves failed to score in 4 of these 11 outings, losing 0-1 to WBA, Villa and Chelsea in the process.

1955/56

The 1955/56 season saw the birth of the European Cup, but the short-sighted Football League Management committee refused English Champions Chelsea the opportunity to compete. Chelsea Chairman Joe Mears was very enthusiastic about this new European competition, and sent a delegate to the April 1955 meeting of the organising committee in Paris. In the first round Chelsea were drawn against Djurgarden of Sweden. However, the powers that be were hostile and suspicious of European football. They were also concerned about potential fixture congestion, and 'strongly advised' Chelsea to withdraw. The Blues reluctantly gave way, their place being taken by Gwardia Warsaw. The only British club to enter this first-ever European Cup was Hibernian. Despite only finishing fifth in their domestic league the Edinburgh club was considered to be Scotland's top team. Hibs did themselves proud, reaching the semi-finals, where they lost 3-0 to French club Reims. The inaugural competition kicked off with sixteen teams, and strangely in those days it wasn't deemed necessary to have won the previous season's Championship in order to enter. It's come full circle, hasn't it? By the way, Real Madrid won the first five European Championships.

In April 1955, during his fourth game for his country, Dennis Wilshaw scored a record-breaking 4 goals for England in the 7-2 demolition of Scotland at Wembley, playing in an England team that also included Billy Wright and Bert Williams.

Dennis Wilshaw was born in Stoke-on-Trent in 1926, signing professional forms for Wolves in 1944. After a successful loan spell with Walsall in 1946/47, he was recalled to Molineux in 1948, scoring 11 that season, including a hat-trick on his first-team debut in the 3-0 defeat of Newcastle United on 12 March 1949. In all for Wolves he scored 112 goals in 219 games before transferring to Stoke City in 1957/58, going on to score another 49 goals for them until, in 1961, a broken leg forced him to retire from the game. He played in 12 full England internationals, including the 1954 World Cup Finals in Switzerland.

In the summer of 1955 Wolves played and lost two friendlies in Moscow. Spartak got their revenge by beating Wolves 3-0 on 7 August. Then Wolves went down 3-2 to Moscow Dynamo five days later. In that match, Dennis Wilshaw scored both Wolves goals, becoming the first Englishman to score in Russia, another record to add to his four against Scotland. Now Wolves had their chance to avenge the latter defeat, as Dynamo came to Molineux.

Above: Billy Wright leads out Wolves for the match against Dynamo in Moscow, 12 August 1955. (Picture supplied by Graham Hughes at Wolves)

Left: Cover of programme from the Wolves v. Moscow Dynamo match.

Opposite: The cover of an unofficial 'pirate' programme for the same match.

Wolves 2 Moscow Dynamo 1
Floodlit Friendly at Molineux

Along with Spartak, Moscow Dynamo were the pride of Russia; they were the team of the Ministry of the Interior. Dynamo's manager and coach Michael Yakushin brought his classy team to Molineux on Wednesday night, 9 November 1955, to face Wolves' proud 100 per cent home record in the 1955/56 season and in the year 1955 to date. Jimmy Murray made his debut in place of Roy Swinbourne, who had sadly been injured at Luton and then again against Preston, the last time he played for the first eleven; he was only 27 years of age.

Roy Swinbourne had been hailed the new king of Molineux following his 24 goals for the 1953/54 Championship-winning team and his two against Honved. A product of Wolves' nursery club Wath Wanderers, Roy's popularity was further cemented in the 1955/56 season, when he scored 17 goals in the first 12 games. His exploits included scoring four in the 7–2 home destruction of Manchester City in August, plus hat-tricks in the record 9–1 away win against Cardiff City in September, and in the 4–0 annihilation of Huddersfield at Molineux. Incidentally, Cardiff later got their own back by beating Wolves 2–0 at Molineux in December that year. There seems little doubt that an injury-free Roy

Swinbourne would have gone on to be an even greater all-time legend. In all, he scored 114 goals in 230 games, including seven hat-tricks.

I read somewhere that Jimmy Murray found out that he'd been selected to face Dynamo when he read it in a newspaper whilst he was in the Whittingham barracks in Lichfield – he was stationed there for his National Service. Jimmy went on to score a total of 166 goals for Wolves in 299 appearances.

Over 55,000 screaming fans, me included, yelled their hearts out in anticipation of another wonderful win under our 'lucky floodlights'. On their tour of England, Dynamo had already beaten two First Division teams and Wolves were determined not to be the Russians' third victims. On the way to Molineux I bought the official programme, plus a 'souvenir' pirate programme, in which there were certainly a number of discrepancies in the spelling of the Russian players' names. The atmosphere inside Molineux was electric, the scene illuminated by the floodlights, mirroring the brightness of Wolves early play. After 14 pulsating minutes of this marvellous match, Wolves took a deserved lead from a corner on the right. Johnny Hancocks sent over a dangerous ball which reached the feet of Jimmy Mullen who instinctively shot for goal. Bill Slater lunged forward, managing to divert the ball wide of Yashin into the Dynamo net. This appeared to stun the Russians, who now seemed strangely subdued. On 27 minutes Hancocks broke free of the Russian defence and crossed to Mullen who met the ball with a first-time half-volley that fully

Wolves and England goalkeeper Bert Williams in action.

deserved a goal, but this time Yashin pulled off a glorious double save. Mullen's shot ricocheted off the big keeper and bounced towards the line; somehow Yashin recovered to smother the ball. Four minutes after half-time Yashin was powerless to keep out Mullen. The Wolves left-winger received the ball from Murray, strongly held off Rodionov and Yashin before smashing a well struck shot into the empty goal. Mullen was having a great game, terrorising the Russian right-back, regularly getting round him to create chances. Jimmy Murray hit the bar with a fine header before the visitors staged a second-half rally, finally beginning to play some of the impressive football we had expected of them. Feodosov had earlier seen a headed goal disallowed for offside by enigmatic Halifax referee Arthur Ellis, a decision that the Russians weren't at all happy with, continuing with their protests long after the event. Wolves' Manager Stan Cullis was later fined £50 by the FA for what he said in response. Eventually Dynamo's precise footballing technique paid a dividend and they pulled a goal back through Ilyin. The remainder of the game continued in fine style; excellent textbook football, with both teams attacking at every opportunity. Towards the end, the visitors began to run out of steam; not so super-fit Wolves, who kept going right up to the final whistle. A valiant effort by the Russians, but not enough, and so Wolves won 2-1, becoming the first British team to beat the crack Russian side. In goal Dynamo boasted the immortal Lev Yashin; he certainly lived up to his reputation as one of the world's finest goalkeepers. Yashin seemed to have a number of nicknames: sometimes he was known as 'The Cat' or 'The Black Cat'; at other times as 'The Lion'. The first of these may have had the power to confuse some people, but not the Molineux faithful, who knew that the real 'Cat' was Bert Williams.

> Wolves' team at Molineux: Williams; Stuart, Shorthouse; Slater, Wright, Clamp; Hancocks, Broadbent, Murray, Wilshaw, Mullen.
> Dynamo: Yashin; Rodionov, Krizhevsky, B. Kuznetsov; Boykov, Sokolov; Sabrov, Feodosov, Y. Kuznetsov, Ilyin, Ryzhkin.
> Referee: Mr Arthur Ellis (Halifax)
> Score: Wolves 2, Moscow Dynamo 1
> Wolves' scorers: Bill Slater, Jimmy Mullen
> Scorer for Dynamo: Ilyin
> Attendance: 55,480

Apparently around this time, managers of the town's cinemas complained that Wolves' night matches were adversely affecting their business; a bit daft considering Wolves only played the occasional mid-week game.

A second Argentinian First Division team came to Molineux in the new year, and there's no doubt that San Lorenzo wanted to avenge the defeat of their 'cousins' a year earlier. They had recently toured Spain prior to their trip to England, emerging with a series of impressive results in a 6-game unbeaten run. Beating Espaniol of Barcelona 3-1, Valencia 4-2, Deportivo La Coruna 3-0, Real Oviedo 4-1 and Seville 3-1, the only side to hold them were Real Madrid in a thrilling 2-2 draw. Wolves had been knocked out of the FA Cup in round 3 at the first time of asking, and so this match was arranged for the afternoon when others were playing their fourth round ties. It's not strictly a floodlit night match, but the lights were switched on at half-time, (otherwise we wouldn't have been able to see a flippin' thing!) so I have included it.

Wolves 5 San Lorenzo 1
Friendly at Molineux

Four-time Champions of the Argentine First Division, San Lorenzo boasted seven full internationals in their team and were brimful of confidence following their successes in Spain. The match was played at Molineux on Saturday 28 January 1956, kick-off 3 p.m. A bit cold for the 'Argies' from Buenos Aires, we all thought. Billy Wright won the toss and straight from kick-off, the cheeky Argentinians took the lead. Inside-forward Sanfilippo swerved past Wright as if he wasn't there, to put the visitors one-nil up after only 90 seconds. Blimey, this wasn't going to be as easy as we thought! Wolves dug deep and pulled a rabbit from the hat — or should I say, referee Mervyn Griffiths did, when on 6 minutes he awarded us a penalty. Norman Deeley headed against the bar and full-back Martina stupidly handled the rebound, bringing a welcome sharp blast from the referee's whistle. Up stepped penalty king Johnny Hancocks, but young Argentinian goalkeeper Galelli guessed right, diving sideways to push out Hancocks's shot, not many keepers saved one of Johnny's penalties. Unfortunately for Galelli, the referee adjudged that he had moved before the ball had been struck, and ordered the penalty to be retaken. This time Hancocks made no mistake, levelling the scores at one each. Eleven minutes later Wolves went one better. Peter Broadbent controlled a long throw from Hancocks before cutting inside to score with a narrow-angle shot; now Wolves were motoring. Dennis Wilshaw got Wolves third 3 minutes later with a right-foot lob from way out on the left wing. Then Broadbent drove in a fierce shot from beyond the visitors' penalty area for Wolves' fourth. Blazina replaced goalkeeper Galelli at in an attempt to prevent a rout. In the second half Wolves opened up with a series of fierce attacks in which Broadbent was outstanding. Then in the 55th minute Wilshaw jumped over a ball that Hancocks pulled back almost from the bye-line, and Broadbent smacked it home, the crowd rising to him as he completed his hat-trick. In the 58th minute Castillo came on for Saba, and 4-minutes later Torres replaced Benavidez. The game started to get a bit rough: Eddie Stuart had to be treated for injury, then the referee took the number of one of the Argentinians after three of them had lunged at Eddie Clamp. Jimmy Mullen replaced Broadbent after 74 minutes, and Faina took Martina's place. It was a pity that Broadbent picked up his injury as there was no doubt he had been the star of the show. When the referee awarded Wolves a second penalty, this time for a foul on Norman Deeley, pandemonium broke out. Sanfilippo rushed at the referee, and together with his colleagues began pushing, poking and prodding the official, before finally grabbing the ball and booting it into the crowd — amazingly he wasn't sent off. Blazina saved Hancocks' spot kick with his foot; we couldn't believe it — two Hancocks penalties saved in one match! (Although to be precise, one was retaken.) And, by different goalkeepers! San Lorenzo may have been one of the top teams in Argentina, but at times, on the sticky Molineux surface they looked very ordinary. They were far too temperamental, exemplified by their all-too-frequent displays of petulance, which punctuated the second half and climaxed with the sorrowful scenes of their protests to the referee. Several of them should have been sent off. In the end Wolves won easily. San Lorenzo's first-half goalkeeper Galelli was just 17 years of age, and already the understudy goalie for the full Argentinian national team. Shame the poor kid and his mate Blazina had to pick the ball out of their net five times, wasn't it?

Wolves' team at Molineux: Williams; Stuart, Shorthouse; Slater, Wright, Clamp; Hancocks,
    Broadbent (Mullen), Murray, Wilshaw, Deeley.
San Lorenzo: Galelli (Blazina); Martina (Faina), Basso; Requin, Saba (Castillo), Pizzarro;
    Jofre, Martinez, Benavidez (Torres), Sanfilippo, Gutierrez.
Referee: B. M. Griffiths (Newport)
Score: Wolves 5, San Lorenzo 1
Wolves' scorers: Peter Broadbent (3), Johnny Hancocks, Dennis Wilshaw
Scorer for San Lorenzo: Sanfilippo
Attendance: 32,408

Under a new league directive, floodlights were allowed to be used for Football League fixtures in the 1955/56 season. The first floodlit game was played at Fratton Park, where Portsmouth took on Newcastle United on 22 February 1956. The failure of a fuse delayed the game for nearly 30 minutes, but that little mishap didn't dampen interest or enthusiasm for this new venture. Clubs soon realised that floodlit extravaganzas were real money-spinners, and therefore loved them. The fans loved the special atmosphere that was created. The floodlights and the white ball somehow made everything much more dramatic and faster – floodlit league football had arrived and was here to stay. Wolves weren't slow in staging the first floodlit league match at Molineux, taking on Tottenham Hotspur at 7.30 p.m. on Wednesday 18 April 1956. The bright lights certainly arrived for Wolves that night, but went out for Spurs as we murdered them 5-1, with Bill Slater scoring two from the penalty spot, plus one each from Broadbent, Murray and Wilshaw – a truly memorable occasion.

Prior to the Tottenham game Wolves found themselves at the centre of a controversy. The next floodlit friendly at Molineux against foreign opposition should have been against Spanish Cup holders Atletico Bilbao, a match scheduled for Wednesday 14 March 1956. In the week before the game, the Players Union decided to step up the pressure in their battle with football's governing bodies for overtime payments for floodlit football, by announcing a ban on all floodlit and televised games. The ban was due to commence on 13 March 1956. Wolves were shocked, the Bilbao party were due to arrive in Wolverhampton the following Monday. Following a two-hour meeting with Union Chairman Jimmy Guthrie after a training session, the Wolves players pledged their support to the Players Union. Wolves' directors and management wanted to pay, most clubs did, but their hands were tied by the official FA and Football League rules. The Players Union had submitted a proposal to radically change the existing wage and bonus structure, which included such things as a minimum wage of £416 per year for a full-time pro, compared to the £7 10s per week in the playing season, and £5 10s per week in the close-season for players aged 20 and over. They also demanded that the then-present bonus system, which paid £2 for a win and £1 for a draw, should be doubled to £4 and £2 respectively. The next day, the decision was ratified, and the game with Bilbao, which had been scheduled to be televised, was cancelled. Clubs earned a great deal from floodlit games, and from television, but none of this money was passed on to the players, surely one of the most archaic and unfair rules in the feudal regime that pervaded English football at that time. Players argued that constant midweek fixtures gave them no time to recover from injury. Following the agreement of the Football League to hold talks with the Players Union, the ban was lifted on Sunday 11 March 1956. Had this agreement come sooner, Wolves game with Bilbao could still have gone ahead. The whole affair left a nasty taste in the mouth. Subsequently Wolves' players wrote to their

From the first floodlit League Division 1 game at Molineux: Wolves v. Tottenham Hotspur, Wednesday 18 April 1956.

Union to protest about the handling of the ban, and the suddenness with which it had been imposed, which had placed them in the invidious position of having to choose between supporting their Union and their desire to play football against top-class opposition. There seems little doubt that they were being used as pawns in a much bigger game.

1956/57

The following season Wolves took on Luton Town on a lovely evening at Molineux under the new rule, whereby games were to begin in daylight but could be completed under floodlights if the referee thought they were necessary. On Wednesday evening, 29 August 1956, a crowd of almost 47,000 was enthralled by a thrilling eight-goal first half, unfortunately followed by only one more in the second period, Wolves running out winners 5-4 in what was one of the best games ever witnessed at Molineux. Wolves' scorers were Murray (2), Broadbent, Mullen and Slater.

On the world stage, trouble was brewing in the Middle East following the nationalisation of the Suez Canal by Egypt's President Abdul Nasser, resulting in a military confrontation from October to December 1956. Since its opening, the canal had brought in a profit of around £267 million, most of which was shared by Britain and France, with Egypt getting only a minuscule portion. Israel sent in a force, followed by troops from Britain and France, in an attempt to reopen the canal. The Suez Crisis, as it was called, was universally unpopular, resulting in international censure, which eventually forced the withdrawal of the invasion forces, and the resignation of British Prime Minister Anthony Eden.

After the skilful Argentinians, next up for a floodlit friendly at Molineux was another team from behind the Iron Curtain: the pride of Roumania, leaders of their league, Roumania C.C.A. – it was another floodlit thriller.

Wolves 5 Roumania C.C.A. 0
Floodlit Friendly at Molineux

C.C.A. had already drawn with Arsenal and Sheffield Wednesday, and beaten Luton Town, so once again, as it had been with Honved, the task of upholding the prestige of English football was left to Wolverhampton Wanderers. Mind you, the Luton game had been a close one. Luton had gone 3-0 up before the Roumanians had got into their stride, then the visitors had found their form, scoring four to run out 4-3 winners; the last shot by Constantin was so fierce that it broke the Luton net. Wolves were also currently on a roll, having scored 12 goals in the previous 3 league games. So it came as no surprise that on the night of Monday, 29 October 1956, Wolves' whirlwind attackers and staunch defenders walloped the Roumanian Army team, in which every player was a full international, 5-0. It was a 90-minute exhibition of typical high-power soccer. In the face of Wolves' rousing display of non-stop attacking football, C.C.A., playing a system of 3 backs plus 2 half-backs, were fortunate to have escaped with only a 5-0 thrashing. Wolves dictated the play from start to finish, moving fast and tackling hard, the latter being particularly well performed by Bill Slater and Ron Flowers. Early on in the game Jimmy Murray opened the scoring with a fine goal – a mere taster of the delights to follow. In the first 19 minutes Harry Hooper's lightening pace caused Apolzan so many problems that eventually he ran out of ideas, and so to stop him just stood in the winger's path; Hooper himself slotted home the resultant penalty. Wolves' trademark, swift incisive wing-to-wing passing by Mullen and Hooper, was a joy to behold, and although both wingers played well, Murray was the pick of Wolves' forward line, working tirelessly throughout the 90 minutes. Wilshaw started well until receiving a kick on his thigh in the 28th minute, which meant he had to be withdrawn, Peter Broadbent substituting. On 62 minutes, Murray's fabulous slide-rule pass split the Roumanian defence for Broadbent to score Wolves' third; then eleven minutes later another decisive ball from Murray put Colin Booth in the clear. The young inside-forward made no mistake. How fitting it was that Murray himself got Wolves' fifth and final goal on 78 minutes to crown a great individual performance.

The Roumanian club president said that his team had been well beaten, and had been impressed by Wolves' skill and speed, as well as their tackling, which had been hard, but fair. He rated Wolves alongside Moscow Spartak, whom C.C.A. had beaten under the Moscow floodlights, and was also greatly impressed with the Molineux floodlighting system.

Wolves' team at Molineux: Finlayson; Stuart, Harris; Slater, Wright, Flowers; Hooper, Booth, Wilshaw (Broadbent), Murray, Mullen.
C.C.A.: Toma; V. Zavoda, Apolzan, Ivanescu; Onisie, Bone; Moldovan, Constantin, Alexandrescu, F. Zavoda, Tataru.
Referee: Mr R.J. Leafe (Nottingham)
Score: Wolves 5, Roumania C.C.A. 0
Wolves' scorers: Jimmy Murray (2), Harry Hooper (penalty), Peter Broadbent, Colin Booth
Attendance: 47,284

In the wake of the Hungarian uprising, Wolves agreed to host a benefit match against Red Banner of Budapest, a team laden with Hungarian internationals, and who now expressed their wish to be known by their original name – M.T.K. The proceeds of the match, £2,312 3s 0d, were to be donated to the Hungarian Relief Fund.

Wolves 1 Red Banner (M.T.K.) 1
Floodlit Friendly (Benefit) at Molineux

The game was played on the night of Tuesday 11 December 1956, kick-off 7.15 p.m. At the pre-match banquet the Hungarians had pledged to play the very best football they could in honour of their gracious hosts. Responding, Wolves Chairman Mr James Baker told his guests that Wolverhampton's and Wolves' motto was 'Out of darkness cometh light' and hoped that very soon that would be the way in their native land. M.T.K.'s team was

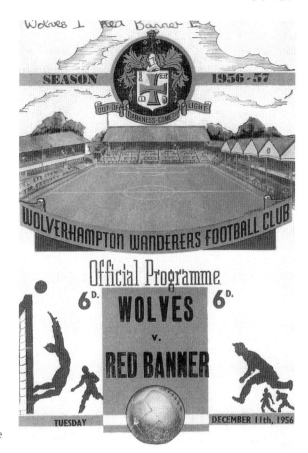

Front cover of the official programme
from Wolves v. Red Banner.

packed with Hungarian internationals, three of whom had played in the humiliating victories over England a few years earlier. They became only the second team to escape floodlit defeat at Wolves' Molineux lair, demonstrating a brand of top-class individual football artistry. In the game itself, Wolves gave the impression of holding something back. Certainly they didn't unleash the kind of power we had witnessed on previous occasions, and particularly as they had against C.C.A. The rather subdued Molineux crowd, sensing this, produced what can only be described as 'the Molineux murmur' instead of the customary 'roar'. The biggest cheer from the crowd came when Johnny Hancocks replaced Jimmy Murray 8 minutes from time. Everyone was looking for the little magician to provide a fairy-tale ending, but the winger only touched the ball 3 times. If this had been a boxing match, I suppose you would say that Wolves just about won the first half on points after they had smashed three good shots against goalkeeper Veres' body. Aside from this, they couldn't break down the visitors defensive system, which was one of the coolest under pressure ever seen at Molineux. The Hungarians took the lead in the 6th minute, Palotas whipping the ball past the diving Bert Williams following some excellent work by world-famous centre-forward Hidegkuti. In the end, it was left to a young amateur, Portsmouth schoolboy Pat Neil, making his debut for Wolves, to save Wolves' blushes and their proud unbeaten record under the Molineux floodlights. He scored the equaliser 10 minutes after the visitors had gone one up. Hooper took a corner, which Veres palmed away, but only to the unmarked Neil, who had drifted outside the goal-area: his smartly hit shot passed through the ruck of players to beat Veres to his left. Neil scored again the following Saturday in the 3-2 win over Manchester City at Maine Road. He played in only three more first-team games, his final appearance coming against Everton on 29 December 1956. The cool, calculating football of Red Banner saw them all too frequently guilty of trying one pass too many; clever stuff, but too slow for our tastes. At half-time, the talented Hidegkuti was replaced by Karasz. The game wasn't exactly dull; there were chances at both ends. Both goalkeepers acquitted themselves well, making a string of acrobatic saves, but I guess that the solemnity of the occasion, set against the backdrop of the Russian crushing of the Hungarian uprising, was really responsible for the fare served up that night. The day after the match, the Hungarians were on their way to Vienna, where their future movements would be dictated by the course of political events in their stricken country.

Wolves' team at Molineux: Williams; Showell, Harris; Slater, Wright, Flowers; Hooper, Mason, Murray (Hancocks), Broadbent, Neil.
Red Banner (M.T.K.): Veres; J. Kovacs, F. I. Kovacs; I. Kovacs, Borzsei, Sipos; Sandor, Palotas, Hidegkuti (Karasz), Molnar, Szimcasak.
Referee: Mr Arthur Ellis (Halifax)
Score: Wolves 1, Red Banner 1
Wolves' scorer: amateur Pat Neil
Red Banner scorer: Palotas
Attendance: 43,540

Molineux, with North Street in the foreground.

Five days earlier, on 5 December 1956, Molineux had played host to a World Cup qualifier, England versus Denmark, which England won 5-2. I watched this wonderful game from the South Bank, along with 54,082 others, sometimes perched precariously on the wall near the refreshment kiosk. It was great to see many of the Busby Babes playing, all 5 England goals coming from two of the Red Devils: Tommy Taylor with 3, and Dudley-born Duncan Edwards with 2. On their way to winning their group, England also beat Ireland 5-1 at Wembley and Denmark 4-1 in Copenhagen, and drew 1-1 with the Republic of Ireland in Dublin to qualify for the 1958 World Cup Finals, which were to be held in Sweden.

The 1956/57 season became infamous for a bizarre Molineux incident, when in the 6th minute of their FA Cup 4th-round clash with Third Division (South) Bournemouth on 26 January, Wolves' Eddie Stuart and opposing left-winger Reg Cutler crashed into a goalpost, snapping it clean in two. The game eventually restarted after running repairs had been carried out, Wolves lost 1-0 and, yes, it was Reg Cutler that scored Bournemouth's goal; the fans all thought the game should have been abandoned – Wolves might have won next time. Apparently before their next-round match against Spurs, Bournemouth manager Freddie Cox received a warning letter telling his team to 'cut out the commando stuff you used against Wolves – or we will do the same to you and your boys'. They beat Tottenham 3-1 to reach the quarter-finals, only to lose 2-1 to 10-man Manchester United, and as far as I know the threatened rough stuff never materialised. The goalposts collapsed again a few years later on 25 August 1973. This time it was Norwich goalkeeper Kevin Keelan who knocked them down, in the process getting himself in a right tangle, net-wise.

Programme from England v. Denmark.

An interesting piece was included in the programme notes for Wolves' game against Manchester United on 16 March 1957, the day I first entered Molineux via the front door. The article was headed: ENTERTAINMENT TAX. It informed the fans of the following:

> The Football League has made representations to the Chancellor of the Exchequer for the abolition or reduction of duty on Football Matches. The following is where the money you pay for your football, goes. From every £100 taken at Molineux:

ENTERTAINMENT TAX	£18	0	0
Referee and Linesmen	£1	0	0
Printing, Posting & Advertising	£1	0	0
Checkers and Gatemen	£2	0	0
Police	£2	10	0
Visitors Share	£17	0	0
Football League Share	£3	0	0
	£44	10	0

THE CLUB IS LEFT WITH ONLY £55 10s 0d of every £100

Only one match is staged each fortnight, but the club has to pay weekly, Wages, Rates and all the administration expenses involved in running a Football League Club. During the last three years Wolves have paid in Entertainment Tax:

1953–54	£24,027
1954–55	£28,645
1955–56	£23,989
GRAND TOTAL	£76,661

That was the end of the piece! No further comments or any other form of statement. It's interesting to get this small insight of the club's 1957 finances.

In March 1957, Wolves travelled to Spain for the first time. They were to take on Valencia in their Mestella Stadium on the 19th in the first leg of a two-legged friendly. The game kicked-off in front of 65,000 screaming Spaniards, all celebrating the St Joseph's Day festival. Valencia F.C. were 3-times Spanish Cup Winners, and finalists a total of 7 times, the last time having been 3 years earlier when they beat Barcelona 4-2. They had also won the Spanish League on four occasions, so they certainly had a top-draw footballing pedigree. A bone-dry bumpy pitch and a light ball provided a couple of headaches for Wolves, along with the fact that the temperature was in the high eighties. The Spaniards played a slick brand of football, full of fast interchanges between players well-versed in the skills of moving into space created by their superb positional intuition – hot stuff in more ways than one! Wolves were thumped 3-1, Peter Broadbent scoring Wolves' equaliser after Pla had put the home team in front after 36 minutes. After the break, Argentinian trialist Seaone scored in the 68th minute, Mano wrapping it up for Valencia on 72 minutes. As I said, it was the March fiesta in Valencia, and the locals certainly were celebrating before, during and after this game. Stan Cullis remarked that the standard of refereeing was ridiculous, complaining that the Spanish referee had blown his whistle for any heavy bodily contact or when a foot was raised above knee-height.

Wolves' team in Valencia: Finlayson; Stuart, Harris; Clamp, Wright, Flowers; Hooper, Broadbent, Murray (Bonson), Booth, Deeley.
Valencia: Eizaguirre; Marital, Quincoces; Pasieguito, Sandra, Puchades; Mano, Suertes, Wilkes, Pla (Padron), Segui.

The next floodlit spectacular at Molineux came five days later.

Wolves 4 Borussia Dortmund 3
Floodlit Friendly at Molineux

Wolves took on and beat German aces Borussia Dortmund 4-3 in a thrilling game on Wednesday 27 March 1957, kick-off 7.15 p.m. Borussia came to Molineux with a reputation as one of the best teams in Europe for coming from behind to win a game, and nearly did so on this occasion, their *blitzkrieg*-style finish raising all kinds of worries for the home team and supporters. Borussia sometimes attacked at breakneck speed, timing many of their runs to near-perfection. In the final half-hour they played a gorgeous combination of slick football, penetrative one-touch passing, and an unbelievable speed of movement, coupled with an at times astounding degree of intuitive anticipation. The marvellous interplay between their players was certainly fascinating to watch. I guess it was characteristic of the continental style of football – dangerous and often audacious. The Germans pulled back from 4-1 down to 4-3. Only an unlucky rebound from a post preventing them from earning a draw. Despite being good in the closing stages of matches, Borussia didn't start too well. Two minutes after the start Peter Broadbent's marvellous run took him between two defenders, allowing him to calmly slot the ball home. Soon afterwards, centre-half Michailck headed Mullen's goal-bound effort off the line with Kwiatkowski beaten. It was one-way traffic towards the visitors' goal. Then the big keeper saved Broadbent's fine shot to surprisingly keep the score at the interval to 1-0. Totally against the run of play, and in only their second attack of the game, Borussia equalised. Billy Wright's attempted headed clearance failed to reach Eddie Stuart, allowing Niepieklo to dart in to clip the ball past Bert Williams. That was the signal for Wolves to step on the gas. Playing in their white reserve shirts, plus white shorts borrowed for the night from Birmingham City, Flowers, Wilshaw, and then Hooper, all brought excellent saves from the Borussia goalkeeper. Kwiatkowski was playing a blinder, but even he couldn't keep out Jimmy Murray's delicate 38th-minute lob or Dennis Wilshaw's sublime effort for Wolves' third after a shrewd short-range pass from Murray had put him through. What happened next was a first at Molineux: a series of odd events involving substitutions. Bobby Mason replaced Murray at half-time, but only lasted 10 minutes. A stud in his leg forced him to leave the pitch, to be replaced by Mick Lill. The visitors also made a change at half-time, Schmidt coming on for the injured Priessler. Moments later, Kelbassa was carried off, and Preissler returned to play out the remainder of the game, Harry Hooper having already made it 4-1 to Wolves. The change of line-up seemed to spur on the Germans. In the 62nd minute Schmidt beat Stuart and swept the ball into Wolves net to make it 4-2. On 70 minutes Niepieklo scored his second of the night, and suddenly it was 4-3; twenty minutes left and Wolves had definitely taken their foot off the pedal. Peters silenced the crowd when he crashed in a fierce goal-bound shot. For a split-second we held our breath, and then breathed a sigh of relief as the ball smashed against the inside of Bert's far post. Fortunately, the ball rebounded into Williams' arms as he turned to follow the flight of the ball. (Many years later, in the 1972/73 FA Cup semi-final at Hillsborough, John Richards' shot was almost a replay of this.) Wolves ran out 4-3 winners in what was a hugely entertaining game, worthy to be remembered as one of Wolves' great floodlit encounters. I dread to think what might have happened if the Germans had occasionally slowed down the pace of their attacking, they might have managed to round off some of their exquisite play with goals – at times they were probably moving too fast to score! But then again, their dash and artistic use of the ball might have suffered, and they might have beaten us, and that wouldn't have done at all, would it?

Wolves' team at Molineux: Williams; Stuart, Tether; Slater, Wright, Flowers; Hooper, Murray (Mason, Lill), Wilshaw, Broadbent, Mullen.
Borussia Dortmund: Kwiatkowski; Burgsmuller, Sandmann; Schlebrowski, Michalick, Bracht; Peters, Preissler, Kelbassa (Schmidt), Niepieklo, Kapitulski.
Referee: Mr Mervyn Griffiths (Wales) who cut a sartorial dash by wearing an all-maroon strip.
Score: Wolves 4, Borussia Dortmund 3
Wolves' scorers: Peter Broadbent, Jimmy Murray, Dennis Wilshaw, Harry Hooper.
Scorers for Dortmund: Niepieklo (2), Schmidt
Attendance: 26,900

Now for the Molineux leg against the footballing Señors from Valencia.

Wolves 3 Valencia 0
Floodlit Friendly at Molineux

The return match against the Spanish Grandees from Valencia was played at Molineux on the night of Wednesday 10 April 1957, kick-off 7.15 p.m. Apparently, referring to the previous month's game, the Spanish newspapers had proclaimed, 'Buena victoria del Valencia', and 'Leccio teorica de futbol de los Ingles'. I'll leave it to each reader to make his or her own translation. When the Valencia officials and players had inspected the Molineux pitch, they were amazed and a little dismayed to see the sprinklers in full flow. After receiving assurances that the pitch would be in perfect condition for the game they were placated, but probably not entirely convinced that their hosts weren't up to something. This was Wolves thirteenth match under floodlights – 'unlucky for some' and all that – 'no problemento!' After a brief scare in the first minute there were no worries this time as Wolves ran out 3-0 winners. A mistake by Ron Flowers almost got the Spaniards off to a great start; his under-hit back-pass let in Iborra, who somehow contrived to miss from close range. The skilful Spaniards flattered to deceive, primarily Spanish internationals Mano and Fuertes who combined well on the right a number of times, but to little effect. Valencia had possession of the ball for long periods, particularly in midfield, but like Borussia Dortmund, tended to over-pass the ball when a through ball might have been a more positive choice. Unlike the game in Spain, when almost every attempt at a tackle was given as a foul, this time a good referee was in charge, Arthur Ellis deeming that Wolves' hard but fair and generally uncompromising tackling

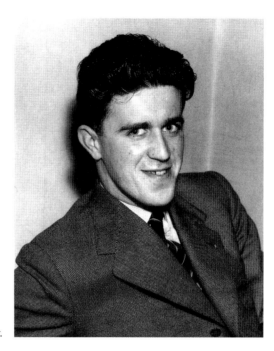

Wolves winger Harry Hooper.

was definitely legal. The ferocity of some of the tackles that went unpunished probably owed a great deal to the determination of the Wolves players to reverse the previous result against Valencia. Young Scot Bobby Thomson made his first-team debut at inside-right, heading in Wolves first on 9 minutes with a lovely flick, then scoring his second just before the interval. Eddie Clamp wrapped up the game and the tie for Wolves with an excellent shot from a 77th-minute free-kick that was rolled back to him by Peter Broadbent. With a little more luck Wolves might have scored more goals. Goalkeeper Eizaguirre made a couple of saves from Harry Hooper, and both Norman Deeley and Dennis Wilshaw went close to adding to the home side's tally. Broadbent claimed that one effort had in fact crossed the line before Areta cleared. George Showell, standing in for Eddie Stuart, had another steady game, and of course, as ever, Billy Wright was commanding at the heart of Wolves' defence. I guess the fans would have preferred the Spaniards to provide a little more excitement, but in the end we were happy with a 3-0 victory on the night and a 4-3 aggregate win over the two legs.

Incidentally, Bobby Thomson scored again 3 days later, in the 2-0 win over Newcastle, but never played for Wolves' first team again.

Wolves' team at Molineux: Williams; Showell, Harris, Clamp, Wright, Flowers; Hooper, Thomson, Wilshaw, Broadbent, Deeley.
Valencia: Eizaguirre; Piques, Mestre; Pasieguita, Quincoces, Sendra; Mano, Fuertes, Iborra, Areta (Pla), Vila.
Referee: Mr Arthur Ellis (Halifax)
Score: Wolves 3, Valencia 0
Wolves' scorers: Bobby Thomson (2), Eddie Clamp 1
Attendance: 25,310

In the close-season, Johnny Hancocks retired; he was 38 years old. Sad for me, because he was one of my all-time favourite players. In 1956/57 Harry Hooper had taken over Johnny's right-wing berth in the first eleven, but the little man wasn't through yet, I remember watching him play for the reserves, still the darling of the fans, scoring 24 goals in the Central League that season. At 5ft 4in, Johnny Hancocks was one of the smallest players around; however, he packed an explosive shot in his size 4 boots. Johnny's record was incredible for a winger. In all competitions he scored 168 goals in 378 senior games for Wolves. He joined Walsall just before the start of the Second World War, and signed for Wolves in May 1946 for a fee of £4,000. This great player won three full England caps, scoring twice on his international debut. He finally left Wolves at the age of 38, when he moved to Wellington Town as player-manager in the 1957 close-season. Johnny Hancocks died 19 February 1994, 2 months short of his 75th birthday.

In the same close-season, Bert Williams, Wolves' marvellous and ever-popular keeper, affectionately nicknamed 'The Cat', hung up his gloves after making 420 senior appearances. Another Walsall Town find, the acrobatic Bert joined Wolves for a fee of £3,500 in September 1945, making his debut that month. He played in goal for England in 24 internationals, including at the 1950 World Cup Finals, where he lined up with Billy Wright. Bert kept goal in all 3 of England's group matches, including the ill-fated and humiliating 1-0 defeat by the USA.

Another Wolves stalwart, centre-half and left-back Bill Shorthouse, decided to retire through injury in the summer of 1957. Bill had been Wolves' captain before Billy Wright took on the role, playing in 376 senior games and scoring 1 goal. A member of the British Expeditionary Force, he was wounded in the Normandy D-Day landings. In his long career at Wolves he had the distinction of never having been dropped. He went on to become coach of the England Youth team, and in 1980 coached Aston Villa to their FA Youth Cup triumph.

1957/58

In 1957 Wolves' Board decided that a new set of floodlights was to be installed, the old lights going to a local non-league club; this time the cost was £25,000. In the course of the previous four years, Wolves had proudly established themselves among the leaders in the presentation of floodlit football. It was time to once again demonstrate that Wolves were in tune with the changing times and fresh ideas coming into the game. Additionally, the demand for even better standards of lighting was at the forefront of their thinking – therefore, as you would expect, a lot of serious thought went into the development of the new lighting scheme. Wolves' directors were confident that the four new and taller towers, each holding a battery of 48 lamps – the original towers had proved to be a little too low – would provide lighting comparable with the best in the country – they were right. Tottenham Hotspur had the honour of becoming Wolves' first victims under the new lights when they came to Molineux on Wednesday evening, 2 October 1957. The match kicked-off at 7 p.m. with a rampant Wolves winning 4-0.

Two weeks later, Wolves fans were licking their lips at the prospect of seeing the mighty two-times European Champions Real Madrid at Molineux; we didn't mind paying a little extra for this one.

Wolves 3 Real Madrid 2
Floodlit Friendly at Molineux

Spanish champions Real Madrid, with their mouth-watering team of Spanish, French and South American footballing wizards, were entertained on Thursday 17 October 1957. The Spanish giants had dominated the first two years of the European Champions Cup, and so would be a stern test for Wolves. Real Madrid had been developed into a truly huge club by Señor Santiago Bernabeu, whose vision transformed a club with 16,000 supporters into a footballing colossus. It was he that spotted the vast money-making potential of a premier European competition, and he set out to develop the financial clout required to buy the top players in the world. European Champions two years running and also holders of the Latin Cup – a competition between the champions of Spain, Portugal, Italy and France – Real were also holders of the Spanish League Cup. So, a bit good, then! Missing from the Wolves line-up would be Billy Wright, who was due to skipper England against Wales two days later. The honour of filling his vacant

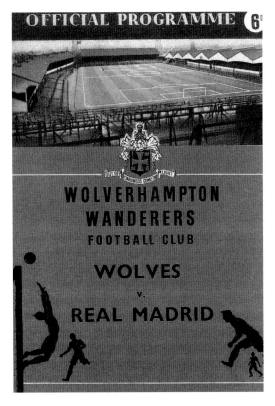

Programme from Wolves v. Real Madrid.

MOLINEUX GROUNDS, WOLVERHAMPTON

Thursday, October 17th, 1957 : Kick-off 7·35 p.m.

WOLVES v. REAL MADRID

Other players on whom our visitors can call for tonight's game include:
Dominguez (goalkeeper), Atienza (back), Santamaria (centre-half back),
Marsal, Ruiz and Santisteban (half backs), and Joseito (winger).

Referee—M. GUIGUE (France)

Linesman—Yellow Flag   Linesman—Red Flag
P. N. CARR (Redditch)   A. SMITH (Stoke-on-Trent)

position fell to George Showell. Sadly, or should I say, thankfully, the legendary Ferenc Puskas hadn't yet joined Real. In one of the most thrilling games witnessed at Molineux – it had everything but the kitchen sink – Real's footballers unveiled their wonderful silky skills. Their sheer artistry with the ball was fabulous to see as they gave a display of precision football that was up to slide-rule standards. Add to this the controlled athleticism of their body swerves, coupled with the marvellously intuitive runs off the ball to create space for their colleagues to move into – and you have a recipe for heady stuff indeed. However, it was not enough! Wolves came from behind to beat the Spanish maestros with a display of accurate long-range precision passing and much faster attacking and approach play – the comparison between the two very different styles was a delight to witness. Wolves started in fine fettle, going into the match in confident mood after their recent victories over foreign opposition. Unfortunately, as with Honved, Wolves allowed the Spaniards to get into the game, playing some excellent football in the process. The visitors probed away at Wolves' defence and finally got their reward when Joseito's corner was powered home by the impressive Marsal after 25 minutes; his bullet-like header would have done justice to Roy Swinbourne. The Molineux faithful were soon back in good voice when 7 minutes after the break Broadbent equalised to make it 1-1. Finlayson punted an enormous kick almost to the Real penalty area, which Murray headed on for Broadbent to lob home. On the hour, Wolves took the lead. Norman Deeley took a corner from which Murray scored Wolves' second with a brilliant downward header. However, Wolves' fans had a nervy final 20 minutes after Marsal scored a second for Real, sending the ball past Finlayson in fine style with a rasping shot on 71 minutes. Fortunately the game turned out to have a happy ending when Dennis Wilshaw calmly lifted the ball over the goalkeeper from Mullen's corner with 10 minutes remaining. Wolves' trademark solid defending was rewarded when French *gendarme* referee Monsieur Guigue blew the final whistle, the Molineux side running out 3-2 winners, having beaten the pride of Europe to win respect and enhance their growing reputation as one of the greatest club sides around at that time. On that notable evening, George Showell, playing in place of Billy Wright, pretty much subdued the famous Alfredo Di Stefano, marking the Argentine out of the game for long periods. However on the occasions when Di Stefano got the ball in space he showed all of his magnificent ball-skills – worth every penny of the entrance money on their own. His best goal efforts were a superb volley that narrowly cleared the bar, and a shot that brought a diving save from Malcolm Finlayson.

> Wolves' team at Molineux: Finlayson; Stuart, Harris; Clamp, Showell, Flowers; Deeley, Broadbent, Murray, Wilshaw, Mullen.
> Real Madrid: Dominguez; Atienza (Marquitos), Lesmes; Santisteban, Santamaria, Zarraga (Ruiz); Joseito (Kopa), Kopa (Marsal), Di Stefano, Marsal (Rail), Gento (Joseito).
> Referee: M. Guigue (France)
> Score: Wolves 3, Real Madrid 2
> Wolves' scorers: Peter Broadbent, Jimmy Murray, Dennis Wilshaw
> Scorer for Real Madrid: Marsal (2)
> Attendance: 55,169

1957/58 was the season that Wolves provided the entire England half-back line for a friendly against Russia in Moscow: Eddie Clamp, Billy Wright and Bill Slater. Yes! Half-back lines – remember them?

The next three matches against non-English opposition were all played away from home, the first against top Belgian team Anderlecht, who showed Wolves a thing or two as they won 2-0 in Brussels on 20 October 1957. After this setback, Wanderers travelled to Scotland for a tilt at Hibernian on 28 October 1957, winning 3-2 in Edinburgh to regain some of their lost pride. Then it was off to Spain for the return match against Real Madrid under the fantastic Bernabeu floodlights. Talk about the rain in Spain, it absolutely chucked it down for the whole game. Wet or not, having been beaten at Molineux, the Spanish champions were out for revenge. On the memorable night of 11 December 1957, in the Bernabeu Stadium in Madrid, Wolves withstood heavy pressure, producing a fighting performance that saw them hold the mighty Real 2-2. Once again it was George Showell, a 50th-minute substitute for Eddie Clamp, who shackled the great Di Stefano. The home team's proud five-year record of being unbeaten in Madrid was in danger of going out the window. With a little more luck Wolves might have won this meeting of football giants. The only goal of the first half came when Bobby Mason put Wolves in front just before the half-hour with a powerful header. Twenty-five minutes after the restart the Spaniards got the benefit of a crazy decision from the match officials. Mateo was at least three yards offside when he grabbed the equaliser – obviously shades of 'homer' refereeing. However, the next goal was a product of real skill, Alfredo

Real Madrid rosette.

Di Stefano putting Real ahead in the 70th minute after running into a gap in Wolves' defence to slot home Kopa's defence-splitting cross. Suddenly, things began to look good for the home team, until fittingly, Jimmy Mullen's cross was diverted into the net by a defender's boot to ensure that justice was well and truly done – an honourable draw in every sense. In the opinion of everyone, except maybe the Real Madrid supporters, the European Champions were lucky to get away with a draw. Biased refereeing plus a rank offside goal robbed Wolves of outright victory; instead they were forced to settle for a moral victory. Wolves' team in Madrid was Finlayson; Stuart, Harris; Clamp (Showell), Wright, Flowers; Deeley, Broadbent, Murray, Mason, Mullen.

The tragic scenes of the Munich air crash on 6 February 1958, brought tears to many a football fan's eye. To lose so many young and gifted stars and starlets from one club in a single disaster was devastating. Playing in their second European Cup, Manchester United's 'Busby Babes' had again won their way through to the semi-finals, beating Red Star Belgrade in Yugoslavia. After landing in Munich to refuel, the twin-engined Elizabethan aeroplane carrying them home from Belgrade failed in its third attempt to get airborne in a snowstorm. The plane was unable to gain altitude, left the runway, hit a house and burst into flames. A tragedy for the whole country as well as for the world of football.

On 5 April 1958, Wolves entertained Portsmouth at Molineux on their way to the First Division title. Playing at number 9 for Pompey was a young Irishman by the name of Derek Dougan. Wolves won 1-0, courtesy of an Eddie Clamp goal. Earlier in the year, Dougan had played at inside-left for Portsmouth in the 5-1 FA Cup 4th-round thumping dished out by Wolves on 15 January 1956. The following season, as Wolves retained their Championship title, Dougan again played at centre-forward for Portsmouth, this time catching Wolves in real festive spirit on 27 December 1958. All Wolves gave them was a good pasting, as they hammered Pompey 7-0. Hat-tricks from Colin Booth and Norman Deeley, plus a goal from Des Horne emphasised Wolves' superiority. Twenty-four hours before, on Boxing Day, Wolves had thumped Portsmouth 5-3 at Fratton Park, with goals from Peter Broadbent, who bagged a hat-trick, and one each from Colin Booth and Norman Deeley. I wonder if the Doog remembered these results when he signed for Wolves in March 1967. Incidentally, Portsmouth were relegated at the end of this season, and Wolves were Champions for the third time.

Wolves, minus Wright, Slater, Clamp and Broadbent, who were all on England duty, headed for Belgium again in May 1958, this time to play in the International Soccer Tournament in Brussels. In the opening game on 14 May, Anderlecht thrashed Juventus 4-1. On the same Wednesday, Wolves met Beerschot in Antwerp and were beaten 2-1 in a poor game that they should have won, Booth netting for Wolves. The next day they faced Juventus in the play-off for third place. This was the first time that they were to play against the Italian giants. Wolves lost 5-1 in Brussels' Heysel Stadium having had an abundance of excellent chances which they failed to take, in contrast with Juve who showed real class in front of goal, Welsh legend John Charles scoring for the Italians after 10 minutes, Sivori grabbing a hat-trick, and Hamrin getting the other. Wolves' goal was scored by Colin Booth. The match took place on 15 May. Wolves' team for the Juventus match was Finlayson; Jones, Harris; Howells, Flowers, Thomson; Deeley, Booth, Murray, Henderson, Mullen. Anderlecht beat Beerschot 2-0 in the final – Wolves came last!

Wolves won the First Division title for the second time in season 1957/58. The following season would see Wolves accept an invitation to play in the European Cup.

In the summer of 1958, the World Cup Finals were hosted by Sweden. Again Wolves provided players for the England squad: captain Billy Wright at the heart of the defence, naturally, but now he was flanked by his two Molineux teammates: Eddie Clamp at right-hal, and Bill Slater at left-half. In this tournament each nation played three group games, with these three Wolves stalwarts playing in each England game: 8 June, 2-2 against the Soviet Union in Gothenburg; 11 June, 0-0 against Brazil, also in Gothenburg; and 15 June, 2-2 against Austria in Boras. After three draws, England had to play the Soviets in a play-off for a place in the quarter-finals. Sadly, Eddie Clamp missed this game, being replaced by Ronnie Clayton; however, Wolves were still represented by three players when Peter Broadbent took Bobby Robson's place at inside-right to win his first of 7 full caps. Unfortunately, England went down 1-0 and were eliminated; what might have happened if England had not been deprived of the skills of the Manchester United players tragically killed or injured in the Munich air crash.

Meanwhile, back at Molineux nine months later, Wolves were scheduled to entertain the South Africans once again.

Billy Wright in action in the 1950s.
Johnny Hancocks looks on.

1958/59

Wolves 1 South Africa International XI 0
Floodlit Friendly at Molineux

The night of Monday 29 September 1958 saw Wolves take on a South African international XI at Molineux for the second time. Billy Wright and Peter Broadbent had been selected by England for the match with Northern Ireland in Belfast, and so had to miss this re-enactment of Wolves' first-ever floodlit match at Molineux, 5 years ago almost to the day, or more correctly, to the night. An extremely low and long-suffering crowd witnessed a disappointing and one-sided game. Many left before full-time, others stayed on the terraces after the final whistle to vent their feelings at Wolves' poor performance, many by cheering the Springboks. The Wolves players certainly didn't have on their shooting boots as shot after shot hit the woodwork, legs, bodies and various other barriers. Goalkeeper Smith earned some applause with a display of acrobatic skill; even so, one would have expected any one of Wolves' Central League team to score against him. Wolves had three South Africans in their team: Des Horne, Eddie Stuart and Cliff Durandt, and it was Horne who scored Wolves' goal with a fine left-foot volley. Otherwise, miss after miss by a failing Wolves forward line conspired to frustrate the home fans. Even wing-halves Bill Slater and Eddie Clamp missed chances to score in dramatic fashion. Called upon to make a rare save, Malcolm Finlayson took a kick on the head from Salton for his trouble. Later in the game, little Warren should have done better with the two golden chances that came his way; he really ought to have put at least one of them away. This was one of the few occasions when the crowd didn't go home happy. Not a good night at all!

Wolves' team at Molineux: Finlayson; Stuart, Jones; Slater, Showell, Clamp; Lill, Durandt, Murray, Mason, Horne.
South Africa: Smith; Williams (Martin), Dennyschen; Hauser, Petersen, Rufus; Hurly, Scott, Salton, Warren, Barratt.
Referee: Mr W. Clements (West Bromwich)
Score: Wolves 1, South Africa 0
Wolves' scorer: Des Horne
Attendance: 13,511

By winning the First Division Championship in 1957/58, Wolves qualified to play in the European Champions Cup, the Football League having overcome their previous aversion to this competition a couple of years earlier. This would be the first time that Wolves were to play in a knockout European competition – they didn't start too well! Details of away legs are now included in addition to the games at Molineux.

Wolves 2 FC Schalke 04 2
European Champions Cup, 2nd round, 1st leg, home

In the 1958/59 European Cup, Wolves received a bye in the first round, and so went into the hat for the second-round draw that pitted them against FC Schalke 04 of West Germany, who had beaten Boldklub of Copenhagen in the preliminary round. The first leg was played at Molineux on Wednesday, 12 November 1958, in front of a good-sized crowd of almost 46,000 fans. Wolves had been disappointed that all of the tickets hadn't been sold prior to the game, therefore, in view of this, a number of cash turnstiles were opened for payment on the night; their decision proved to be a shrewd one. UEFA had appointed a trio of Belgians to officiate at the match, but on the way to Wolverhampton they were involved in a car accident; fortunately none were injured.

The best word to describe this game from Wolves' point of view was frustrating! Schalke were a very beatable team despite being champions of their country, and there is no doubt that Wolves should have won handsomely. Instead, in 90 action-packed minutes, where they had at least 80 per cent of the play, they squandered chance after chance in the manner of the game against South Africa six weeks earlier. Some poor early defending allowed Schalke to grab a shock lead through centre-forward Gunther Siebert; his goal lit a fire under Wolves' attacks. In the first 10 minutes the crowd witnessed two misses each by Mullen and Jackson, followed by one each from Deeley and Flowers, as Wolves launched attack after attack but nothing got past the reserve German goalkeeper, thus, at the interval, Wolves went in 1-0 down. Three minutes after the break, Peter Broadbent thankfully equalised to put Wolves back in it. Ron Flowers then had two good attempts smothered by Loweg before Allan Jackson headed narrowly over. In previous games that season, Wolves had already tried Henderson, Murray and Showell as leader of their attack, now 20-year-old Allan Jackson became the fourth, and most surprised, player to pull on the famous number 9 shirt, having started the season as seventh-choice centre-forward. In another series of onslaughts, first Bobby Mason and then Norman Deeley dragged shots across the German goal. The tense crowd began to wonder if it wasn't another of those nights when Wolves wouldn't score more than once, until up popped Broadbent to capture the lead with a well-taken header. Now surely the floodgates would open, but no, Deeley lifted an easy chance high into the terraces, missing the goal completely when it was easier to score. And so it continued, until late in the game when the Schalke captain Berni Klodt slipped a clever ball to Willi Koslowski, who scored a priceless second away goal with comparative ease, and that, as they say, was that! Once again Wolves had completely dominated a match, but this time, could only manage a 2-2 draw, a disappointing result that made the second leg in West Germany a very tough proposition. One which would surely result in the kind of fight for survival that everyone had hoped to avoid.

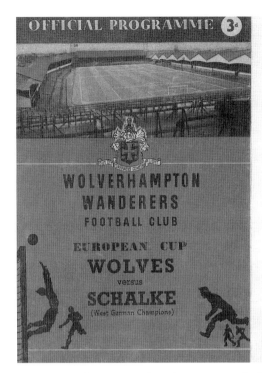

Front cover and teams page from the programme for Wolves v. Schalke.

Wolves' team at Molineux: Sidebottom; Stuart, Harris; Slater, Wright, Flowers; Deeley, Broadbent, Jackson, Mason, Mullen.

Schalke 04: Loweg; Brocker, Laszig; Borrutta, Kreuz, Karnhof; Koslowski, Koerdel, Siebert, Jagielski, Klodt.

No substitutes were allowed in the European Cup at this time.

Referee: Monsieur Albert Alsteen (Belgium)

Score: Wolves 2, FC Schalke 04 2

Wolves' scorer: Peter Broadbent (2)

Scorers for Schalke: Siebert, Koslowski

Attendance: 45,767

FC Schalke 04 2 Wolves 1
European Champions Cup, 2nd round, 2nd leg, away

Reports stated that 1,000 extra police had been called in to control traffic and prevent congestion on the roads around the stadium in Gelsenkirchen, near Essen, West Germany. The town is known in the area as 'The City of a Thousand Fires,' and is the home of Schalke 04. Wolves' away leg with Schalke was played there on Tuesday 18 November 1958 – it wasn't a good night for us. Our beloved Wolves were about to play a game in which their 'luck' had already burned away. Bill Slater was busy with his duties at Birmingham University and couldn't make the trip so Ron Flowers deputised. Schalke scored two goals

73

from only four chances before the interval as Wolves woefully rued their ill fortune, first on 12 minutes when the ball ricocheted off Harris into the path of Heinz Koerdel, who made no mistake from close-range, then in the 39th minute, when the ball span out of Finlayson's arms for Siebert to slip the ball into the net. Jimmy Mullen and Bobby Mason both unluckily hit the post, and watched as other almost certain goal-bound efforts were scrambled off the line, to leave Wolves two down at the break. Apparently, the Gelsenkirchen tradition was to create 'The Ceremony of The Thousand Fires'. All the lights in the stadium were switched off, and in the ensuing darkness, to the sound of the local miners' band playing traditional hymns, all of the crowd lit a match or lighter to produce what must have been a truly magical effect. Maybe it was this magnificent spectacle that inspired Wolves, because within 3 minutes of the restart, Norman Deeley crossed the ball, and Allan Jackson took Mason's subsequent pass in his stride before striking the ball home beautifully. Now captain Billy Wright, along with Ron Flowers and a reported 3,000 cheering British servicemen drove Wolves on in a magnificent assault on the German goal. Unfortunately, the Germans responded with a display of outstanding defending. Wolves just couldn't find the move that would open up the home team's stout defence for the equaliser. And so, Wolves, their hopes of European glory extinguished at the first hurdle, departed from this competition, losing 2-1 on the night, 4-3 on aggregate, having put on a second-half show to bring credit to the name of Wolves. Really, the tie had been lost in the first-leg at Molineux, so Wolves couldn't complain.

Billy Wright was due at Buckingham Palace two days later – no, not to explain the reason for Wolves' failure to the Queen, but for a formal luncheon. The Schalke camp accused Wolves' players of over-physical play, and in a tit-for-tat, Wolves complained about the Germans' almost constant time-wasting.

> Wolves' team in West Germany: Finlayson, Stuart, Harris; Clamp, Wright, Flowers; Deeley, Broadbent, Jackson, Mason, Mullen.
> Schalke 04: Loweg; Brocker, Laszig; Borrutta, Kreuz, Karnhof; Koslowski, Koerdel, Siebert, Jagielski, Klodt.
> Referee: M. Versypp (Belgium)
> Score: Wolves 1, FC Schalke 04 2 (Wolves lost 3-4 on aggregate)
> Wolves' scorer: Jackson
> Schalke scorers: Koerdel, Siebert
> Attendance: 40,000

So, Wolves first 'official' trip into Europe was a disaster, but would the lessons learned from this disappointing experience be of use in the future? The final of the competition was played in Stuttgart's Neckarstadion in front of a crowd of 72,000, Real Madrid beating French aces Reims 3-0 to retain the trophy.

The 1958/59 league season itself was another great success for the Molineux marvels, with Wolves again finishing as champions.

On the left-wing of Wolves' famous teams of the 1950s was Newcastle-born Jimmy Mullen, born 6 January 1923. In his Wolves career he made 486 appearances, scoring 112 goals. Jimmy also won 12 full England caps. He made his Wolves debut on 18 February 1939 at the tender age of 16 years and 43 days. Jimmy scored against Switzerland in the 1954 World Cup Finals, and had the distinction of being England's first-ever substitute against Belgium in Brussels in 1950; he scored 15 minutes after coming on. He died in October 1987 aged 64, a true gentleman in every sense of the word.

1959/60

The start of the 1959/60 season was marred when Wolves legend Billy Wright dropped a bombshell by announcing his retirement, aged 35. He reputedly told a reporter, 'Yes, this is it. I have had a wonderful run with a wonderful club and I want to finish while I am still at the top.' Stan Cullis was reported to have said that under no circumstances would he ask Billy to play in the Central League team, he wanted him to finish as a first-team player. Billy played his farewell match at Molineux in Wolves colours in the pre-season charity practice match on Saturday, 8 August 1959. Although Billy's news was bad for Wolves it was good for charity, as a larger-than-usual crowd was expected to turn out in honour of their captain. In fact 20,000 fans, twice the usual number, came to Molineux to witness Billy's swansong. The game was an emotional affair, with the players forming a guard of honour. As a mark of respect, Billy was switched from the whites - the second XI – to the colours – the Championship-winning side – for his last Molineux match. The whites won 4-2. Bobby Mason and Jimmy Murray put the colours 2-0 up, but before the interval Barry Stobart pulled one back for the whites. After the break, Des Horne levelled with a penalty, then scored the goal of the match, after Colin Booth had given the whites the lead. The whites' half-back line of Slater, Showell and Kirkham looked every bit as good as the colours' England trio of Clamp, Wright and Flowers. In a later interview Billy Wright acknowledged that he had told reporters the previous April that he reckoned he was good for another season at least, but added that since he had got his England hundred, and had been awarded the CBE, he had thought it over and decided now was the time to quit. He reminded people that Wolves' policy was based upon the development of younger players, and felt that the time had come to make way for George Showell to take his place in the team. He added that one thing he was certain about was that George would make a good job of it. Stan Cullis wanted Billy to take over as his chief coach, with specific responsibility for coaching the club's youngsters. Billy hadn't yet decided, but had confirmed that he would not move to another club. 'How can I play for anyone else after Wolves?' he said. Billy's third benefit cheque, this time for £1,000, was due in October.

What can be said about Billy Wright CBE that hasn't already been said? Another true gentleman, he always had time to sign autographs, always had time for the fans. Voted 'Footballer of the Year' in 1951/52, and runner-up 'European Footballer of the Year' in 1956/57, Billy won everything and achieved everything in his long and illustrious career. He was the rock that Stan Cullis built his team around. Billy Wright died aged 70 on 3 September 1994, a great loss to England and sport in general.

Billy Wright in action for Wolves.

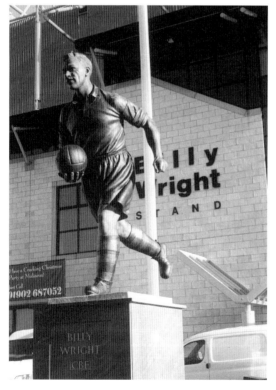

The statue of Billy Wright CBE in front of the Billy Wright Stand, Waterloo Road.

By virtue of having retained the First Division title in 1958/59, Wolves again qualified for the European Champions Cup, this time hoping to recapture some of their devastating league form against foreign opposition – 14 days earlier they had beaten Fulham 9-0 at Molineux. However, after their disappointing performance the previous year they were forced to play a preliminary round before entering the competition proper. This time around, they did a lot better:

A.S.K. Vorwaerts 2 Wolves 1
European Champions Cup, preliminary round,
1st leg, away

In the preliminary round Wolves embarked on a trip behind the Iron Curtain to face A.S.K. Vorwaerts of East Berlin; the initials represent Armeesportklub. This match had been transferred to the spacious and very grassy pitch of the Walter Ulbricht Stadium in East Berlin, as East German Champions Vorwaerts' own ground was deemed to be too small for such a prestigious match. The sell-out 65,000 partisan crowd, including around 1,000 British troops from West Berlin, hoped for good weather as there were no stands to give shelter. Wednesday 30 September 1959, was the eve of the sixth anniversary of Wolves' first floodlit match at Molineux, and coincidentally the eve of the tenth anniversary of the founding of the German Democratic Republic (GDR). Vorwaerts had done their homework after watching Wolves wallop Fulham, and they played a nine-man defence, a formation that Wolves weren't able to cope with. The highly mobile Germans worked hard to keep possession of the ball to deny their opponents the opportunity to show their attacking flair. As part of their plan, Meyer, the Vorwaerts centre-forward, constantly dragged Showell out of the middle, whilst his colleagues prevented Flowers playing his normal attacking game by forcing him to defend. Despite facing this unusual formation, Wolves took the lead after 16 minutes when goalkeeper Spickenagel dropped a long-punt upfield by Gerry Harris. Peter Broadbent out-thought the German defenders and quickly latched on to the loose ball; he moved it to his right and cracked it into the net. The Germans recovered their composure with a display of close marking coupled with some sharp tackling, and Wolves found themselves having to defend fiercely. In the 24th minute the Germans got their reward. Flowers lost possession, allowing Neoldner to race onto the subsequent through-ball to score. Vorwaerts went two-up when Kalinke sent Wirth away on the right wing, his chest-high cross was inch-perfect as Kohle beat Finlayson to the ball to flick it past the big keeper. Midway through the second half Wolves' cause was not helped when Eddie Stuart had to be carried off for treatment after receiving a nasty kick on the shin. He eventually returned, but was limping badly, and was forced to limp along on the touchline. After the game Stuart's leg was X-rayed, and fortunately his injury was less serious than first thought. Norman Deeley tried hard for Wolves, as did Broadbent and Murray, all having good shots well saved by Spickenagel. On the whole though, Wolves' forward play was disappointing. Even so, with a little bit of luck they might have broken through the Germans' resolute defence, which constantly frustrated Wolves with back-pass after back-pass. Even the crowd whistled their disapproval at this tactic. Neither side managed another goal, and so Wolves disappointingly lost this away leg 2-1.

> Wolves' team in East Berlin: Finlayson, Stuart, Harris; Clamp, Showell, Flowers; Lill, Mason, Murray, Broadbent, Deeley.
> Vorwaerts: Spickenagel; Kalinke, Kiupel; Krampe, Unger, Reischelt; Wirth, Meyer, Riese, Neoldner, Kohle.
> Referee: M. Van Nuffel (Belgium)
> Score: Wolves 1, Vorwaerts 2
> Wolves' scorer: Peter Broadbent
> Attendance: 65,000

Wolves 2 A.S.K. Vorwaerts 0
European Champions Cup, preliminary round,
2nd leg, home

The return match was played at Molineux on Wednesday 7 October 1959, in front of an excellent crowd. Having lost the away leg 2-1, fortune favoured the brave when Peter Broadbent and Bobby Mason scored the goals in a 2-0 win to give Wolves the tie 3-2 on aggregate. Wolves' forwards again had no problem hitting the woodwork, several efforts cannoning to safety, none going into the net. The first half proved to be a tense affair, with the Germans determined to hold onto their slender one-goal advantage. The breakthrough eventually came 9 minutes after the break. Wolves started the second half in true aggressive style, snarling with renewed vigour. Spickenagel brought off a great save from Mason, but couldn't hold the ball, which Broadbent smacked home with glee. The Germans decided to change the script and began to attack with some flair, but brave Finlayson was having none of it, saving everything that they fired at him. Somehow we knew Wolves would do it, but had to wait until the 76th minute for the second goal. Broadbent passed to Murray whose lovely crossed ball was easily tapped in by Mason. After the game manager Stan Cullis singled out Malcolm Finlayson for particular praise following the goalie's outstanding display of saving goal-bound shots. The following Saturday saw a tired Wolves team lose 5-1 at Tottenham in the League. Seven days later, Wolves recovered their winning ways, beating Manchester United 3-2 at home.

> Wolves' team at Molineux: Finlayson, Stuart, Harris; Slater, Showell, Flowers; Lill, Mason, Murray, Broadbent, Deeley.
> Vorwaerts: Spickenagel; Kalinke, Kiupel; Krampe, Unger, Reischelt; Wirth, Meyer, Vogt, Neoldner, Kohle.
> Referee: M. Versypp (Belgium)
> Score: Wolves 2, Vorwaerts 0 (Wolves won 3-2 on aggregate)
> Wolves' scorers: Peter Broadbent, Bobby Mason
> Attendance: 55,747

Before the first round proper, Wolves were once again entertained in Glasgow by their old adversaries Celtic – yet another match in their series of games. Played in Glasgow on Monday 12 October 1959, Wolves managed to repeat their earlier victory by winning 2-0. Wolves' scorers that day were Peter Broadbent and Jimmy Murray. Many Wolves fans

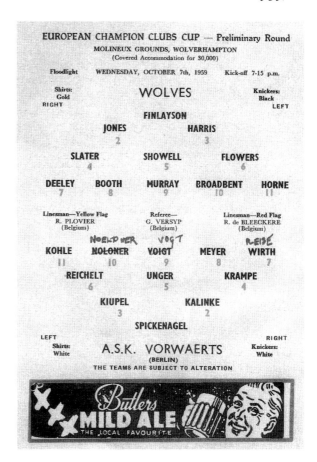

Teams page from the programme
for Wolves v. A.S.K. Vorwaerts.

believed that it was folly to play this friendly just 2 days after emphatically losing 5-1 to Tottenham, especially with the next important match in the European Champions Cup against Red Star Belgrade coming up.

Red Star Belgrade 1 Wolves 1
European Champions Cup, 1st round, 1st leg, away

In the first round proper Wolves faced a 1,300 mile trip to Belgrade, having been drawn against the Yugoslavian champions Red Star. The first leg was played in the aptly named Partizan Stadium, Belgrade, on Wednesday 11 November 1959, kick-off 7.30 p.m. Once again it was left to Wolves to restore English pride on a ground where the previous year Yugoslavia had beaten England by five clear goals. On a brilliant sunny day, another massive crowd watched as Wolves showed tremendous fighting spirit to earn a creditable 1-1 draw. Prior to the match a touch of controversy was added by Red Star's decision to include Dragon Sekularac in their starting line-up at outside-right. Sekularac was currently serving a suspension from Yugoslavian league and cup games for arguing with a referee, although he had played in his customary left-wing position in an international match whilst still under suspension. For some reason Wolves didn't protest about the inclusion of this talented player. This decision nearly backfired on Wolves when in the 7th minute Sekularac brought a good save from Malcolm Finlayson in Wolves goal. The Scot pushed the ball out for a corner, from which Ivan Popovic saw his shot cleared off the line by Eddie Stuart, and then the same player smashed a powerful header against Wolves' bar. These narrow escapes seemed to sting Wolves into action. Red Star weren't ready for the resulting display of aggressive power-play by wing-halves Eddie Clamp and Ron Flowers as Wolves turned up the heat to stun the partisan crowd. George Showell was solid in the middle of defence, and Eddie Stuart and Gerry Harris tackled like demons as Wolves drove on. On 28 minutes Jimmy Murray sent Des Horne clear, and the South African winger centred beautifully for Norman Deeley to score with a neat header. Inevitably, Red Star came back at Wolves. They won a direct free-kick outside the right-hand corner of Wolves' penalty area, which Kostic took. His swerving shot spun out of Finlayson's hands for Red Star's equaliser. This was a tough game, but Wolves determination carried them through. In the second period Spajic almost scored an own-goal when he turned a fierce Horne cross inches past his own post. Horne's speedy wing-play was tremendous, often turning full-back Durkovic inside-out. The match was marred from Wolves' point of view by the controversial performance of the West German referee. Some of his decisions were beyond belief. However, Wolves accepted and overcame this whistle-happy official's 'homer' style of refereeing. Stan Cullis called his handling of the game 'deplorable' after the German had given a foul against Wolves for almost every tackle.

> Wolves' team in Belgrade: Finlayson, Stuart, Harris; Clamp, Showell, Flowers; Deeley, Mason, Murray, Broadbent, Horne.
> Red Star: Beara; Durkovic, Stojanovic; Tasic, Spajic, V. Popovic; Kostic, Sekularac, Zebec, I. Popovic, Rudinski.
> Referee: Herr Wilhelm Omerbann (West Germany)
> Score: Wolves 1, Red Star Belgrade 1
> Wolves' scorer: Norman Deeley
> Scorer for Red Star: Kostic
> Attendance: 45,000

Wolves 3 Red Star Belgrade 1
European Champions Cup, 1st round, 2nd leg, home

The return leg at Molineux was played on Tuesday 24 November 1959. The good news was that there was a change of referee, Herr Asmussen taking over this game. It turned out to be a one-sided affair, with Wolves easily overcoming their Yugoslavian opponents 3-0. The North Bank was lit up by an illuminated red star, borrowed for the occasion from a local cinema and attached to a floodlight pylon. Wolves carried on from where they left off in Belgrade two weeks earlier. To be fair, this was not one of their best performances, but there's no doubt that they once again demonstrated their stamina and fitness with a gutsy display full of determination. Wolves' tough tackling and pursuit of the ball denied Red Star the space they needed to get their slick passing game going. Wolves began

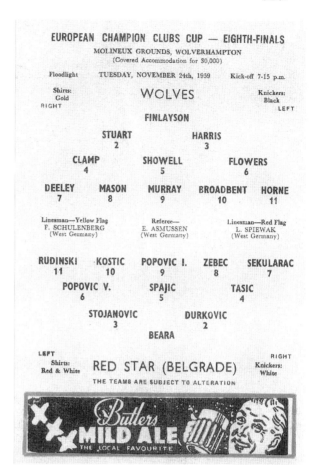

Teams page from the programme for Wolves v. Red Star.

superbly, going ahead early in the game with a bit of a freak goal. On 7 minutes Jimmy Murray latched onto a throw-in from Des Horne, and lofted the ball towards the Yugoslavian goal. The Red Star goalkeeper Beara misjudged this speculative lob and could only watch in horror as the ball bounced behind him and into his net off the upright. Red Star rallied to the attack, Kostic looking particularly dangerous as the home defence made a number of saving tackles. The visitors were looking as if they might yet come out on top. On 25 minutes Malcolm Finlayson showed that he had learned from his mistake in Belgrade. Judging the flight of the ball perfectly, he pulled off a fantastic flying save from another swerving free-kick from Kostic, the ball deflecting high into the South Bank. That's how it stayed until the final 5 minutes of the game, when Bobby Mason netted from a Horne cross following Murray's excellent pass, the little Tipton-born inside-forward calmly side-footing the ball past the goalkeeper. The Yugoslavians now had to throw caution to the wind, leaving big gaps in their defence for Wolves to exploit. Murray had a goal disallowed for offside, again from a cross by Horne. For a time it looked as though Wolves wouldn't score again, but in the last minute Broadbent centred, and there was Mason, virtually unchallenged, to head the ball into the net. Wolves were through to the next round, the quarter-final, after an overwhelming second-half display of power play in which every member of the team fought to win. Tackling, challenging, and blocking every time Red Star tried to get back into the game.

> Wolves' team at Molineux: Finlayson; Stuart, Harris; Clamp, Showell, Flowers; Deeley, Mason, Murray, Broadbent, Horne.
> Red Star: Beara; Durkovic, Stojanovic; Tasic, Spajic, V. Popoviv; Stipic, Maravic, Sekularac, Zebec, Kostic.
> Referee: Herr Erik Asmussen (West Germany)
> Score: Wolves 3, Red Star Belgrade 0
> Wolves' scorers: Bobby Mason (2), Jimmy Murray
> Attendance: 55,519
> Wolves won 4-1 on aggregate.

C.F. Barcelona 4 Wolves 0
European Champions Cup, Quarter Final,
1st leg, away

It was bad luck for Wolves to be drawn against Barcelona at a time when the Spaniards were almost invincible. They'd already beaten CDNA Sofia by an aggregate score of 8-4 in the preliminary round, and AC Milan 7-1 in round 1. The first leg was played at Barcelona's Nou Camp stadium on Wednesda, 10 February 1960, kick-off 7.30 p.m. Barcelona fielded a team of many nationalities: their five principal forwards hailed from Paraguay, Uruguay, Hungary, Brazil and Spain. This contest developed into a pre-match war of nerves as both team managers kept their match tactics to themselves. Despite strong cajoling from the press, neither would announce their team selection until the very last moment – mind you nobody expected Cullis to spring any surprises as Wolves' team generally picked itself. Barcelona played with three backs and two half-backs. If the game in Belgrade had been a 'Battle', this one would turn out to be much more 'Balletic'. Wolves started brightly, but missed a hatful of chances. Bobby Mason slipped when he looked as though he was about to score. Deeley also missed a good chance. Then Broadbent headed narrowly wide and the Spaniards had weathered the early storm. Now they scored with their first real attack, Villaverde heading in a cross from the 'idol of Spanish football', Juan Suarez. The versatile Spaniard raided down the right wing and sent an exquisite centre across Wolves goal Finlayson was caught in two minds: he didn't know whether to come or stay. In the end he stayed, allowing speedy left-winger Villaverde to head past him. In what was only their third attack, Barcelona stylishly added to their lead on 18 minutes, with the industrious and elusive Suarez again the provider. Repeating his earlier right-wing raid he accurately slipped the ball through to Kubala, whose first-time shot beat Finlayson despite the big keeper getting his hand to the ball. Wolves were still having the majority of possession, but couldn't find the spark that would lead to a goal. Barcelona were giving Wolves a tactical lesson in controlled football, despite an injury to right-back Flotats in the 34th minute which saw the full-back limping through two-thirds of the game on the wing. Barca's forwards cleverly switched around, running into space and retaining possession of the ball – it was magnificent. All over the pitch they played an immaculate brand of football that was alien to English players. Wolves tried to play their normal power game, but each attack fizzled out all too early. On the few occasions they threatened, Barca's goalkeeper Ramallets held Wolves at bay, saving well from Flowers and collecting dangerous centres from Mason and Horne. In the 65th minute, centre-forward Evaristo finished off a glorious five-man move for the home team's third. Then 9 minutes from full-time, the mobile Villaverde got his second and Barca's fourth to bring Wolves down to earth with a bump, beating them 4-0. Evaristo had the ball in Wolves net for a hat-trick, or so he thought, and was disappointed, as were the crowd, when the referee brought play back for an earlier infringement. Jimmy Murray was the pick of Wolves' attack; he worked tirelessly against the tall and commanding Gensara. The skill of Barcelona's players in eluding Wolves tackling was at the heart of the gulf in class between the two teams. They moved the ball around the pitch so fast that they couldn't be caught in possession. With their accurate passing and running into space, Barcelona made the game look simple. The Spaniards must have expected a tougher game in view of Wolves' reputation for hard tackling, which on the night had proved ineffective. That Wolves' forwards had a rare off night in front of goal was plain to see; they had chances, but failed to take them. Murray shot wide following a marvellous run from his own half, and there were times when Broadbent and Flowers showed their class. Stan Cullis acknowledged that his team had been beaten by a better side and hoped that they would play better at Molineux. A mountain to climb? Remember, Hungarians Czibor and Kocsis hadn't made the starting line-up, the latter having broken his leg the previous August.

Worse was still to come as Wolves were to also lose the return leg at Molineux.

> Wolves' team in Barcelona: Finlayson; Stuart, Harris; Clamp, Showell, Flowers; Deeley, Mason, Murray, Broadbent, Horne.
> Barcelona: Ramallets; Flotats, Gracia; Segarra, Gensana, Vergeni; Martinez, Kubala, Evaristo, Suarez, Villaverde.
> Referee: M. Versypp (Belgium)
> Score: Wolves 0, Barcelona 4
> Scorers for Barca: Villaverde (2), Kubala, Evaristo
> Attendance: 95,000

Wolves 2 C.F. Barcelona 5
European Champions Cup, Quarter Final,
2nd leg, home

The Molineux faithful knew that Wolves would never throw in the towel despite the walloping received in Spain. We packed into the stadium for the return leg in Wolverhampton on Wednesday 2 March 1960, hoping and praying for a miracle. The Wolverhampton Police were on the alert after reports of black-market stand and terrace tickets had been received. Thorough inspections were carried out, causing unexpected delays at the turnstiles. As far as this match was concerned, Wolves had a few injury problems to contend with: Gerry Harris had had flu all week, and only just made the starting line-up; club captain Eddie Stuart didn't make it, the reliable George Showell deputising, with Bill Slater taking over as captain; and Malcolm Finlayson hadn't recovered from injury, so in came Geoff Sidebottom to take his place. The remainder of the knocks

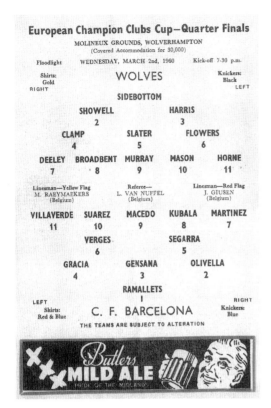

Teams page from the programme for Wolves v. Barcelona.

Front cover of a 'pirate' programme for Wolves v. Barcelona.

that other players had been carrying all improved sufficiently for Wolves to field nine of the eleven that had played in Spain. Barca's coach Señor Herrera made four changes. The brilliant Sandor Kocsis hadn't played in the Nou Camp, and unfortunately he was fit for this return leg; boy, did he make an impression, replacing Evaristo. Coll came in for Kubala. Rodriguez was brought in at centre-back to combat the threat posed by Jimmy Murray, Gensana reverting to his customary position on the left of the defence in place of Vergeni. Flotats was still injured so Oliverta came in at right-back. Facing an uphill struggle of Everest-like proportions, needing four goals just to draw level, Wolves went for it, no holding back, all-out attack, with both wing-halves fully committed to going forward, joining the attack at every opportunity. Inevitably, this left many holes at the back, which the speedy Barca forwards were only too pleased to exploit. Goalkeeper Ramallets was again in outstanding form, commanding his area to claim the numerous potentially dangerous crosses that Deeley and Horne put over. Geoff Sidebottom showed that he wasn't about to be outdone, getting down smartly to keep out Coll's snapshot. Barcelona produced a world-class display of attacking football to steal Wolves' proud record of never having been beaten under home floodlights, in the process astonishing the capacity crowd with their slick, stylish brand of football. Because of their all-out attacking formation, Wolves' defensive frailties were seriously exposed in a repeat of their display in the Nou Camp. With each attack, the Spanish Champions threatened to slice straight through what was normally a resolute last line. On this March night, Wanderers were simply outplayed. Our boys fought valiantly, but it was not enough, and in their most humiliating defeat, Wolves were thrashed 5-2. The fabulous Hungarian Sandor Kocsis, a player of infinite footballing ability, scored four of Barcelona's goals that night, in the 29th, 42nd, 60th and 74th minutes. One wonders how many he would have scored in Barcelona had the Magyar Magician played. His first warning of what was to follow came when Martinez put him through with an immaculate pass for the Hungarian ace to dispatch into the net. This was still relatively early in the game, and Wolves quickly showed that they weren't about to give up the fight. Five minutes after going behind, Jimmy Murray was well placed to latch onto a rebound, which he hammered into the Barca net for the equaliser. For a moment, we thought Murray was going to score a second, but the centre-forward was too static as the ball sped past him across Barca's goalmouth. Then in the 42nd minute up popped Kocsis to once again emphasise his class in a repeat of his first goal to make it 2-1 to Barcelona at the break. Both teams had given their all in an absorbing and exciting first 45 minutes. I guess Wolves were the happier to hear Mr Van Nuffel's whistle. The players needed a rest and so did the fans – time for a quick Bovril. In the second half, Wolves' task went from extremely difficult to virtually impossible. Kocsis' injured shoulder needed pain-killing injections at half-time, but this didn't slow him down one bit. After the break Wolves renewed their vigorous assault on the visitor's goal, but again found the excellent Ramallets barring their path, his best save from a ferocious shot from Eddie Clamp that he gathered at the foot of his post. In front of him his confident defence showed no sign of panic or gave any indication of capitulating under the pressure Wolves were putting them under. Quite the opposite, they played with an abundance of calm not previously seen under the Molineux lights. On the hour, the inventive Martinez lifted the ball over Gerry Harris only to see it hit the bar before luckily rebounding to him; he stabbed it across Wolves area for Kocsis to complete his hat-trick with a smart header. Sixteen minutes from time a little bit of Suarez magic put Coll clear. His pass found Kocsis, who made no mistake, dispatching the ball into the net for his fourth goal. Still Wolves wouldn't give up, despite being down

4-1 on the night, 8-1 on aggregate, and Bobby Mason reduced the arrears 12-minutes from the final whistle – a consolation? – not really. A minute later Villaverde held off a couple of defenders to score Barcelona's fifth, and as they say, that was that, our kid – 5-2! We couldn't believe it – it was like being shell-shocked. On the trolley-bus back to Darlaston en route for home the atmosphere was eerie to say the least – no one spoke. Standing in the bus stop in Darlaston, waiting for the one to Wednesbury, somebody asked how they'd got on, eventually after a silent pause an answer containing several swear words plus the result was shouted out – the enquirer muttered, 'I only bloody well asked, mate!' Bill Slater, playing at centre-half had turned in an almost faultless performance, but even he proved to be powerless to halt the fantastic flair of Kocsis and his pals. Sadly this was the last time Wolves would play in the premier European club competition. This match marked the end of an era as Wolves lost their coveted and hard-won record of 'unbeaten under Molineux floodlights' to a team of soccer Señors, who in a wonderful exhibition of running off the ball to create space for their colleagues to move into, out-thought and out-played the best team in England. Incidentally a daily newspaper explained the gulf in pay between the Spanish and English Leagues. Apparently Alfredo Di Stefano of Real Madrid was paid the equivalent of £30,000 a year, whereas the Maestro, Stanley Matthews, only earned £1,000 a year – enough said?

Wolves lost by a staggering 9-2 aggregate score.

> Wolves' team at Molineux: Sidebottom; Showell, Harris; Clamp, Slater, Flowers; Deeley, Mason, Murray, Broadbent, Horne.
> Barcelona: Ramallets; Oliverta, Rodriguez, Gracia; Segarra, Gensana; Coll, Kocsis, Martinez, Suarez, Villaverde.
> Referee: M. Van Nuffel (Belgium)
> Score: Wolves 2, Barcelona 5 (Wolves lost 9-2 on aggregate)
> Wolves' scorers: Bobby Mason, Jimmy Murray
> Scorers for Barcelona: Kocsis (4), Villaverde
> Attendance: 55,535

There is no doubt that a huge gulf existed between the tactical sophistication of the top continental teams, as compared to their English counterparts. In the two legs against Barcelona, Wolves traditional tactics of muscular power-play coupled with a long-ball game, which had proved so successful in domestic competitions, had been emphatically exposed by intelligent and thoughtful defending behind inventive and speedy counter-attacking. Bravery and effort were no longer the weapons with which to fight against the European style. Patience was needed when probing for an opening, guile much more effective than mere enthusiasm; the future in European competition would be fascinating. In the semi-final, Barcelona were beaten 6-2 by eventual winners Real Madrid.

Obviously there was more of a knack to playing these two-legged ties than had previously been figured. Unfortunately, Wolves hadn't yet learned how to do it. However, 1959/60, still turned out to be another vintage season as Wolves went desperately close to being the first club to win the magical double, winning the FA Cup for the fourth time in their history, beating Blackburn Rovers 3-0 on 7 May 1960, but sadly being pipped to the First Division title by Burnley by a single point; Wolves would have been champions three years running if we'd won.

My Wolves mates and me, along with the rest of the faithful, firmly believed that in 1959/60, Wolves would be the first club in modern times to win the elusive double. When we didn't, we just couldn't figure out how we'd lost the league title, and with it the double. It wasn't a case of Burnley winning the title so much as Wolves throwing it away. With just 2 league games left to play, Wolves were sitting pretty at the top of the table, three points ahead of Tottenham and Burnley, the latter having two away games in hand. The Wolves wheels didn't exactly come off, but far too often in the run-in they failed to fire on all cylinders. It's quite often the hectic round of Easter matches that decide championships, promotions and relegations, and this was certainly true in 1959/60. Wolves played 3 games in 4 days, losing 3-1 away to Newcastle on 16 April, recovering to beat Nottingham Forest 3-1 at home on 18 April, then drawing 0-0 at Forest on 19 April, earning only 3 points out of 6. On Saturday 23 April Wolves faced second-placed Spurs at home only to lose 3-1 in front of a crowd of 56,283 to a team that hadn't won a league match at Molineux since before the war. Fortunately Burnley had also been dropping a few points along the way, but to have any chance of the title we needed a good result at Stamford Bridge a week later. Wolves turned on the style in their final game of the season, walloping Chelsea 5-1 in front of 61,569 people to finish the season on 54 points, still one ahead of their two rivals. Sadly it wasn't enough. In their final game, Burnley beat Manchester City 2-1 at Maine Road to deny Wolves a history-making moment. It seemed unfair; Wolves thumped Burnley 6-1 at the end of March to show our superiority. 'Fix!' we all cried, but in the end, they got one more point than we did. Possibly some players may have had their eyes on the FA Cup Final, who knows? At least Wolves had the bottle to go on and win the Cup.

The 'gold'-coloured *Sporting Star* Souvenir Edition for Saturday 7 May 1960, proudly proclaimed 'OURS AGAIN' as it's headline, following the even 'golder', Cup Special Edition of eleven years earlier, which had borne the headline 'IT'S OURS', celebrating Wolves 3-1 FA Cup victory over Leicester City on Saturday 30 April 1949. Both of my copies are fading a little, but they still make fascinating reading.

In the 40th minute of the 1960 FA Cup Final, Blackburn Rovers' left-back Dave Whelan, these days better known as the founder of JJB Sports, was seriously injured in an incident that saw left-half Mick McGrath deflect Barry Stobart's cross into his own net to give Wolves the lead. Whelan was unable to continue and was carried off a few minutes later. He was taken to Wembley Hospital where it was learned that he had broken his leg. Leading the Blackburn attack was none other than Derek Dougan who, with immaculate timing had controversially put in a transfer request on the morning of the game. Ten-man Rovers couldn't prevent a Wolves victory Norman Deeley scoring Wolves' two other goals in the 67th and 80th minutes to bring the Cup back to Wolverhampton for the fourth time. Wolves' team that day was Malcolm Finlayson; George Showell, Gerry Harris; Eddie Clamp, Bill Slater, Ron Flowers; Norman Deeley, Barry Stobart, Jimmy Murray, Peter Broadbent, Des Horne. Unfortunately, I didn't get a ticket for the final. My application, along with over 20,000 other loyal fans, lost out in the ballot.

The European Cup Final of 1960 was played at Hampden Park, Glasgow, on 18 May 1960 in front of a capacity crowd of 138,000. Real Madrid, with Puskas, Di Stefano *et al*, beat Eintracht Frankfurt 7-3 in what was a most memorial final.

By virtue of winning the FA Cup Wolves qualified for the brand-new European Cup Winners Cup; the Molineux fans couldn't wait for another tilt at a European crown. For many years the national press had called Wolves' style of attacking football 'Power-Play', a convenient tag for, 'the systematic bombardment of the opposition's goal, with long balls accurately delivered at pace, allied to fierce but fair tackling.'

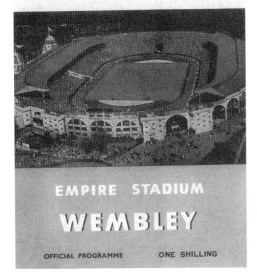

THE FOOTBALL ASSOCIATION CHALLENGE CUP COMPETITION

FINAL TIE
BLACKBURN ROVERS
V
WOLVERHAMPTON WANDERERS

SATURDAY, MAY 7th, 1960   KICK-OFF 3 p.m.

EMPIRE STADIUM
WEMBLEY

OFFICIAL PROGRAMME   ONE SHILLING

Left: Front cover of the FA Cup Final programme for 1960, when Wolves played Blackburn Rovers.

Below: Wolves shoot for goal in the 1960 FA Cup Final.

Left: Bill Slater on his teammates' shoulders holding the FA Cup. *Right*: A mounted policeman patrols Broad Street, Wolverhampton, as happy Wolves fans wait for their 1960 FA Cup-winning heroes to arrive.

Wolves' 1960 FA Cup-winning side parade the trophy in Broad Street.

1960/61

The end of 1960 saw the discontinuation of National Service in the armed forces for 18-year-olds; 21 if you were an apprentice as I was. Not many of the people I knew fancied joining up, but many young Wolves players had no choice, serving their 2 years with pride.

Wolves fans went into the 1960/61 season full of anticipation of even more success, and the lads didn't disappoint us, opening up their League season with five wins and a draw – then both Everton and Leicester beat us, before Blackburn held us to a 0-0 draw. For some inexplicable reason, Wolves' forwards suddenly seemed over-anxious in front of goal. What followed next was the stuff of dreams. The next match was away to Manchester United at Old Trafford, and 20-year-old debutant Ted Farmer was brought in as Murray's replacement; the young centre-forward scored two in Wolves 3-1 win. Farmer's scoring record was to become legendary at Molineux. In time for this new season, and following the current trend, the seating in the Molineux Street Stand had been extended over the enclosure. Another new feature was the Molineux Street scoreboard, which now had its own frame, theoretically making it easier to read.

Secretary to the FA, Sir Stanley Rous, renewed his war-cry for a European League, which at the time was felt to be inevitable by many soccer pundits. This season also marked the start of a new competition – the League Cup. However, Wolves, in company with Spurs, Albion, Arsenal and Sheffield Wednesday, declined to take part. I can't say what was behind the reasoning of these other clubs, but Wolves didn't want the added distraction and fixture build-up, because they were about to compete in the European Cup Winners Cup.

F.K. Austria 2 Wolves 0
European Cup Winners Cup, quarter-final,
1st leg, away

Wolves were given a bye in the qualifying round of this brand new competition, coming in at the quarter-final stage because only 10 teams entered. Their opponents were to be F.K. Austria of Vienna. The away leg was staged in the stadium where Nat Lofthouse had earned the accolade 'The Lion of Vienna' – the famous Rater Stadium, Vienna, on Wednesday 12 October 1960. Wolves were unlucky. Having played some excellent football, they should at least have earned a draw, but conceded two sloppy goals to leave them with it all to do in the second leg. Wolves' power-play threatened to overwhelm the home side; they hit the Austrian woodwork five times. However, there were a few moments when they didn't have it all their way. In the second minute Geoff Sidebottom was called upon to make an excellent save from the Austrians' giant centre-forward Nemec, who cleverly latched onto the ball before hooking his shot at Wolves' goal. Spurred on by this, Wolves stepped up their attacks, but it was F.K. that took the lead, not Wolves. On 19 minutes the referee awarded the Austrians a direct free-kick outside Wolves' penalty area. Riegler's strong shot found a gap in the wall, the ball passing the stranded Sidebottom to squeeze just inside his near post and Wolves were a goal down. A bizarre incident occurred after another Austrian attack: Geoff Sidebottom was accidentally kicked by a ball boy as he attempted to retrieve the ball; he was able to resume after treatment. Wolves pressed hard up to and after the break, but still couldn't stick the ball away. This pattern continued until the 85th minute when the Austrians scored a second goal, one that had more than an element of luck to it. A harmless-looking centre from the right eluded all Wolves' defenders to fall into the path of lunging left-winger Huschek; the ball somehow diverting into the net to make it 2-0 to the Austrian Cup holders. I'm sure Wolves couldn't figure out how exactly they had lost this match. Eddie Stuart had been commanding in the centre of defence with Irish international Phil Kelly and Mr Dependable, George Showell, playing well at right and left-back respectively. Their performances, added to those of wing-halves Johnny Kirkham and Ron Flowers, gave Wolves' defence a secure look. Ted Farmer had hit the inside of the upright, Peter Broadbent had seen his shot rebound from the goalie's face, Gerry Mannion smacked a header against a post, but Wolves couldn't score. They left Vienna no doubt frustrated at their inability to finish effectively, also the German referee didn't help much, allowing far too much body-checking to go unpunished. Thankfully it would be a different ref for the second leg at Molineux.

> Wolves' team in Vienna: Sidebottom; Kelly, Showell; Kirkham, Stuart, Flowers; Mannion, Murray, Farmer, Broadbent, Deeley.
> F.K. Austria: Gartner; Fischer, Swoboda; Medweth, Stotz, Paproth; Hirnschrodt, Riegler, Nemec, Fiala, Huschek.
> Referee: Herr Deusch (Germany)
> Score: Wolves 0, FK Austria 2
> Scorers for FK: Riegler, Huschek
> Attendance: 25,135

We could hardly wait for the second leg. First up though was another floodlit friendly, and it turned out to be a cracker:

Wolves 5 Dynamo Tbilisi 5
Floodlit Friendly at Molineux

Somewhat surprisingly, Wolves decided to sandwich this friendly fixture in between the two legs of the European Cup Winners Cup. Even more surprising was that it was to be against Dynamo Tbilisi (known also as Tiflis Dynamo) of Southern Georgia instead of Moscow Dynamo, who Wolves had originally expected to be their opponents. Apparently the other Dynamo were touring Africa. Paraphrasing the Duke of Wellington's reported comment following the Battle of Waterloo, 'This was a close run thing!' On the evening of Thursday 10 November 1960, a crowd of 35,000 turned out to watch this thrilling 5-5 draw with another top-class Russian team. The foxy Russians led 5-2 until the 80th minute, when Wolves' South African winger Cliff Durandt popped up to score, thus beginning the pride-driven grand finale that ultimately saved Wolves' blushes. Many of the crowd had either already left the ground or were heading towards the exits and missed the fun. Prior to the game Wolves fans had expected a goalfest from Wolves; after all, Sheffield Wednesday had beaten the Georgians 5-0 on the previous Monday night (or was it Sheffield Monday on Wednesday?). The soccer Tsars had other ideas, producing a display of excellent football to take a 3-1 lead at the interval. The danger signs were there for all to see as on 2 minutes Melashvili and Barkaya exploded down the right wing, combining well before sending in a great centre that reached Russian international winger Meskhi, who smacked home a wonderful shot to give the Russians the lead. Straight from the restart Ted Farmer latched on to a misplaced back-pass to steer the ball into the net for the equaliser. The cheers of the Wolves fans were silenced as the Tbilisi captain Gogoberidze headed the visitors back into the lead. Wolves roared back, getting back into the game with periods of good possession, seemingly abandoning their usual power-play style of bombardment in favour of numerous passes, far too many of which failed to find their intended target. This build-up was sometimes slow and laborious and didn't produce the means to break through the ball-playing Russian defence. Any further first-half goal attempts were acrobatically dealt with by goalkeeper Kotrikadze, who at times flung himself about his goal area quite spectacularly, especially in one save from Ron Flowers. We were certain that a second Wolves goal must come soon, when Tbilisi scored again. The impressive Yamanidze drove on his attack and with an inch-perfect pass put Meskhi away; the winger played the ball to skipper Gogoberidze whose fierce shot off the underside of the crossbar bulged the Wolves net for a 3-1 lead. Cullis knew he had to do something if Wolves were to retain their 'unbeaten in friendlies under Molineux lights' record, and after the interval sent on Durandt in place of Norman Deeley. The presence of the speedy winger certainly had a positive impact on Wolves' play, resulting in a fine goal, scored by Bobby Mason with a smart shot to make it 3-2 and thus restore some of our confidence. This feeling wasn't long-lived, as 2 goals in as many minutes had the home side reeling with shock. The first was scored by Meskhi for 4-2, the second by Barkaya to make it 5-2 to the Russians. We couldn't believe it – 5-2! Barcelona again? – impossible! Wolves didn't lie down and die; they renewed their efforts, fortunately reverting to their traditional style of all-out attack. This tactic worked when Durandt scored a fine individual goal to bring back a measure of hope. The home side stormed forward to besiege their opponent's goal, but it was Lady Luck that eventually provided the breakthrough. An uncharacteristic misunderstanding between left-back Chohely and his goalkeeper let in Farmer who calmly dispatched the ball into the net for his second of the night. Time was running out for Wolves when Kotrikadze made amends for his earlier mistake by saving Farmer's wicked shot at point-blank range. The 88th minute was sweetest. Jimmy Murray rose to loop a header over the goalkeeper and defenders to give us the equaliser we had prayed for. In the dying seconds of the match Farmer almost won it for Wolves. He challenged the Tbilisi goalkeeper and his centre-back and cleverly took the ball away from the now nervous-looking Kotrikadze, but unluckily his momentum took him wide of the goal and off balance; he couldn't recover to slot the ball home from such an acute angle. What a finish that would have been. Those of the crowd who were already outside were halted in their tracks by the huge shouts and cheers that greeted these two face-saving goals. Five-all, what a game!

Wolves' team at Molineux: Finlayson; Stuart, Showell; Clamp, Slater, Flowers; Mason, Murray, Farmer, Broadbent, Deeley (Durandt).
Tbilisi: S. Kotrikadze; B. Sichinava, E. Toradze, G. Chohely; V. Voronin, S. Yamanidze; T. Melashvili, S. Barkaya, Z. Kaloev, A. Gogoberidze, M. Meskhi.
Referee: R. H. Davidson (Scotland)
Score: Wolves 5, Dynamo Tbilisi 5
Wolves' scorers: Ted Farmer (2), Murray, Mason, Durandt
Scorers for Tbilisi: Meskhi (2), Gogoberidze (2), Barkaya
Attendance: 35,000

Wolves now had to get back to the Cup Winners Cup. One could almost sense that they felt that had a firmer grip on European tactics, and this, coupled with their recent impressive form in the league – in the seven games played since losing in Vienna Wolves had won five, drawn one, and lost one, scoring 24 goals in the process – meant that they fully expected to be able to overturn the Austrians' two-goal advantage – and they did.

Wolves 5 F.K. Austria 0
European Cup Winners Cup, quarter-final, 2nd leg, home

In the second leg of this tie, played on Wednesday, 30 November 1960, Wolves were an absolute delight. Playing majestic football, they murdered the Austrians 5-0. Strangely enough, five was exactly the number of times they'd hit the woodwork in Vienna. Wolves started like an express train. Wednesbury-born Johnny Kirkham stepped in at the last minute as replacement for Ron Flowers, who had a heavy cold, and gave Wolves a great start by scoring in the first minute with a hopeful long-range effort. Like Jimmy Murray's goal against Red Star Belgrade a year earlier, the goalkeeper misjudged the flight of his lofted long ball, allowing it to drop into his net. In the 26th minute, Kirkham got his second of the night to bring the aggregate score level, when he managed to get his head to a Cliff Durandt shot-cum-centre to deflect the ball passed the stranded Gartner. The visitors' keeper made some good saves as Wolves dominated; however, in the 35th minute he let in Wolves again when he mistakenly threw the ball out straight to the feet of Bobby Mason, who lobbed it into the Austrians' net to put Wolves into a 3-2 aggregate lead at half-time. At the start of the second-half the Austrians pressed for an equaliser, but with Bill Slater in magnificent form Wolves easily contained the visitors. On 70 minutes Gartner flung himself sideways to hold a Broadbent header, then seconds later could only watch as the same Wolves player headed the ball past him. Peter Broadbent was playing superbly, and fired home his second, Wolves fifth, a couple of minutes later before again being denied by the enigmatic Austrian keeper to prevent the schemer's hat-trick. This was undoubtedly one of Wolves' finest performances, one that deserved many more goals. On a luckier evening Ted Farmer would have scored a couple; he had three good efforts ruled out by the referee. But still, the fans were happy, no – ecstatic would be more accurate!

Into the semi-final, would this be Wolves year? We had to wait nearly 4 months for the match against Rangers, the team who had reached the semi-final of the previous season's European Cup.

> Wolves' team at Molineux: Sidebottom; Stuart, Harris; Clamp, Slater, Kirkham; Deeley, Mason, Farmer, Broadbent, Durandt.
> F.K. Austria: Gartner; Loesner, Swoboda; Medweth, Stotz, Paproth; Hirnschrodt, Riegler, Nemec, Fiala, Schlieger.
> Referee: Herr Josef Gulde (Switzerland)
> Score: Wolves 5 FK Austria 0 (Wolves won 5-2 on aggregate)
> Wolves' scorers: Peter Broadbent (2), Johnny Kirkham (2), Bobby Mason (New discovery Ted Farmer had 3 disallowed)
> Attendance: 31,669

In the meantime, Jimmy Hill, he of beard and pointy chin fame, was leading the PFA in its long-running dispute with the Football League over the maximum wage and terms of contract. In 1960 the maximum wage was £20 per week in the season and £17 in the summer. The widely-held view amongst footballers and their union was that they were being exploited by their clubs. This was a time of great turmoil in English football; the tension between players and their clubs must have been difficult to overcome. The purse-holding directors of football clubs had always had complete control over their players, paying them a pittance by comparison to many other forms of entertainment, and preventing them from moving to a club of their choice on the expiry of their contract. The players had had enough. PFA Chairman Hill called it a 'slave contract' – a change had to come sooner rather than later. With a strike only days away the Football League finally backed down, and on 9 January 1961, the maximum wage was abolished. The League however, steadfastly refused to budge on the issue of player's contracts. England inside-forward George Eastham's contract with Newcastle ended and he wanted to join Arsenal – his club refused, so he decided to challenge the legitimacy of his contract in court, arguing that it was a restraint of trade. Three days before the footballer's strike – it was still scheduled for 21 January – the League capitulated. An agreement was reached to abandon the regulations that effectively tied a player to one club for life unless they wanted to transfer him. Eastham's PFA-backed challenge regarding his contract went to the High Court, who ruled in his favour.

Glasgow Rangers 2 Wolves 0
European Cup Winners Cup, semi-final, 1st leg, away

In a major European semi-final for the first time, Wolves fans were hoping for a display that matched the Molineux leg against the Austrians; unfortunately it was not to be. In front of a crowd of almost 80,000 baying Scotsmen at Ibrox Park in Glasgow on Wednesday 29 March 1961, Wolves pretty much flopped against a below-strength Rangers. Broadbent had been injured and was not available; he was badly missed by Wolves. In the 17th minute Rangers' right-half Harold Davis took a knock which had him limping along on the wing for the rest of the game. In the opening exchanges, honours were just about even, then Wolves experienced their first slice of bad luck, as on 23 minutes Jimmy Murray intuitively ran on to George Showell's delightful pass. His surging run took him past a number of Rangers' defenders, through the heart of their defence and into the penalty area. With only the goalkeeper to beat he hit an 'almost precise' shot that looked a goal all the way, but which unfortunately struck the crossbar to rebound clear of danger. Then in the 34th minute, a mistake by Ron Flowers gave the home side a chance. His attempted headed clearance was latched onto by winger Alex Scott, who from the right of the area unleashed a terrific cross-shot that flew passed Malcolm Finlayson in Wolves' goal. Rangers besieged Wolves' goal for the next 50 minutes looking for a second. There were only 6 minutes of the match remaining when Eddie Clamp's intended clearance was intercepted, and with Wolves' defence caught square, Brand was put through to score a second goal for Rangers. It was a dreadful blow. Sluggish Wolves had been beaten 2-0. Rangers' defence, marshalled by big Bill Paterson, was well organised and tight. Ted Farmer tried hard against the giant centre-half, but got little change. Cliff Durandt was well shackled by right-back Bobby Shearer, resulting in a distinct lack of quality balls being delivered from the left. Of Wolves' front-line only Jimmy Murray and Norman Deeley looked anything like themselves. In defence, Bill Slater restricted Baillie to a few efforts, and Showell played solidly. Despite having overcome a two-goal deficit against F.K. in the previous round, it was obvious that Rangers would be a much tougher proposition than the Austrians' had been. Only Showell, Clamp, Slater, Deeley and Murray had shown anything of their class; the rest strangely seemed to lack heart. We would need to see a 100 per cent improvement if Wolves were to progress in this competition.

> Wolves' team in Glasgow: Finlayson; Stuart, Showell; Clamp, Slater, Flowers; Deeley, Murray, Farmer, Mason, Durandt.
> Rangers: Ritchie; Shearer, Caldow; Davis, Paterson, Baxter; Scott, Wilson, Baillie, Brand, Hume.
> Referee: Jonni Cesare (Italy)
> Score: Wolves 0, Glasgow Rangers 2
> Scorers for Rangers: Scott, Brand
> Attendance: 79,229

Before the second leg, Wolves might have gained a psychological advantage over certain Rangers players following England's impressive 9-3 win over Scotland on the previous Saturday — we all hoped so.

Wolves 1 Glasgow Rangers 1
European Cup Winners Cup, semi-final, 2nd leg, home

The return leg of this semi-final was played on Wednesday 19 April 1961. Wolves had won three out of the last four league games before this match, and so a two-nil deficit in the return leg at Molineux was deemed redeemable by most Wolves fans. After all, in Glasgow the Wolves attack had looked woefully short on confidence, now they'd got it back. The bad news was that Ted Farmer wasn't fit and therefore wouldn't be playing in the return; what might have happened had he played? Rangers were pleased to have their star schemer Ian McMillan back in their starting line-up. Wolves turned on the power straight from the kick-off, Rangers' defence holding out in the face of a tremendous onslaught, forced to dig ever deeper into their reserves of strength and dogged defiance. Apart from the opening 10 minutes when Wolves power was operating at maximum-strength, Scottish international full-backs Bobby Shearer and Eric Caldow played as if they had something to prove after their recent poor display at Wembley. Together with Bill Paterson they formed a substantial solid human barrier to Wolves' progress in this new competition. In the opening period all the luck went the way of the Scots. After only 17 seconds Norman Deeley hooked in a shot that went high and wide. Two minutes later, Ritchie kept out Jimmy Murray's goal-bound shot with his legs. On 8 minutes Eddie Clamp curled in a great free-kick and Murray headed the ball across the goalmouth to Deeley, but the little winger mis-timed his header, allowing the Scots to escape again. Wolves' poor finishing saved the Scots yet again in the 14th minute, when Broadbent's cross rebounded off Ritchie to Murray, who put his shot wide. Four minutes later a Bobby Mason effort was cleared off the line by Davis. Had Wolves scored at this time I think they'd have got a hatful. As it was, they grew more frustrated with every miss. Rangers seemed to sense a change and seized the opportunity to go on the offensive for almost the first time in the match. Now it was Wolves' turn to defend. There was a heart-stopping moment when Wolves' back-four watched helplessly as Davis sent a stinging shot narrowly wide of the post. This helped Rangers regain their composure following their earlier backs-to-the-wall effort. Now they began to play some delightful stuff, the excellent McMillan spraying the ball around at times quite beautifully and Wilson, Brand and Scott all combining well in several penetrating moves. Then came the moment we were dreading. Scott and Brand again fashioned a goal that knocked the stuffing out of Wolves, whose all-out attacking style had invariably left a few gaps at the back. When the bounce of a high-clearance deceived Bill Slater, Brand grabbed the chance to play in Scott, who really couldn't miss – he didn't, and Wolves were one-nil down on the night. Ron Flowers drove forward and taking aim for the corner of Rangers' goal let go a 20-yard screamer, which the agile Ritchie tipped wide. Wolves went in 3-0 down on aggregate. After the restart, Wolves didn't let up in their quest for the goal that would provide the springboard for victory. We thought we had it when Mason ran clear of the Gers' defence. Like Murray in Glasgow, he had only Ritchie to beat, but chose to take the ball round the keeper. This proved to be the wrong option when Ritchie, with excellent timing, grabbed the ball without giving away a penalty. The breakthrough finally came in the 64th minute from a corner on the right, Peter Broadbent cleverly flicking the ball home; it was a start and brought loud cheering from the crowd. Heartened by this long-awaited success, Wolves signalled another round of all-out attacking. Davis broke Wolves' hearts again when he cleared off the line for the second time in the game, before Scott almost finished the job off and murdered any hope we still had; fortunately Finlayson managed to grab the ball as the winger bore down on goal. Then 3 minutes later Finlayson turned Wilson's shot over the crossbar. In the final phase of the match Wolves had a number of efforts blocked or saved, but the second goal just wouldn't come. Despite playing well, Wolves couldn't overturn the Scots' two-goal advantage and ultimately were forced to settle for a 1-1 draw; it was not to be. For a time, getting to the final had not seemed altogether impossible, but in the end we had to face the reality of the situation – we had lost! The Scots' brand of fast-running, free-flowing football was probably the main difference between the two sides. All too frequently Rangers had the Wolves defence back-pedalling as well as acting out the title of a Chuck Berry song – 'Reelin' And Rockin', particularly in the first leg. A few bottles were thrown inside Molineux, just to add to the ambience, and there were a few disturbances in the town centre. In fact, Wolverhampton came in for quite a battering from the hordes of Rangers fans that descended upon the town. I dread to think what would have happened if the Scots had lost – rowdy? boisterous? – yes, the pubs did a roaring trade. Anyhow, Rangers had qualified for their first European final – Wolves would have to wait their turn, which we all felt must come soon – how wrong we were!

Wolves' team at Molineux: Finlayson; Stuart, Showell; Clamp, Slater, Flowers; Deeley, Mason, Murray, Broadbent, Durandt.
Rangers: Ritchie; Shearer, Callow; Davis, Paterson, Baxter; Wilson, McMillan, Scott, Brand, Hume.
Referee: George Dienst (Basle, Switzerland)
Score: Wolves 1, Glasgow Rangers 1 (Wolves lost 1-3 on aggregate)
Wolves' scorer: Peter Broadbent
Scorer for Rangers: Scott
Attendance: 45,163 (allegedly including 10,000 Rangers fans)
Rangers subsequently lost to Fiorentina in the final.

In 1960/61, Wolves finished 3rd in Division 1 behind champions and first double winners Tottenham, with Sheffield Wednesday claiming 2nd place.

1961/62

Eddie Clamp was transferred to Arsenal in November 1961 for a huge £35,000 fee. Nicknamed 'Chopper' by a large section of the fans because of his often uncompromising style of play, Eddie was a hero on the terraces. I remember one powerful shoulder-charge on Albion's darling Johnny Nicholls, when Clamp knocked the WBA starlet off the pitch, lifting him into the air and into the crowd in the Molineux Street Paddock; Eddie stood no messing, that was sure. However, his hard-man image sometimes belied the skill that he definitely possessed; you didn't get picked for England if you couldn't play. Eddie Clamp won four full England caps, all in 1958 as part of England's all-Wolves half-back line with Billy Wright and Bill Slater. For Wolves, he made 241 appearances, scoring 25 goals in a career that saw him win two First Division Championship medals and the FA Cup in 1960.

The wheels definitely came off in season 1961/62, Wolves slipping to 18th in the First Division, their first time out of the top six in 10 seasons; only 14,597 watched the final match of the season against Chelsea.

By the summer of 1962, the talented multi-trophy-winning Wolves squad had all but broken up. The quality of the reserves coming through was unfortunately not up to the standard of the glory years. Four more Wolves greats left the club that year.

Little Norman Deeley was transferred to Leyton Orient for £12,000. Norman was marginally taller than Johnny Hancocks, and started out as a wing-half before switching to the wing to eventually take Johnny's place. He won 2 full England caps against Brazil and Peru, and for Wolves made 237 appearances, scoring 75 goals, including 2 in the 1960 Cup success. Equally at home on either flank, Deeley's characteristic style of running, chin forward, chest out, was sorely missed when he was transferred in February 1962.

Inside-forward Bobby Mason was a slightly-built lad from Tipton, who scored 54 goals in 173 games, winning championship medals in 1957/58 and 1958/59. One of the burning, and as far as I know unanswered, questions is why did Stan Cullis *really* leave him out of Wolves' FA Cup-winning team in 1960 in favour of 18-year-old Barry Stobart? Stobart got his chance in Wolves' final game of the 1959/60 season against Chelsea, doing well in a 5-1 win, so maybe it was just a case of preferring the younger man. Mason had virtually been an ever-present in the side that season, playing in 37 league games and scoring 13, although 11 of these were netted before Christmas. Mason played in every round of the Cup except the final, scoring twice in the 5th-round victory at Luton. He had also played in all six European matches, scoring 4 goals, the last on 2 March against Barcelona. The final part of the mystery is that Bobby Mason retained his place in the starting line-up for the following season's campaign, scoring 6 in 28 games, with Stobart no more than a reserve player. In May 1962 Mason was transferred to Leyton Orient for £10,000.

South African-born Eddie Stuart also left Wolves, transferring to Stoke City in July 1962 for a fee of around £8,000. Eddie made his Wolves debut at centre-forward against the Albion at Molineux on 15 April 1952, scoring in a 4-1 defeat. However, he didn't get a first-team game in the following season, and it was February 1954 before we saw him again in a league match, this time in the number 2 shirt, which, apart from injuries, he pretty much made his own from then on. Stuart also played sometimes at centre-half, and had the distinction of captaining Wolves against his home country in the inaugural floodlit match at Molineux in 1953, Bill Shorthouse standing down so that the young man could have this honour. In a long and distinguished career, Eddie Stuart made 322 appearances for Wolves, scoring his only goal on his debut at centre-forward against West Bromwich Albion. He was another who was left out of Wolves' 1960 FA Cup Final line-up.

In the summer of 1962 it was World Cup Final time once again, and this time Chile were the hosts. Ron Flowers was the only Wolves representative to play in these finals, and distinguished his performances with goals from the penalty spot in each of England's first two group games, becoming the first non-forward to score in four successive internationals. England lost 2-1 to Hungary in their opening game, then beat Argentina 3-1 and drew 0-0 with Bulgaria to reach the quarter-finals, where sadly they faced the holders Brazil, losing 3-1.

James Marshall succeeded long-serving James Baker as Chairman of Wolves. Mr Baker decided to step down in 1962 after 16 glorious years at the helm of the club.

1962/63

Wolves, with Ted Farmer back at number 9, kicked off the 1962/63 season in fine style, thumping Manchester City 8-1 at Molineux. Farmer scored 4 that day, and their swash-buckling style saw them topping the First Division when they were unbeaten after their first eleven fixtures. In that time this youthful team scored 31 goals and conceded only 13 in a sequence of 8 wins and 3 draws. Farmer scored 8 in 9 games, missing only 2 matches until he received another injury in September 1962. He would only recover in time to play in the final three matches of the season. By then the title had been lost and Wolves finished fourth. Disappointing, but a lot better than the previous season. One of the highlights was the 7-0 Molineux thrashing handed out to the Albion on 6 March 1963.

In December 1962, Wolves once again entertained Honved at Molineux

Wolves 1 Honved 1
Floodlit Friendly at Molineux

This time there was no clamour for tickets like there had been 8 years earlier. Admission for this match, played on Monday 3 December 1962, would be pay-on-the-night. The Hungarians were no longer the pride of Europe. Gone were the likes of the legendary Ferenc Puskas, Sandor Kocsis and their talented countrymen. Nonetheless, Honved, currently second in Hungary's top division, would still prove to be excellent opposition for Wolves. Ujpest Dozsa were occupying top spot in Hungary, with another of Wolves' old adversaries, M.T.K. (Red Banner) in third place. Flowers, Slater and Broadbent of Wolves' 1954 team were happy to renew old friendships, pleased that two members of the famous Mighty Magyar team would be at Molineux: Jozsef Bozsik was now club president, and Gyula Lorant was club coach. One player Wolves weren't so happy to see lining up against them was goalkeeper Lajos Farago, who as understudy to the great Grosics had played an absolute stormer on his previous Molineux appearance, and yes, he was going to be between the sticks again. The game itself bore scant resemblance to the 1954 classic. The fans must have sensed this because they stayed away in their droves, obviously preferring the warmth of their firesides over the rigours of the English winter weather; it was a bitterly cold night. In the 1954 epic Farago had been magnificent; tonight he had decided to go one better, without doubt earning the accolade, 'Star of the Show'. He was quite literally brilliant, stopping everything Wolves threw at him, except one effort from Wednesbury lad Alan Hinton, who on another night would have probably got at least a hat-trick before the game reached the hour mark. Farago's save of the night must be the point-blank effort from Chris Crowe, one of the finest saves ever seen at Molineux. Jimmy Murray had been recalled in place of cold victim Barry Stobart, and missed a hatful of the kind of chances he used to have no trouble putting away. But then again, his fellow forwards were just as guilty of glaring misses. Ten minutes from time, with the frustrated crowd growing ever more concerned, Honved's speedy winger Vagi broke away dangerously. For a moment all seemed lost, but fortunately he fluffed his chance; suddenly the omens were not good. Next it took an excellent off-the-line headed clearance by Bobby Thomson to keep the visitors out. Then with only 5 minutes left the fans' worst fears came true. Komora chipped the ball over magnificently for George Nagy to score what he must have thought was the winner, so enthusiastic was his celebration. Fortunately the excellent Hinton was on hand to crash home a terrific equaliser with only 3 minutes to spare, thus saving Wolves' blushes and earning a 1-1 draw. Bozsik announced that he wanted to make this fixture an annual event, and sure enough, a year later the teams met again, this time in Budapest.

Wolves' team at Molineux: Davies; Showell, Thomson; Kirkham, Slater, Flowers; Wharton, Crowe, Murray, Broadbent, Hinton.
Honved: Farago; Levai, Morosi, Dudas; Perecsi, Kotasz; Nagy, Komora, Nogradi, Tuschinger, Vagi.
Referee: J. Finney (Hereford)
Score: Wolves 1, Honved 1
Wolves' scorer: Hinton
Scorer for Honved: Nagy
Attendance: 13,914

The winter of 1962/63 was very bleak indeed. It was described by one pundit as 'the modern ice-age'. Many games had to be cancelled, resulting in chaos and subsequent severe fixture congestion. FA Cup 3rd-round day on 5 January 1963 was devastated when only 3 of the 32 ties were able to take place. Then on Saturday 9 February 1963 only seven Football League games could be played. Wolves' League game with Nottingham Forest was postponed five times, eventually being played on 29 January 1963; Forest won 4-3.

At Molineux, the almost invincible Wolves had completed 10 years of floodlit friendlies, September 1953 to December 1962, in that time playing a total of 17 games, winning 13 and drawing 4, all against foreign opposition except the match against Glasgow Celtic. Also in this period Wolves lined up at Molineux in six home ties in European competitions, winning 3, drawing 2 and losing only once – to Barcelona. A grand total of: played 23, won 16, drawn 6, lost 1. A record to be well and truly proud of!

The summer of 1963 saw Wolves embark upon a tour of North America, playing a number of games against Canadian, American and Brazilian teams, plus one against a Mexican international team. At the Downing Stadium, Randalls Island, New York, Wolves met again their first European Cup opponents, Schalke 04 from Germany, and beat them 4-2.

Also that summer, Alf Ramsey replaced Walter Winterbottom as England Manager and Billy Wright was appointed manager of Arsenal.

1963/64

Wolves travelled to Budapest to play a friendly against Honved on Wednesday 6 October 1963, unfortunately losing 2-1 to the Hungarian aces in the People's Stadium. In fine weather, a near 31,000 crowd witnessed a quiet game that Wolves were lucky to only lose by the odd goal, Tuschinger and Komora netting for Honved before Ray Crawford pulled one back for Wolves.

> Wolves' team: Davies; Thomson, Harris (Showell); Goodwin, Woodfield, Flowers; Wharton, Crowe, Crawford, Murray, Hinton.
> Honved: Takacs; Dudas, Mihalecz; Kotasz, Tuschinger, Nogradi; G. Nagy, Balogh, A. Nagy, Komora, Kotona.

1963/64 again saw many changes at the club: Ted Farmer and Jimmy Murray requested transfers, and ultimately Wolves plummeted to 16th place in Division 1. We had to face the obvious fact that our current team without the old stars just wasn't good enough. Finlayson retired, Farmer's career was cut short by injury, Murray and Hinton left for pastures new, and despite the 26 goals from 38 games from new signing Ray Crawford, Wolves only managed 70 goals in total that season.

Malcolm Finlayson had briefly taken over in Wolves' goal from 'The Cat' in September 1956, Bert Williams returning to the team in early December of that year and playing in the remainder of Wolves' games except the final match of the season, when the big Scot from Dumbarton finally took over as Wolves' number one goalkeeper. Cullis had bought the agile keeper in August 1956 for £4,000 from Millwall, for whom he had played 299 times; Finlayson went on to make 203 appearances for Wolves. In June 1982, now a successful businessman, he was appointed Vice-Chairman of Wolves when the new regime took over.

A few words about goalscoring phenomenon Ted Farmer, who sadly only played 62 times for Wolves first XI. In those games Ted scored 44 goals, including one hat-trick and nine braces, and twice getting four goals in one match, a fantastic strike rate. Farmer burst onto the scene at Old Trafford on 24 September 1960, scoring two in Wolves' 3-1 defeat of Manchester United. It was a pity he hadn't arrived a year earlier, maybe Wolves would have won the title that year with his goals. Who knows, Wolves might have even matched Barcelona goal for goal? In his first season Ted forged a great partnership with Jimmy Murray, scoring 28 league goals in 27 starts while Murray got 23 in 31 appearances.

Wolves' 103 goal tally fired them to a third-place finish. Unfortunately, not having yet fully compensated for the loss of Billy Wright, the defence leaked in 75 goals; in the title-winning seasons they had conceded less than 50. Ted Farmer suffered many injuries in his short career, eventually losing his fight to overcome a serious knee problem that had originally been inflicted by Dave Woodfield in a practice match. Ted played twice for England Under-23s, scoring against Israel on his debut, and also getting a hat-trick against Holland. I'm certain that he would have played for the full England team had he not been injured. One interesting statistic is that on 21 January 1961, Ted played for Wolves against Everton – his 21st appearance. In the match he scored his 21st goal for Wolves on his 21st birthday! No, not in the 21st minute, he couldn't wait that long, that would be too much of a coincidence wouldn't it? In his first season his 28 goals meant that he finished as fourth top goalscorer in the league. In 1958 he was a member of Wolves' FA Youth Cup-winning team. His full Wolves record is:

1960/61	28 goals in 32 games
1961/62	5 goals in 11 games
1962/63	9 goals in 13 games
1963/64	2 goals in 6 games

1964/65

The fortunes of Wolves now took a distinct turn for the worse as money-spinning European qualification became just a dream. The team's performance got worse, culminating in relegation at the end of the 1964/65 season. The end of an era was about to shatter the lives of the fans. First Chairman James Marshall handed over the reins to John Ireland. Then 2 months later, at the end of a long illness, the greatest Wolves manager of all time, Stan Cullis, was sacked by new Chairman John Ireland. This black day was 15 September 1964. The team had lost their first three matches, drawn the fourth, then proceeded to lose the next three, so it was against the backdrop of this disastrous start that the knives were being sharpened for Stan. Additionally, attendances had dropped significantly compared to those of Wolves' rivals; something had to give. In their eighth match, Wolves reversed the trend by beating West Ham 4–3 at Molineux; that was on 14 September 1964, the day before Cullis left his beloved Wolves. For many years Stan Cullis *was* Wolverhampton Wanderers. A proud and dedicated man, one of the small breed of outstanding footballing giants who achieved greatness both as a player and manager; even fewer have achieved both with the same club. Stan was born in Ellesmere Port, Cheshire, on 25 October 1915, and joined Wolves in February 1934. As a player he was a great centre-half, tough-tackling, good in the air, and a shrewd and thoughtful passer of the ball. A born leader, he captained Wolves before his nineteenth birthday, and England a few years later. The outbreak of war restricted him to 12 full England caps, plus 20 wartime international appearances. He was a member of Wolves' losing FA Cup Final team in 1939, when the popular opinion was that Wolves only had to turn up to win; Portsmouth beat them 4-1. When the great man prematurely hung up his boots in May 1947 after making 171 appearances for Wolves, he accepted the post of assistant manager to Ted Vizard, and at age 32 he became the youngest man to manage at this level. A year later, on 23 June 1948, he took over as manager to begin an era of success. As the architect of Wolves' triumphs, his record as manager was three League Championships, in 1953/54, 57/58 and 58/59, and two FA Cups, in 1949 and 1960, the latter being the year Wolves almost won the double, finishing as runners-up by one point to Burnley.

Stan Cullis' full managerial record in 16 years at Wolves was:

> FA Cup Winners - twice
> League Division 1 Champions – 3 times
> Runners-up – 3 times
> Third place – 3 times

Fifth place – once
Sixth place – twice
Fourteenth – once
Sixteenth – twice
Eighteenth – once
Losing FA Cup Semi-Finalists - once

Success under Stan Cullis wasn't restricted to the first XI. Under his guidance, the reserves were Champions of the Central League 5 times, in 1950/51, 1951/52, 1952/53, 1957/58 and 1958/59. The youth team won the FA Youth Cup once, in 1957/58, and were beaten finalists on 3 other occasions, in 1952/53, 1953/54 and 1961/62.

The following year, Stan Cullis was appointed manager of Birmingham City, and in November 1964 Andy Beattie was appointed caretaker-manager of Wolves.

On 22 December 1964 came another bombshell: news that the great Major Frank Buckley had died at his home in Walsall at the grand old age of 91. Frank Buckley was born in Urmston, Manchester, on 9 November 1883. He enlisted in the British Army and served in the Boer War, 1899-1902. Buckley started his footballing career playing centre-half for Aston Villa in April 1903. In 1905 he moved to Brighton & Hove Albion for a year before joining Manchester United. He subsequently played for Manchester City, Birmingham City, Derby County – with whom he won a Second Division Championship medal in 1911/12 – and finally Bradford City in May 1914. He won one England cap in 1914 against Ireland. The outbreak of the First World War put his footballing career on hold. He joined the 17th Middlesex Regiment, commanding the 'Footballer's Battalion', which as its name suggests was comprised of professional footballers. In 1916 he was promoted to the rank of Major. At the end of hostilities, Major Buckley returned to football as player-manager of Norwich City from March 1919 until July 1920 when, after difficulties at the club, he drifted out of the game, working as a commercial traveller for 3 years. The call of football was strong, however, and in July 1923 he returned to his first love, as manager of Blackpool Town. On 27 June 1927, Major Frank Buckley was appointed manager-secretary of Second Division Wolverhampton Wanderers, where he stayed until March 1944, a tenure of almost 17 years. He became known as the 'Master of Molineux', indisputably exerting a major influence on the club, shaping it to suit his style. Buckley arrived at Wolves at a time when the club was desperately short of money and going nowhere fast, taking over from dismissed previous incumbent Fred Scotchbrook on a 3 year contract. It took him four seasons to establish a decent team, which in 1930/31 he guided to 4th place in Division 2. The following season, 1931/32, Wolves won the Division 2 Championship, and again he set about building a side that would be strong enough to compete with the best sides, and challenge for top honours. Wolves reached 5th spot in Division 1 in 1936/37, were runners-up in 1937/38, and again in 1938/39 in a season that saw them reach the FA Cup Final only to be beaten 4-1 by lowly Portsmouth (no disrespect to them). Then came the outbreak of war, which halted Wolves' revival, but the groundwork had been done. In his time, Buckley brought to the club and developed some great players, a number becoming Wolves legends – Stan Cullis, Dennis Westcott, Billy Wright, Jimmy Mullen, Dennis Wilshaw, Dicky Dorsett, Tom Galley, Joe Gardiner, Billy Hartill, Reg Hollingworth and Bryn Jones to name but a few. In 1938 Buckley's contract was renewed for another 10 years, but in March 1944 he sensationally quit, citing private and personal matters as the reason; maybe we'll never know the real truth of what happened, and why he decided to leave the club he loved at such a moment. After leaving Wolves he managed Hull City from May 1946 to March 1948; Leeds United from May 1948 to April 1953, during which time he signed the legendary genial Welsh giant John Charles for the club; and finally Walsall Town from April 1953 to September 1955. He retired from the game at the age of 71. Major Buckley never again repeated his success with Wolves, and never really saw the job through to the end. During the war years Wolves won their only trophy under Buckley's tutelage, the 1942 Wartime Cup.

Back in 1965, new Manager Andy Beattie couldn't keep us up, and down we went into Division 2. Wolves may have been relegated at the end of 1964/65, but still held a top-flight record to be proud of. From 1936/37 to 1964/65, in 22 seasons, excluding the break for the Second World War, Wolves were Champions three times, runners-up five times, 3rd four times, strangely never 4th, 5th three times and 6th twice. In that time Wolves finished lower than 6th on only five occasions, also winning two FA Cups and making one losing Cup Final appearance.

1965/66

In the 2nd Division in season 1965/66 we witnessed the then worst result in living memory (Chorley was yet to come!). The 9-3 defeat handed out by Southampton at the Dell on 18 September 1965 was an all-time low for the faithful, even worse than the 7-4 mauling handed out by Spurs at White Hart Lane the season before on 27 March 1965. After the turmoil of Cullis' sacking and relegation from the top flight, team confidence was understandably at rock bottom, Andy Beattie decided he'd had enough and resigned. Ronnie Allen, who had joined Wolves as coach in August 1965, now took over as caretaker-manager. He was not the most popular appointment amongst Wolves fans, because of his previous long association with West Brom. However, Allen managed to somehow instil confidence in the players. They overcame the ignominy of the 9-3 thrashing to embark on a 10-match unbeaten run, eventually finishing the season in 6th place. In the process Wolves handed out a pasting of their own, murdering Portsmouth 8-2 at Molineux in November. It was an entertaining season of extremes; either we got thumped or we walloped some team or another. In 1965/66 Wolves scored 87 and conceded 61. In March 1966, Allen bought a man who was to have a major influence on the coming years: Mike Bailey was signed from Charlton for £40,000. His job was to stiffen up the Wolves midfield. Now maybe we had the makings of a reasonable team? Many fans' main gripe that season was the adoption of gold shorts and socks to go with our gold shirts. As Wolves traditionalists we hated it. Sadly, Peter Broadbent left the club in January 1965 when he joined Shrewsbury Town.

The silky skills of inside-forward Peter Broadbent had graced the Molineux stage for 14 years. Cullis signed him from Brentford for £10,000 in February 1951, calling it one of his finest ever signings. A magical playmaker, a great passer of the ball, and a brilliant goalscorer, his delicate touch and outstanding body-swerve rivalled anything seen in continental football. Peter Broadbent's style of play attracted numerous admirers, including the illustrious George Best. In Joe Lovejoy's book *Bestie*, Wolves fan George says that he didn't have an individual hero, but supposed that Broadbent was close. Yes, as a boy George Best supported Wolves! Broadbent won 3 First Division Championships and 1 FA Cup with Wolves, plus 7 full international caps with England, including playing in the 1958 World Cup. Peter made 497 senior appearances for Wolves, scoring 145 goals.

Whilst we were waiting for the new season to start, there was the little matter of the 1966 World Cup Finals to be sorted out, hosted in England as we all know. Ron Flowers was selected for the England squad, but sadly didn't play in any of England's games. Ron's 49th and final full cap had been won on 29 June 1966 against Norway in Oslo. Alf

1966 England World Cup rosette.

Ramsey's wingless wonders were great; the two Bobbys, Charlton and Moore, were truly world-class; Peters and Hurst were a revelation, as in that glorious summer of 1966, England won the World Cup, beating West Germany 4-2 in the final, after extra-time.

Front cover of the 1966 World Cup souvenir programme.

1966/67

As his reward for halting the slide, Allen had been confirmed as full-time manager in July 1966 in time for the new season. And 1966/67 didn't go too badly. We'd already handed out a few wallopings, beating Blackburn 4-0, Cardiff 7-1, Northampton 4-0, Derby 5-3 and 3-0, and Bolton 5-2, when in March 1967 Ronnie Allen produced a stroke of genius by signing Derek Dougan from Leicester City. 'The Doog' knocked in 9 goals in 11 games, amidst a great attacking line-up: Terry Wharton, Ernie Hunt, the Doog, Peter Knowles and Dave Wagstaffe. Their goals brought to an end Wolves' two-season stay in League Division 2. We finished second to Coventry to win promotion back to the top flight. On a sad note, the wonderful floodlit friendlies had now become a thing of the past. Incidentally, 1966/67 was the first season that Wolves had entered the League Cup, which had been inaugurated in 1960. Mind you they needn't have bothered! Entering the competition in round 2, they failed to even make it through the third round. Sammy Chung joined as trainer-coach in July 1967.

Jock Stein's Celtic won the 1967 European Cup, beating Inter Milan 2-1 to become the first British team to succeed in this competition.

In the summer of 1967, Wolves accepted an invitation to play in an International Soccer Tournament in America. Wolves played under the name of Los Angeles Wolves against teams from Brazil, Holland, Italy, Scotland and Uruguay. After a gruelling series of matches, Wolves emerged as winners, beating Aberdeen 6-5 in the final. Ball juggling Dave Burnside scored three for Wolves. Guess who got 3 for Aberdeen? None other than the fantastic, soon-to-be-transferred-to-Wolves, Frank Munro. Frank joined Wolves from Aberdeen in January 1968 for a fee of £55,000. In those days Frank played in midfield, not in the centre of defence where ultimately he was to be outstanding for Wolves and Scotland.

1967/68

Ron Flowers, the last of Wolves' great players of the title-winning era left the club in September 1967. Another product of Wath Wanderers, Ron played 512 first team games for Wolves, scoring 37 goals and winning three Championships and one FA Cup. The first of his 49 England caps came in 1955, the last 11 years later, a true testimony to the ability and longevity of this wonderful wing-half.

Wath Wanderers was an amateur club from Wath-on-Dearne in Yorkshire, which Major Frank Buckley took on as a feeder club for Wolves. Run by former Wolves player Mark Crook, this little club produced a number of promising players in what Buckley recognised as being a hugely cost-effective way of finding and blooding players. Revolutionary in its day, the idea has since been adopted by many top clubs. Along with Ron Flowers, Wath Wanderers produced Roy Swinbourne, Peter Knowles, Alan Sunderland and Steve Daley to name but a few.

Back in the First Division once again, Wolves conceded too many goals and didn't score enough. Now where had we seen this before? They finished a lowly 17th in 1967/68. I have to mention one Molineux match from that season because of the anger it generated among Wolves fans at the time. The date was 23 August 1967. Our opponents – the Albion. The 51,438 gate generated a lot of noise in our first home game of the season after winning promotion. Big Phil Parkes had already saved a 6th-minute 'Bomber' Brown penalty, and Wolves were subsequently cruising along 2-0 up, when a linesman, who must have been seriously challenged sight-wise, persuaded the referee that an Albion effort had in fact crossed the Wolves goal line – rubbish! Then at 3-2 in a whirlwind finish, the ball was crossed from Albion's right and Brown punched the ball into Wolves' net with only a couple of minutes to go. I'm sure that everybody in the ground saw it – 'as plain as the nose on yer face mate!' Even my mate Mick saw it, and he's an Albion supporter! The only blokes not to see it were the ref and his linesman. Phil Parkes was sent off for protesting too vehemently, and the game finished 3-3. Two extremely doubtful decisions and one diabolical one cost Wolves a well-deserved victory. This was a match lit up by the fireworks on the pitch!

Frank Munro in the 1970s.

FOOTBALL LEAGUE — FIRST DIVISION

AT MOLINEUX, WOLVERHAMPTON
WEDNESDAY, AUGUST 23rd, 1967
Match No. 2.   Kick off 7.30 p.m.

WOLVES   WEST BROMWICH ALBION

Shirts : Gold. Shorts : Gold.	Shirts : Blue and White. Shorts : White
1. PARKES	1. OSBORNE
2. TAYLOR	2. FRASER
3. THOMSON	3. WILLIAMS
4. BAILEY	4. HOWSHALL
5. WOODFIELD	5. COLQUHOUN
6. HOLSGROVE	6. TALBUT
7. WHARTON	7. FOGGO
8. HUNT	8. ASTLE
9. DOUGAN	9. KAYE
10. BURNSIDE	10. BROWN
11. WAGSTAFFFE	11. CLARK
Substitute : **KNOWLES**	Substitute : **COLLARD**

Linesman—Red Flag	Referee—	Linesman—Yellow Flag
J. F. ORPIN	J. E. CARR	K. HARRIS
(Cardiff)	(Sheffield)	(Chester)

Teams page from the programme for Wolves v. West Brom, 23 August 1967.

1968/69

In a nondescript next season Wolves again couldn't seem to score on a regular basis, but still progress was being made; we were 14th in the League in November 1968, when all of a sudden Ronnie Allen resigned, and we had a new manager, Bill McGarry. On the field, things stayed pretty much the same except the manager sold Frank Wignall and brought in Hugh Curran. By the end of that season, Wolves had managed to finish one place better than the previous year, in 16th spot. Then we were up to 13th in 1969/70, a season that saw them vie against foreign opposition for the first time in nearly ten years. But at least they changed back to the traditional black shorts! Yep, the coming season, 1969/70, was awaited with eager anticipation. Once again we had a European competition to look forward to. True, it was only the Anglo-Italian Cup, but never mind, as far as all loyal Wolves supporters were concerned, the good times were on the way back.

The team flew to Baltimore on 30 April 1969 for an 8-match, month-long tour of the United States of America. They returned with another trophy for the cabinet after winning the 5-team mini-league championship. The other teams were West Ham, Aston Villa, Kilmarnock and Dundee United. During the tour Bill McGarry tried Frank Munro in the centre of the back four, and lo! it came to pass, that he unearthed a defensive diamond – Frank was superb. McGarry admitted that Frank had often said that he fancied playing a defensive role, so he decided to give him a try; at the time Frank still wore the number 8 shirt. Captain Mike Bailey wrote an interesting 6-page diary of the USA adventure for the *Molineus* match day magazine. (It's in Volume 2, No. 1, Wolves v Stoke City).

The details of the 8 matches Wolves played are as follows:

May 2nd v West Ham; Wolves lost 2-3, scorers: Bailey, Knowles
May 4th v Dundee United; Wolves won 4-2, scorers: Knowles 2, Wilson, Bailey
May 8th v West Ham; Wolves won 4-2, scorers: McAlle 2, Curran, Bailey
May 11th v Kilmarnock; Wolves won 3-2, scorers: Curran 2, Farrington
May 14th v Aston Villa; Wolves won 2-1, scorers: Knowles (pen.), Dougan
May 16th v Kilmarnock; Wolves won 3-0, scorers: Dougan, Wagstaffe, Curran
May 24th v Aston Villa; Wolves won 5-0, scorers: Curran 2, Dougan, Knowles, Woodfield
May 31st v Dundee United; Wolves lost 2-3, scorer: Dougan 2

Mike wrote that the lads wanted to win their final game. However it was not their day, and in any case they had already won the championship.

Wolves were back home well in time to see those monumental TV pictures of Apollo 11, as Neil Armstrong and Buzz Aldrin landed on the surface of the moon and hopped about a bit. Five more moon landings followed in the Apollo project that had been announced by President John F. Kennedy in 1961, the last in 1972. The total cost added up to $24 billion. Gosh! Wouldn't that buy a few players?

Wolves played the Inter City Fairs Cup qualifiers Kilmarnock again three months later, the Scots being referred to in the programme notes as 'one of Scotland's big four'. This Molineux meeting was on Saturday 2 August 1969, a warm-up game for the 1969/70 season.

1969/70

On Wednesday 27 August 1969, Wolves unveiled their new £20,000 floodlights in a League game with Brian Clough's Derby County. Apparently the new lights, among the finest in the country, were so powerful they caused many press photographers to over-expose their films. On 3 September the new floodlights had the distinction of lighting the first-ever floodlit game to be televised in colour. This was the 2nd-round League Cup clash against Tottenham, which Wolves won 1-0. A friend of mine claims that Grimsby bought the old lights.

The 1969/70 season started magnificentl, and promised so much, Wolves winning their first four games, then bang! another bombshell hit Wolves. Darling of the fans Peter Knowles announced that he was giving up football to devote his life to the Jehovah's Witnesses. He played his last game on Saturday, 6 September 1969, in the 3-3 draw against Nottingham Forest, 24 days before his 24th birthday. In his programme notes for that game McGarry said that he was still hoping for a happy ending where Peter was concerned, that his kit would be laid out on Monday and that he was expected to arrive for training. As we now know, he didn't turn up.

Peter Knowles had seemed destined to become a great footballer. His wonderful skills and special temperament showed in the way that he played the game. Capped four times for the England Under-23 team, he surely would have made it to the big stage. Peter made his Wolves first-team debut in October 1963, a year after signing professional forms, and scoring 4 times in 14 outings. By the end of the following season Peter had established himself as a regular first-teamer and although injuries subsequently restricted the number of games he was able to play, he still managed 84 goals in 188 appearances. A truly precocious football talent like his doesn't come along all that often, so it's understandable how the fans took the news of his announcement. Peter has to be respected for having the courage and moral fortitude to turn his back on the sport he loved, for true to his word, he never came back, despite Wolves holding on to his registration for a number of years. Several years later he did return to the Molineux turf to play in part of a testimonial game.

The season ended disappointingly with four defeats, Wolves losing eight of the final thirteen games and drawing the other five, taking only 5 points from a possible 26. In the process they set a then post-war record of 16 draws in one season. 1969/70 was the first season that all 22 First Division clubs entered the League Cup; Wolves were knocked out in round three.

January 1970 saw the formation of the 'Official Wolves Supporters Club', amalgamating with the existing 'North Bank Away Supporters Club'.

At the end of the season, Wolves qualified to compete in the Anglo-Italian Cup, a competition including six English teams and the same number of Italian teams. Twelve teams divided into three groups, each containing two teams from each country. Group 1 comprised Sheffield Wednesday, Swindon Town, Juventus and Napoli. Group 2 was Middlesborough, West Bromwich, Lanerossi and Roma. Group 3 was Sunderland, Wolverhampton Wanderers, Fiorentina and Lazio. No one that I spoke to knew quite what this competition was really all about, aside from bringing in much-needed revenue. At least it got us back into Europe without having to book with Don Everall Travel! I've included the games, but with only a small amount of detail.

Wolves 2 Fiorentina 1
Anglo-Italian Cup, 1st leg, home

Wolves won 2-1 in the first leg at Molineux on Friday night, 1 May 1970; it was almost like the old days. However, Wolves would need to display much more guile and urgency than they showed in the early part of this game if they were to have any chance of winning this new inter-league competition. A revolutionary format was being tried out with teams awarded points for scoring goals as well as for winning or drawing. So goals equal points, and what do points make? Sorry that's a different game. Back to the rules: 2 points were awarded for a win, 1 point for a draw – so far so good – plus 1 point for each goal scored, none deducted for conceding. Actually, I think I've only just got it! So for this result Wolves got 4 points and Florence only 1. Sunderland beat Lazio 3-1 and so got 5 points. Eventually Wolves got their act together. Hugh Curran went down the left and his super cross was headed home in fine style by the Doog. Did Wolves think this was going to be easy? Who knows? They certainly slowed down the pace of the game. We had to wait another frustrating hour until Waggy got Wolves' second. In the meantime, in the 65th minute John Holsgrove got himself booked. Brazilian Amarildo showed us his skill with a 69th minute screamer that had the crowd on their feet – most of us were standing anyway – fortunately the alert Phil Parkes managed to get down smartly to save his swerving free-kick. Wolves hadn't won since 24 January. This trend looked like it might continue when Holsgrove gave away a gift goal to the Italians in the 83rd minute. Mario Maraschi eagerly latched on to the tall defender's mistake to hammer the ball passed Parkes to give us all another case of jangly-nerves for the final minutes of a game that Wolves desperately wanted to win. Phew! They did it! The Italians had Rogora booked for impeding Curran. Paul Walker had replaced the injured Mike Bailey, who had limped off at half-time, then

Wolves' team at Molineux: Parkes; Shaw, Parkin; Bailey (Walker, then McAlle), Holsgrove, Munro; Lutton, McCalliog, Dougan, Curran, Wagstaffe. Subs: Walker, McAlle.
Fiorentina: Bandoni; Rogora, Longoni; Esposito, Marinelli, Berni; Rizzo, Merlo, Maraschi (Mariani), Amarildo, Chiarugi.
Referee: Fabio Monti (Italy)
Score: Wolves 2, Fiorentina 1
Wolves' scorers: Dougan, Wagstaffe
Scorer for Fiorentina: Maraschi
Attendance: 14,262

Walker too twisted himself and thus the substitute had to be substituted, John McAlle coming on in his place. Would 2-1 really be enough?

Wolves 1 Lazio 0
Anglo-Italian Cup, 1st leg, home

Wolves beat the other Italian club 1-0 in the first leg at Molineux on Saturday, 9 May 1970, kick-off 3 p.m. It was definitely like the old days – two wins against European opposition. Lazio were excellent, showing marvellous technical ability as well as some solid defending, which kept Wolves out for a long time. The Italians' agile goalkeeper Sulfaro ably dealt with most things that came his way, apart from skipper Mike Bailey's 65th-minute shot that fired Wolves into the lead. A section of the crowd had a good-natured go at the Lazio manager, Lorenzo, I guess, just to relieve the boredom. A little later Parkes mishandled and the Lazio forwards claimed the ball had gone over the line, the linesman said no, and so did the referee. All hell broke loose, resulting in Giorgio Chinaglia being dismissed for 'over vehement and physical protesting'. The game finished 1-0 and Wolves earned 3 more points. Now it was a scuffle in the tunnel that provided the final bit of light relief, but Wolverhampton's finest soon calmed things down, although not before Waggy was booked – twice! And Curran – but only once. What a night! I felt like singing, 'Just one Cornetto!'

> Wolves' team at Molineux: Parkes; Shaw, Parkin; Bailey, Holsgrove, Munro; McCalliog, Walker, Dougan, Curran, Wagstaffe. Sub: Richards.
> Lazio: Sulfaro; Papadopulo, Wilson; Governato, Polentes, Marchesi; Massa, Mazzola, Chinaglia, Ghio, Morrone.
> Referee: Senor Carminetti (Milan)
> Score: Wolves 1, Lazio 0
> Wolves' scorer: Bailey
> Attendance: 11,953

One week later Wolves were in Italy for the away legs.

Fiorentina 1 Wolves 3
Anglo-Italian Cup, 2nd leg, away

Wolves continued where they left off against Fiorentina, winning comfortably in the Forte del Marmi stadium, 6 miles outside Florence, on Saturday 16 May 1970, but not before being on the receiving end of a little more Brazilian magic from Amarildo. His 26th-minute surging run took him through Wolves' midfield, body-swerving around two defenders before smashing an unstoppable shot high into Wolves' net. Phil Parkes was in fine form to keep out the home attack. On 35 minutes, John Richards got his first ever goal for the first XI. He managed to steer the ball home after a mix-up in the Italian defence. Wolves were now in command, dictating the play superbly. Fifteen minutes after the restart Hugh Curran converted a neat cross. Then on 83 minutes, Derek Dougan made it three following Curran's good work. Five more points in the bag – great!

Wolves' team in Florence: Parkes; Taylor, Parkin; Bailey, Holsgrove, Munro; McCalliog, Richards, Dougan, Curran, Wagstaffe. Subs: Shaw, Oldfield, Lutton, Walker, McAlle.
Referee: R. Tinkler (Boston)
Score: Wolves 3, Fiorentina 1
Wolves' scorers: Dougan, Curran, Richards
Attendance: 13,120

Lazio 2 Wolves 0
Anglo-Italian Cup, 2nd leg, away

Wolves had won a lot of points, but sadly this trophy was not destined for the Molineux cabinet. On Thursday 21 May 1970, Wolves lost 2-0 to Lazio in Rome and failed to make the final. Over the four games Wolves scored 6 and let in 4, which wasn't good enough. Dave Wagstaffe played well in this game, and Wolves might have scored from two of his corners. From the first, Derek Parkin shot into the side-netting; the second saw Dougan skim the crossbar with a nice header. On 41 minutes Phil Parkes fouled Chinaglia just outside the 18-yard line. Mazzola took the free-kick and sent in a swerving cross which was headed in at the far post by Ghio. On 67 minutes Ghio put Ghenare clear then superbly caressed the return pass into the Wolves net. A minute later McGarry sent on Bertie Lutton for Curran without the substitute having too much effect, apart from being clobbered by the big Italian goalie. Referee Gordon Hill didn't like Sulfaro's heavy challenge on the young Irishman, and the goalkeeper completely lost it when he was sent off. A few afters from the first game must have still been hanging around in the minds of one or two players, because tempers flared and fists were brandished as the Italian team swarmed round the ref like hornets. Holsgrove hit the upright with a header in the dying moments, but it was no good, Wolves were out.

Wolves' team in Rome: Parkes; Taylor, Parkin; Bailey, Holsgrove, Munro; Richards, McCalliog, Dougan, Curran, Wagstaffe. Sub: Oldfield, Shaw, McAlle, Lutton, Walker.
Referee: Gordon Hill
Score: Wolves 0, Lazio 2
Attendance: 43,073

In the First Division Wolves finished 1969/70 in 13th position. The latter part of that season saw Wolves fail to win a single game after beating Ipswich Town 2-0 at Molineux on 31 January. Of the final thirteen games, eight were lost and five were drawn. In April 1970 Wolves embarked on a trip to Yugoslavia, playing three games, winning one and losing two.

1970 was World Cup year. This time it was Mexico's turn to host this wonderful football extravaganza. In the build-up to the competition, England captain Bobby Moore was arrested in Bogota and held in custody, accused of stealing a gold bracelet worth £600. Moore protested his innocence and was eventually allowed to leave Columbia. The whole episode stank! Then when England's goalkeeper, the great Gordon Banks, was taken ill with food poisoning before England's quarter-final with West Germany, the word conspiracy reared its head again. As we know, replacement goalie Peter Bonetti wasn't a patch on Banks and England got beat 3-2, having led 2-0.

Wolves' next venture forth against 'foreign' opposition was to enter the 1970/71 Texaco Cup, sometimes called the British Isles Cup. At last Wolves won another piece of silverware to put in the trophy cabinet. But before that Wolves staged yet another floodlit night match. This time it was the turn of West German outfit Hanover 96 to grace the hallowed Molineux turf.

Wolves 1 Hanover 96 2
Inter-European Challenge Match at Molineux

Wolves played Hanover 96 at Molineux on Monday 10 August 1970, in a pre-season run-out for the 1970/71 season. Stroll around would have been a more appropriate description of this affair. The Germans stroked the ball around, displaying some silky skills and got the win their play deserved. On 12 minutes Jimmy Mac crossed the ball and up leapt the Doog to head it on to Bobby Gould, who drove it home; German skipper Siemensmeyer got both goals for Hanover. Like a great many pre-season friendlies this match lacked action, never managing to invoke the level of commitment or power-play witnessed in years past. But at least I suppose the Germans provided a useful workout for our boys.

> Wolves' team at Molineux: Oldfield; Wilson, Parkin; Bailey, Holsgrove, Munro; Hegan (Walker), McCalliog, Dougan, Gould (Curran), Wagstaffe (Lutton).
> Hanover 96: Podlasly; Stiller, Berg, Anders, Hellingrath, Siemensmeyer (Bandura), Nafziger, Bertl, Reimann (Keller), Weller, Brune.
> Referee: Jack Taylor (Wolverhampton)
> Score: Wolves 1, Hanover 96 2
> Wolves' scorer: Gould
> Attendance: 11,494

And so on to the Texaco Cup, a competition that the top teams weren't allowed to enter – but who cared? These were good nights! The other English teams in the competition were WBA, Stoke, Burnley, Tottenham and Forest.

1970/71

Dundee 1 Wolves 2
Texaco Cup, Round 1, 1st leg, away

Wolves played their hearts out to win the first leg at Dens Park, Dundee, on Wednesday 16 September 1970, to set up an interesting second leg. Two minutes into this game Parkes' long upfield punt found Bobby Gould, who beat a couple of defenders to score with a smart right-foot shot. Then in the 39th minute Jimmy McCalliog ran on to Dougan's pass to belt a 25-yarder past Dundee goalkeeper Donaldson. It looked all over despite the fierce fight put up by the Scots, who were being urged on from the touchline by their manager John Prentice. However, with 3 minutes left, Wallace headed in after a free-kick had rebounded out off big Phil Parkes. In the dying minutes Kenny Hibbitt was kicked in the head by Scott and was carried off with a nasty-looking wound that required ten stitches. The pick of Wolves' players were Munro and McAlle, who formed a solid barrier in the centre of the away side's defence.

> Wolves' team in Dundee: Parkes; Shaw, Parkin; Bailey, Munro, McAlle; McCalliog, Hibbitt, Dougan, Gould, Walker (Richards). Subs: Richards, Charlton.
> Dundee: Donaldson; R. Wilson, Houston; Selway, Stewart, Steele; Gilroy (Duncan), Kinninmeath, Wallace, Scott, J. Wilson.
> Referee: W. Anderson (East Kilbride)
> Score: Wolves 2, Dundee 1
> Wolves' scorer: Gould, McCalliog
> Attendance: 9,892

Wolves 0 Dundee 0
Texaco Cup, Round 1, 2nd leg, home

Wolves' win in the first leg at Dundee paved the way for this two-legged victory, although the Dundee manager John Prentice felt his lads could still win the tie. The Molineux leg was played on Tuesday night, 29 September 1970, kick-off 7.30 p.m. That old Molineux feeling was back at last, even though it was a disappointingly low turnout. Frustratingly, Wolves seemed to take it pretty easy in this game; they appeared to be well satisfied to play for a draw, despite winning lots of corners. To be fair, Dundee goalkeeper Alastair Donaldson played well, saving good headers from the Doog and Jimmy Mac. The pick of Wolves' players were Mike Bailey and Kenny Hibbitt; both passed well as they tried to create clear openings. I would sum the game up as being a bit like a bonfire made of wet leaves; it never really got going, despite there being quite a lot of smoke! Anyway, the draw got us through to the next round.

> Wolves' team at Molineux: Parkes; Shaw, Parkin; Bailey, Munro, McAlle; McCalliog, Hibbitt (Richards), Gould, Dougan, Wagstaffe. Subs: Richards, Oldfield.
> Dundee: Donaldson; R. Wilson, Houston; Selway, Stewart, Steele; Duncan (Johnson), Bryce, Wallace, Scott, J. Wilson.
> Referee: Roger Kirkpatrick (Leicester)
> Score: Wolves 0, Dundee 0 (Wolves won 2-1 on aggregate)
> Attendance: 13,042

Wolves' recent excellent form in the League had seen us collect 14 points out of a possible 16 in a 5-game unbeaten run which gave us all the confidence in the world.

Morton 0 Wolves 3
Texaco Cup, Round 2, 1st leg, away

A great performance at Cappielow Park, Greenock, saw Wolves cruise to a 3-0 victory away to Morton, another fine away result in Scotland. Prior to the game, Wolves had trained at Inverclyde recreational centre, a kind of mini-Lilleshall Hall. They found the facilities very much to their liking, and so, hearts, minds and bodies in the right groove, the team looked forward to this first leg, which was played on Wednesday 21 October 1970. Hugh Curran's troublesome groin injury had again kept him out of contention; he hadn't started for Wolves since 19 September. At the heart of their midfield, Morton had the 39-year-old veteran star Bobby Collins. The ex-Scottish international may have been getting on a bit, but he could still play. The first minutes of the game were even as both teams weighed up each other's strengths and weaknesses. Then Wolves struck in the 19th minute. Jimmy Mac crossed perfectly for the Doog to head the ball down into the path of the onrushing Bobby Gould and the big striker nicked the ball past keeper Neilsen. Dave Wagstaffe was giving Morton's right side a torrid time, sending in a string of dangerous crosses, and it was one of these that provided the ammunition for Wolves' second in the 25th minute. Waggy flighted over the perfect centre and Dougan rose above the defenders to head the ball home. Dougan went close twice more as his speedy and direct runs opened up chances for him. Bobby Collins was showing all his skill, spraying the ball around intelligently, his clever promptings putting Wolves' goal under severe pressure from a number of home attacks. Fortunately Wolves' defence, and in particular Frank Munro and John McAlle, prevented Morton's forwards from scoring, and allowed full-backs Shaw and Parkin to make ground down the flanks. On 86 minutes Bernard Shaw's intelligent run and interchange with Jimmy McCalliog took the full-back deep into the Morton area before he hit a rising shot, which struck the far post and rebounded to him. Unfortunately he was now off balance and put the ball over the crossbar. Wolves were showing a lot of variety in their approach play, sometimes using the long ball to good effect, particularly in the first-half when they had the extra benefit of the wind behind them, but also moving the ball through the midfield well, Mike Bailey prompting his forwards whenever he could. Along with Hibbitt and McCalliog, he was always on the lookout for the killer pass. Morton tried hard, but had no luck against Wolves' defence, the only real danger coming from a swerving shot struck by former Coventry winger Ernie Hannigan. Eight minutes from time, Bobby Gould got his second and Wolves' third following a move of speed and precision. Dougan put Wagstaffe away on the left; again he produced a cracker of a cross, which Gould powered beyond the keeper's reach.

Wolves' team at Morton: Parkes; Shaw, Parkin; Bailey, Munro, McAlle; McCalliog, Hibbitt, Gould, Dougan, Wagstaffe. Subs: Richards, Oldfield.
Morton: Nielsen; Murray, McDerment; Sweeney, Gray, Rankin; Hannigan, Collins, Osbourne, Mason, Clarke (Campbell). Sub: Campbell.
Referee: W. Mullen (Dalkeith)
Score: Wolves 3, Morton 0
Wolves' scorers: Gould (2), Dougan
Attendance: 10,145

Wolves 1 Morton 2
Texaco Cup, Round 2, 2nd leg, home

This second leg was played at Molineux on Tuesday night, 3 November 1970, kick-off 7.30 p.m. It was a good job that Wolves had won the first leg at Morton by 3 goals, because once again they produced a lacklustre performance at home. Time after time Wolves had the nerves of the Molineux faithful jangling in the disappointingly small crowd. Kenny Hibbitt had been injured in the 2-0 defeat by Liverpool at Anfield on the previous Saturday and had been substituted, but was pronounced fit for this game. When no goal came after raiding continuously in the opening minutes, Wolves seemed to be content to sit back on their three-goal lead from the first leg, paving the way for Morton to have a go at them. On 23 minutes the visitors got the reward they deserved for some persistent attacking. Wolves' defence failed to deal with an innocuous ball crossed in from the left wing – a simple case of 'after you old chap' allowed Gerry Sweeney to nip in between them to drive the ball into the net. Amongst Wolves' defenders, one or two exchanged glaring looks. Morton now took the initiative, turning up the volume to pile on the pressure, Bobby Collins again at the heart of most moves. Following a good exchange of passes, the ball was sent through to Campbell and the centre-forward made no mistake with a fierce rising shot that went in off the Wolves crossbar to make it 2-0 on the night. Suddenly there was only one goal in it: 3-2 on aggregate. Half-time came and McGarry knew he had to change things, risking Hugh Curran's injured groin in an attempt to add more firepower to his attack. Dougan came off to make way. In the 67th minute, Curran's promotion from the bench brought the result McGarry had hoped for. Mike Bailey sent over a low centre for the Scot to dive full-length to head home to restore Wolves 2-goal advantage, and salvage a little of Wolves' pride as well as spurring the home side back into

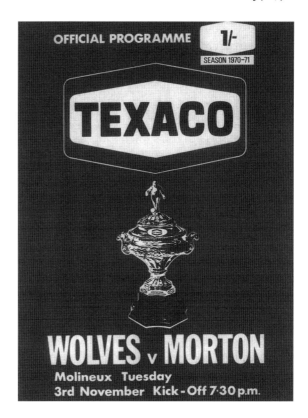

Front cover of the programme for
Wolves v. Morton in the Texaco Cup.

action. Soon after, Jimmy Mac watched in horror as right-back Hale steered his goal-bound header away from the line, then he squandered a couple of good situations that might have resulted in goals. Bailey sent in a cannonball effort as Wolves began to attack in force; it was reminiscent of the old power-play style. Morton's man-for-man marking prevented a number of attacks from developing. When Wolves did get through, the ball would miss the goal by inches, or would be saved by Sorensen. Morton's challenge had fizzled out long before the final whistle was sounded, and Wolves finished the game in complete control, winning the tie with an aggregate score of 4-2 and going through to the third round.

Wolves' team at Molineux: Parkes; Shaw, Parkin; Bailey, Munro, McAlle; McCalliog, Hibbitt, Gould, Dougan (Curran), Wagstaffe. Subs: Curran, Oldfield.
Morton: Sorensen; Hale, McDerment; Sweeney, Gray, Rankin; Hannigan, Collins, Campbell (O'Neil), Mason, Anderson. Sub: O'Neil.
Referee: R. Matthewson (Manchester)
Score: Wolves 1, Morton 2 (Wolves won 4-2 on aggregate)
Wolves' scorer: Curran
Attendance: 13,821

Derry City o Wolves 1
Texaco Cup, Semi-Final, 1st leg, away

This was the first time that Derry City had played an English club in a competitive match. It was no walkover, but on 1 December 1970, it all came good in the end. This competent 1-0 win in Ireland, on a dodgy pitch, was good enough for Wolves in the first leg. Derry's manager Jimmy Hill – no, not the TV pundit, the ex-Everton and Norwich winger – apologised for the state of the playing surface, which was muddy down the centre and greasy on the wings. Bouts of heavy rain earlier in the week had threatened to make this game more like a water-polo match. Wolves, without Bailey, Parkin, Dougan, Wagstaffe and Hibbitt, started like they meant it, but each of their early attacks was repulsed by Derry, who then mounted a counter-attack to earn the first corner of the game, which Hugh Curran easily cut out. The surface was cutting up, making it even harder for players to pass the ball along the ground; route-one should have been the prevailing tactic. However, Wolves still tried the low-road, with some success as Richards was put through on three occasions. He got under the first; the second saw amateur goalkeeper Irwyn McKibbin dive acrobatically to grab the ball; the third was well saved by the young Derry goalkeeper. On 16 minutes Wolves should have nosed in front when Curran teed the ball up for Walker, but the youngster shot wide. McKibbin was playing a blinder, palming away a stinging shot from Paul Walker and handling the ball extremely competently. Finally Wolves managed to win a corner, which was booted away, but only to McAlle, who sent over a dangerous-looking centre; once again McKibbin dealt efficiently with the threat. The fighting qualities of the Irish team, coupled with a worsening pitch, certainly didn't help Wolves' cause. Derry's Brandywell ground, which doubles as a dog-track, is right in the centre of the Bogside area of the city; it certainly lived up to that name. The pattern of the game continued in the second half, Wolves attacking, Derry defending stoutly; it seemed the deadlock would never be broken. Then on 82 minutes Richards got away down the right and put over a great centre that Bobby Gould dispatched with an excellent header. At last, Wolves had the breakthrough, one that I'm sure they expected would bring another before the final whistle, but no, it was Derry that turned on the power. Munro managed to head a Derry corner off the line, then Danny Hale pushed the ball in with his hand when he might just as easily have headed it in. Wolves' class just about told, despite the attempts of their opponents and their pitch to put them out of their stride. Derry tried hard, but too often their lack of stamina in the mud halted their progress. The 1-0 defeat probably flattered the home team.

Wolves' team in Derry: Parkes; Taylor, Shaw; Wilson, Munro, McAlle; Richards, McCalliog, Gould, Curran, Walker. Subs: Holsgrove, Arnold.
Derry: McKibbin; Blake, Maguire; Duffy, White, M. Wood; McLaughlin, O'Halloran, Rowland, Hale, Smith. Sub: McDowell.
Referee: Malcolm Wright (Portadown).
Score: Wolves 1, Derry o
Wolves' scorer: Gould
Attendance: 10,096

At Ibrox Park, Glasgow, the home of Glasgow Rangers, on Saturday 2 January 1971, 66 fans died when a crash barrier collapsed near the end of the traditional Old Firm, new-year fixture with Glasgow Celtic. Around 80,000 fans were packed into the ground, many of whom were leaving following the scoring of the equaliser. Then Rangers scored again ,causing many fans to turn back. In the resultant crush, stairway handrails buckled and a barrier collapsed, killing 66 and injuring many more. There was a public outcry, with many questions going unanswered. This was a subject persistently neglected by the Home Secretary and Parliament alike. There was a distinct need for a higher level of safety standards in football grounds; this tragedy brought the need back into focus. In 1946, 33 fans had been killed and 500 injured at Bolton, caused by a crush of people. In that incident no structures had collapsed. Stanley Rous wrote a letter in March 1948 urging the government to introduce legislation, but nothing much happened. Many recommended the introduction of licensing, but the Home Office constantly rejected all proposals. Now, in the wake of yet another disaster, the public demanded action, but they didn't get it. The 1971 catastrophe was not the first at Ibrox. In 1902, part of the terracing collapsed, killing 24. In January 1970, only a year before this latest tragedy, 24 fans had been injured when railings had given way. In light of more recent calamities it would seem that the public in general, and the victims in particular, were badly let down by the people with the power to make all stadia safe places for those attending.

On an entirely different note, back at Molineux, Wolves had a second leg to win; the omens were good. Three days earlier we'd thumped the Baggies 4-2 at the Hawthorns – and it don't get much better than that, do it?

Wolves 4 Derry City 0
Texaco Cup, Semi-Final, 2nd leg, home

At last, a vintage performance by Wolves as they thrashed Derry 4-0, the home team proving just too good for the Irish League side. This match was played at Molineux on Tuesday 23 March 1971, having been postponed from 8 December 1970. Hibbitt and Dougan were still injured, but Bailey, Parkin and Waggy were back. It was a wet night at Molineux, and for a long time Wolves' forwards were playing the same old song, their shooting boots again seemingly misplaced as we watched chance after chance go begging – talk about frustration! Derek Parkin eventually came to the rescue with a fine run that took him through the heart of the Derry defence, drawing McKibbin and then calmly stroking the ball past the young keeper. Next it was the turn of Bailey and Shaw, again not Wolves' forwards, to provide the thrills, which they did with a couple of excellent shots. Derry defended as well as they could, but undoubtedly would have been swamped if Wolves forwards had got their act together sooner. McKibbin had to be alert to prevent an own-goal by his captain Doug Wood, who surprisingly decided to back-head a harmless-looking ball towards his own goal. With the game heading into the final 15 minutes, Wolves' attackers suddenly came to life. Waggy centred and Curran latched on to the ball after it had been only half-cleared to fire in the second. In the closing stages of the game Bernard Shaw continued his overlapping runs to great effect and provided an astute pass for Mike O'Grady to shoot home; now it was becoming a rout. Shaw again raided down the right, sending over a beautifully flighted cross for Gould to head home powerfully. The miss of the night had been in the 47th minute when Waggy rounded McKibbin and rolled a perfect pass into the path of the advancing Bobby Gould only to

Front cover of the programme for Wolves v. Derry.

watch Wolves' number 9 contrive to miss the simplest of chances. Player–manager Jimmy Hill brought himself on in place of Ward, but it was too late to gain anything more than to add to the pride of his team's energetic performance. Wolves were through to the final, where they would meet Heart of Midlothian for the first time since 1960, earning £7,000 in the process of getting there. Hearts manager Bobby Smith had watched this game intently, no doubt trying to spot the weaknesses in Wolves' tactics and thus plot a strategy to beat us.

Wolves' team at Molineux: Parkes; Shaw, Parkin; Bailey, Munro, McAlle; McCalliog, O'Grady, Gould, Curran, Wagstaffe. Subs: Walker, Oldfield.
Derry: McKibbin; Duffy, McLaughlin; McDowell, White, Wood; Rowland, Hale, Ward (Hill), O'Halloran, Smith. Subs: Mahon, Hill.
Referee: B. Homewood (Sunbury-on-Thames).
Score: Wolves 4, Derry 0 (Wolves won 5-0 on aggregate)
Wolves' scorers: Parkin, Curran, O'Grady, Gould
Attendance: 15,784

Front cover of the souvenir brochure for Wolves v. Hearts in the Texaco Cup Final.

Hearts 1 Wolves 3
Texaco Cup, Final, 1st leg, away

The first leg of this cup final was played on Wednesday 14 April 1971 at Hearts' Tynecastle stadium, Edinburgh, where a gate of 40,000 had been forecast. Obviously Bobby Smith hadn't learned much, because Wolves eventually handed out a right royal drubbing. Again Wolves had a number of injury problems: Shaw was out, Bailey was doubtful with a damaged back, and there was still no Doog, who had missed the previous five league games. The teams were announced and brought good news: Mike Bailey was in fact playing and Dougan would be on the bench. Hearts played well, showing many nice touches, but the game stuttered a bit because of the referee's whistle – it kept blowing! 'Tiny' Wharton, as the 6ft 4in referee was known, booked Curran, Bailey and O'Grady, all three for fouls on Jim Townsend. Mike Bailey produced another classic wing-half performance – thank goodness he'd made the starting line-up. In company with Frank Munro and John McAlle he gave a master-class in tackling and winning the ball. On almost 7 minutes Townsend's cross unluckily flew off McAlle to Ford whose running header left Phil Parkes with no chance. Then it was Wolves' turn to show what they could do. In the 17th minute Mike Bailey equalised. Waggy beat two men and sent in a cross-cum-shot that rebounded to the Wolves captain, who made no mistake with a strong shot that easily beat Cruickshank. Just after the half-hour, Mike O'Grady's good work enabled him to thread a short ball to Curran for the Scottish international to smack home, and it was Curran again who popped up to tap home Wolves' third after the goalkeeper had palmed out O'Grady's thunderbolt. Derek Dougan replaced Gould on 71 minutes; it was good to see him again after his long injury. In the dying minutes Hearts came close to getting a second, but Parkes was up to the task when he dived full-length to tip George Fleming's smart shot onwards to the post and clear. The 3-1 result was fair.

Wolves' team in Edinburgh: Parkes; Taylor, Parkin; Bailey, Munro, McAlle; McCalliog, O'Grady, Gould (Dougan), Curran, Wagstaffe. Subs: Dougan, Oldfield.
Hearts: Cruickshank; Sneddon, Kay; Thomson, Anderson, Brown; Fleming, Townsend, Ford, Wood, Carruthers (Young). Sub: Young.
Referee: T. (Tiny) Wharton
Score: Wolves 3, Hearts 1
Wolves' scorers: Curran (2), Bailey
Attendance: 26,057

So the stage was set for Wolves to crucify their Scottish opponents in the second leg of this cup final at Molineux.

Wolves 0 Hearts 1
Texaco Cup, Final, 2nd leg, home

For the second leg of the final, played on Monday night, 3 May 1971, kick-off 7.30 p.m., Bobby Smith decided to bring in teenage scoring sensation Brian Laing in an effort to claw back a goal or two. Wolves were back to their worst. It was as if there was a script for home games in European competitions, because Wolves once again played out a repetition of previous ineffective football. Those all-too-familiar irksome emotions that pervaded floodlit matches at Molineux with too much regularity – disappointment, frustration and irritation – returned. Fortunately, Wolves had done enough to win the trophy at Tynecastle, but on this showing deserved nothing. One of the stars of Wolves first-leg victory, 2-goal hero Hugh Curran, was dropped in favour of a Dougan-Gould strike force; Curran didn't even make the bench. Having said this, Wolves started the game as though they would definitely add to the three scored in Edinburgh, they certainly had enough chances in the first quarter of an hour. Thankfully, the Hearts forwards hadn't brought their shooting boots either. Frank Munro was once again quite brilliant, but on 25 minutes he was powerless as a mistake at the back gave Hearts the breakthrough they craved, winger George Fleming making no mistake to bring the aggregate score to 3-2. O'Grady came on for Hibbitt on 53 minutes and produced a fine effort that Jim Cruickshank saved well. The hardworking Scots just couldn't come up with the extra bit of spark needed to get a second goal, and near the end it was only Cruickshank's agility that kept out the Doog's header following another excellent cross from Waggy. Ray Tinkler's final whistle was a welcome sound indeed. So that was it, Hearts had won 1-0 at Molineux, but unfortunately for them, that wasn't good enough. Wolves won the final with an aggregate score of 3-2. The Managing Director and Chief Executive of Texaco Limited, Mr Carl D. Hall, presented the Texaco Cup to Wolves' captain Mike Bailey. Apparently this gentleman was American and couldn't understand why he was presenting the trophy to Wolves – the team that had just lost the game! A fair point I suppose!

> Wolves' team at Molineux: Parkes; Shaw, Parkin; Bailey, Munro, McAlle; McCalliog, Hibbitt (O'Grady), Gould, Dougan, Wagstaffe. Subs: O'Grady, Oldfield.
> Hearts: Cruickshank; Sneddon, Kay; Thomson, Anderson, Veitch; Townsend, Laing, Ford, Wood, Fleming.
> Referee: Ray Tinkler (Boston)
> Score: Wolves 0, Hearts 1 (Wolves won 3-2 on aggregate)
> Attendance: 28,462

At last Wolves had won another trophy. In the League they had finished in a creditable 4th place after a disastrous start. Arsenal did the League and Cup double that season, winning the League with 65 points, one ahead of Leeds. Spurs finished 3rd with 52 points, the same as Wolves, but with a better goal difference. In that season, 1970/71, Wolves also did a double of their own, this one over arch-rivals West Brom: 2-1 at Molineux and 4-2 at the Hawthorns – it was a very good year! Wolves' 4th spot in the League meant that they had qualified for Europe once again, this time the UEFA Cup.

As was their customary habit, Wolves played a game against foreign opposition prior to the start of the season; another stroll in the park.

Wolves 2 G.V.A.V. Groningen 0
Inter-European Challenge Match at Molineux

Wolves got a taste of playing against European opposition by taking on newly-promoted Dutch first division team G.V.A.V. Groningen on Saturday afternoon, 7 August 1971, in a warm-up match for the 1971/72 season, rekindling memories of their previous meeting which the Dutch team won. This was the Danny Hegan show; he headed Wolves first at the old 'Cowshed' end and straight from the restart got the second with a smartly struck shot that went in off the post following a strong surging run.

> Wolves' squad at Molineux: Parkes; Shaw, Parkin; Hegan, Munro, McAlle; McCalliog, Hibbitt, Gould, Dougan, Wagstaffe. Subs: Lutton, Wilson, Richards, Daley.
> Groningen's squad: Nordstrom; Schipper, Cornelis; Koeman, Guns, Van Vlierden; Fransen, Hovenkamp, Buijs, Jensen, Oldenburgen. Subs: Visser, Oosterwold, Eimers.
> Referee: Jack Taylor (Wolverhampton)
> Score: Wolves 2, Groningen 0
> Wolves' scorer: Hegan (2)
> Attendance: 8,726.

1971/72

The UEFA Cup, renamed from the Inter-Cities Fairs Cup, was a new competition for Wolves. The fans looked forward to being back in Europe proper for the first time in 10 years. In this competition Wolves took on, and beat, some of Europe's most illustrious names. First up was a Portuguese team from the university city of Coimbra.

Wolves 3 Academica Coimbra 0
UEFA Cup, Round 1, 1st leg, home

In the previous season Academica Coimbra qualified for the UEFA Cup by finishing 5th in the Portuguese First Division; not bad for a team of students. They had also earned the reputation of being difficult to beat in this type of competition; no team had ever managed to score more than one goal against them over two legs in a European tie. Academica's dress code was a little unusual in that they ran out onto the field wearing black cloaks, looking like a squad of vampire bats. Manager Bill McGarry had sold Bobby Gould to West Brom earlier in the day and then left out Hegan and Hibbitt, bringing in Alan Sunderland and Mike O'Grady to replace them. The first leg of this tie was played at Molineux on Wednesday night, 15 September 1971, and Wolves smashed the visitors' proud record by winning 3-0. It could and should have been more. The Portuguese visitors came to defend, their main weapon: frustration; their means of invoking it: the offside trap. The tactic certainly frustrated us fans. However, thankfully, Wolves stuck to their task and did the job. It certainly wasn't pretty to watch, but the atmosphere was tremendous considering the fairly low turnout – on the South Bank we all shouted our heads off, after all, we'd been starved of European action for far too long. Wolves' breakthrough came from an unlikely source, John McAlle scoring only his second-ever goal for Wolves. Strangely, his first goal in 73 outings in the starting line-up had come just seven days earlier in the 4-3 League Cup defeat by Manchester City at Maine Road. This very welcome goal came in the 29th minute when the Wolves number 6 smacked the ball in from close range. Wolves' second came from a Sunderland free-kick, which reached the far post and was steered home by John Richards. In the 80th minute Derek Dougan looked decidedly offside when he received the ball before going on to round the Academica goalkeeper for Wolves' third. The Portuguese quite literally went crackers, slinging their dolly right out of the pram, first crowding round the English linesman (yes,

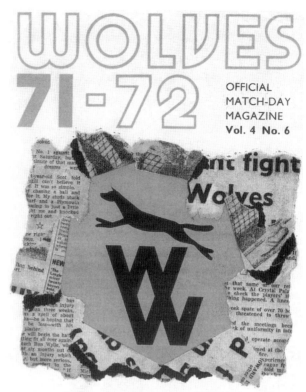

Right: Front cover of programme for Wolves v. Academica Coimbra.

Below: John McAlle scores Wolves' first goal against Academica Coimbra at Molineux.

still linesmen in those days) Mr D. Rogers of Derby, and then the Hungarian referee, protesting like mad. Amazingly, their abusive histrionics fell short of resulting in a couple of sendings-off, as the ref calmly waved away their vociferous objections, but this was short-lived. It only took a minute or so more for the referee to demonstrate his own irritation when goalkeeper Melo's dissent got its richly deserved reward – he was booked, ruining an up till then impressive performance in the visitors' goal. As I said, it wasn't pretty, but the final result was the right one, emphasising as it did Wolves superiority.

Wolves' team at Molineux: Parkes, Shaw, Parkin; Bailey, Munro, McAlle; Sunderland, O'Grady, Richards, Dougan, Wagstaffe. Subs: Oldfield, Taylor, Wilson, Hibbitt, Daley.
Academica Coimbra: Melo, Feliz, Alhinho, Belo, Marques, Gervasio; Mario Campos, Simoes, Manuel Antonio (Duarte), Vitor Campos, Serafim. Subs: Cardosa, Jose Freixo, Fernandes, Gregorio Freixo, Duarte
Referee: Istvan Zsolt (Hungary)
Score: Wolves 3, Academica Coimbra 0
Wolves' scorers: McAlle, Richards, Dougan
Attendance: 23,349.

So far so good. Now it was off to Coimbra, 140 miles north-east of the Portuguese capital Lisbon.

Academica Coimbra 1 Wolves 4
UEFA Cup, Round 1, 2nd leg, away

In Portugal, the second-leg of this European tie was played on Wednesday 29 September 1971, with Wolves going one better than at Molineux as they stuffed their opponents 4-1. The previously proud Portuguese record was really smashed as Wolves scored a total of seven goals against them in the two games. Derek Dougan scored a hat-trick in this match, his second in five days. John McAlle scored his second of the round, his third and last-ever goal for Wolves. The game itself was littered with far too many free-kicks, which interrupted the flow of the play, and it was finally marred by a small amount of crowd trouble as the home fans showed that they didn't take kindly to losing. Academica started positively, moving the ball around well in determined fashion, and 15 minutes of good play brought the breakthrough they had hoped for. Serafim put Manuel Antonio away and his accurate shot went in off a post to bring the Portuguese back into the tie – 3-2 on aggregate. Heartened by this success, Academica pressed forward, inevitably leaving space for the Wolves forwards and the Doog in particular to capitalise upon. In the 23rd minute, Big Phil Parkes' long clearance was misjudged by the Portuguese defenders, and the big Irish centre-forward ran onto the ball, rounding Melo to score with ease in an almost exact replica of his goal at Molineux. Now most members of the home team reverted to spoiling tactics in addition to the offside game they had persisted with from the kick-off. Burly centre-half Marques dished out some pretty violent rough stuff, but the Dutch referee allowed him to get away with it, which was especially surprising as Bernard Shaw had already been booked for retaliating. Wolves were now strong in the tackle, resolute in defence and purposeful when coming forward. A superb Wagstaffe corner from the right

Dougan watches as the ball whizzes past the Academica upright.

Again no luck for Dougan as he is beaten to the ball.

wing was volleyed home by guess who? Yes, that man again, John McAlle, his third in a month and second in this tie to put Wolves 2-1 up on the night. Then sadly, in the 51st minute after being unceremoniously kicked by Vitor Campos, Danny Hegan was sent off for retaliation. Now 10-man Wolves took over completely. Derek Dougan killed off the home side's challenge with successful strikes in the 72nd and 89th minutes. His first was a glorious header from Wagstaffe's pinpoint centre, his second almost a carbon copy of his first. Poor Joao Carlos Melo. The Portuguese goalkeeper was not a happy bunny, and was determined to show it. He started by blatantly upending Dougan in the area, but peculiarly got away with it; the ref didn't give a penalty which would have been the correct decision. Melo writhed around as if he was about to die, obviously tempting the referee's sympathy – he really should have gone off. Well in fact he did, but not because of a red card. His manager decided he'd seen enough and sent on Rogerio Cardosa to take his place in goal for the final part of the game. It had no bearing on the result as Wolves ran out 7-1 aggregate winners. Playing in the centre of defence in place of Munro, Gerry Taylor played well. Mike Bailey was again magnificent, covering every inch of the pitch. The performance of the entire team was great and Wolves were through to the second round.

> Wolves' team in Portugal: Parkes; Shaw, Parkin; Bailey, Taylor, McAlle; Hegan, O'Grady, McCalliog, Dougan, Wagstaffe. Subs: Oldfield, Sunderland, Hibbitt, Daley.
> Academica Coimbra: Melo (Cardosa); Feliz, Alhinho; Simoes, Marques, Gervasio; Mario Campos, Manuel Antonio, Serafim, Vitor Campos, Duarte.
> Referee: Laurens Van Ravens (Holland)
> Score: Wolves 4, Academica Coimbra 1 (Wolves won 7-1 on aggregate)
> Wolves' scorers: Dougan (3), McAlle
> Attendance: 12,000

Wolves eased their way into the second round, where they were to renew their acquaintance with an old adversary of four years earlier: A.D.O. of the Hague. In the close-season of 1967 Wolves had played a number of games in the USA, and one in particular against F.C. Den Hague A.D.O. San Francisco was the setting for a good old fashioned punch-up between these two sides. Goalkeeper Ton Thie, full-back Theo Van Den Burch, half-back Aad Mansveld and forward Piet De Zoete were all involved in the fracas, in which a number of Wolves players were injured. De Zoete had scored the only goal of an ill-tempered game. Les Wilson was hit on the head with a bucket wielded by one angry Dutch official, Derek Dougan was sent off and Dave Wagstaffe went to hospital. Phil Parkes and Gerry Taylor were also involved. So to draw A.D.O promised to be interesting to say the least.

F.C. Den Haag A.D.O. 1 Wolves 3
UEFA Cup, Round 2, 1st leg, away

In Holland on Wednesday 20 October 1971, Wolves took on A.D.O. of the Hague in their Zuyderpark Stadium. Early in the game, Jimmy McCalliog missed a good chance to give Wolves the lead from another excellent Dave Wagstaffe corner. Aside from a couple of attacks, the remainder of the first period was pretty much one-way traffic towards Wolves' goal. No goals at the interval wasn't a true reflection of A.D.O.'s dominance. After the restart, the already at full-tilt A.D.O. stepped on the gas, shots raining in on Wolves' goal from everywhere, but luckily for the visitors there was always someone in the way to make the block. Rudi Pas had replaced Couperus in the 59th minute after the striker had shot wildly over from 6 yards. The Dutch players now began to display signs of becoming a little careless after having Wolves under the cosh for an hour. That was the signal for our lads to produce the goods. Derek Dougan broke free of his marker to latch on to Richard's 61st-minute through ball, side-stepping the keeper to put Wolves one-up. Jimmy Mac had already hit the crossbar with an earlier effort, and headed wide just prior to the break. In the 76th minute he went one better by adding a second for Wolves. Kenny Hibbitt came on as an 80th-minute substitute for McCalliog and scored with his first kick to make it three. The Dutchmen couldn't believe it. Suddenly they were three-nil down in a game they'd pretty much dominated. On 83 minutes Bernard Shaw stuck out a hand to concede a penalty, which Harry Hestad slotted home to pull one back for A.D.O. The Dutchmen pressed, but made little impact on Wolves' resolute defence; they really had themselves to blame for losing this match by such a big score. They had plenty of possession and missed chances galore, three or four of which were excellent scoring opportunities. Norwegian international Harald Berg had cleverly buzzed around, prompting many of the home side's attacks. However the star of the A.D.O. side was undoubtedly the follically-challenged Theo Van Den Burch. This was one game where Wolves had all the luck. They might have taken a bit of a battering, but they won. Gerry Taylor played well in place of Munro, Parkes was superb, McAlle dominant, Parkin and Shaw solid and of course the captain Mike Bailey was his usual influential self. Sadly, near the end Mike O'Grady was booked for retaliation. Still, a great result, one to build upon at Molineux in a week's time.

> Wolves' team in the Hague: Parkes; Shaw, Parkin; Bailey, Taylor (Wilson), McAlle; McCalliog (Hibbitt), O'Grady, Richards, Dougan, Wagstaffe. Subs: Arnold, Wilson, Curran, Hibbitt, Sunderland.
> A.D.O: Thie; Van Den Burch, Weimar; Mansveld, Korevaar, Advocatt; Berg, De Zoete, Roggeveen, Couperus (Pas), Hestad.
> Referee: K. Tschencher (West Germany)
> Score: Wolves 3, ADO 1
> Wolves' scorers: Dougan, McCalliog, Hibbitt
> Attendance: 17,500

Not all the opening matches in this round were as uneventful as Wolves' game. The UEFA disciplinary committee met later in Switzerland and decided to cancel out Borussia Münchengladbach's fantastic 7-1 victory over Inter Milan on 20 October 1971, ordering the match to be replayed. The West Germans were also fined 10,000 Swiss Francs after Inter's centre-forward Roberto Boninsegna was knocked out after being hit by a missile, allegedly a beer can, thrown from the crowd.

Wolves 4 F.C. Den Haag A.D.O. 0
UEFA Cup, Round 2, 2nd leg, home

Molineux hosted the return leg on Wednesday 3 November 1971. Wolves had Frank Munro back at the heart of the defence so we were sure that complacency wouldn't creep into our play. The manager of A.D.O,. Eddie Hartmann, decided to bring in Dutch teenage starlet Aad Kila in place of Jacques Roggeveen, no doubt hoping that his young scoring sensation would do a job on Wolves that matched his descriptive surname – he didn't! The match was pretty much a repeat of the epic in the Hague, Wolves walloping the Dutch masters 4-0. The daft thing about this match is that the Dutch scored three. But unfortunately for them they were all own goals. It's a funny old game! Playing for A.D.O. was a Dutchman who later in his career was to win acclaim as a manager, his name: Dick Advocatt. Whatever the Dutch were hoping for didn't happen; they looked nervous to start with. Sure enough, the wheels started to come off their wagon as early as the 7th minute, when Dougan ran on to a slide-rule pass from Hugh Curran to score Wolves' first on the night. The Dutch did manage to dig in and hold the score to 1-0 at half-time, the excellent Ton Thie in goal saving bravely at the feet of the Doog and generally producing a commanding performance. Inside-forward Harald Berg, the holder of 36 Norwegian caps, was struggling, and was replaced by Roggeveen. In the second half all the Dutch

Hibbitt on the ground after a Wolves goal against Den Haag.

Dougan and McCalliog watch as the ball flies past the diving Dutch goalkeeper.

wheels came off. Four minutes after the restart Weimar headed a Kenny Hibbitt cross wide of Ton Thie to give Wolves a 2-goal lead. Five minutes later following a tremendous left-wing run by Dave Wagstaffe, Dutch skipper Aad Mansveld pushed a Dougan centre into his own net. Wolves now had a 5-goal aggregate cushion and naturally stepped off the gas a little. But if things weren't already bad enough for A.D.O., four-minutes from time up stepped right-back Theo Van Den Burch, whose shiny head somehow contrived to deflect a McCalliog header past his keeper. Three own goals! The Molineux crowd had seen most things, but three own goals? Mike Bailey was inspirational playing his usual captain's role. Frank Munro was great, pointing everywhere, plugging the few gaps that occasionally appeared. Hugh Curran made an impressive return to first-team action. The 'Kila'? – He was taken off in the 74th minute, Van Vliet taking his place to no great effect. And of course, revenge was sweet!

> Wolves' team at Molineux: Parkes, Taylor, Parkin; Bailey, Munro, McAlle; McCalliog, Hibbitt, Dougan, Curran, Wagstaffe. Subs: Arnold, Daley, Sunderland, Wilson, Richards.
> A.D.O.: Thie; Van Den Burch, Weimar; Mansveld, Korevaar, Advocatt; De Zoete, Berg (Roggeveen), Kila (Van Vliet), Couperus, Hestad. Subs: Van Vliet, Ardesch, Wijnaarde, Roodnat, Roggeveen.
> Referee: Medina Iglesias (Spain)
> Score: Wolves 4, ADO 0 (Wolves won 7-1 on aggregate)
> Wolves' scorers: Dougan, Weimar (o.g.), Mansveld (o.g.), Van Den Burch (o.g.)
> Attendance: 20,288

On November 24th Bill McGarry surprised the fans when he announced that Wolves were prepared to listen to offers for seven of his first-team squad: Mike O'Grady, Danny Hegan, Bertie Lutton, Paul Walker, Les Wilson, John Oldfield and Gerry Taylor. Some we could understand, but Hegan – surely not! He was one of the most gifted players ever to grace the Molineux turf, despite his reputation as being difficult to manage.

Carl Zeiss Jena 0 Wolves 1
UEFA Cup, Round 3, 1st leg, away

The away leg was played on Wednesday 24 November 1971, Wolves being entertained behind the Iron Curtain by Carl Zeiss Jena, in Weimar, East Germany. The Zeiss Company make world-famous photographic equipment – I've got one of their old flashguns and very good it is too. This was a side that had beaten Derby County and Arsenal in previous games so it wasn't going to be easy. The snow-covered pitch was reminiscent of an ice-ink and displayed most of its characteristics. A freezing cold wind chilled the crowd to its marrow, but all of these unnatural conditions failed to deter Wolves, who played as though they were born to it. The game was sometimes played at a frenetic pace and although the bounce of the ball was nigh on impossible to predict, Wolves capitalised on this with their long-ball tactics. The Germans too showed great skill in moving over the treacherous surface. Early on, Ducke won a corner which, under pressure, Phil Parkes managed to fist clear before Stein put a header narrowly over Wolves bar from another corner. On 10 minutes Wolves gave notice that they weren't to be taken lightly when Dougan raced through. He was odds-on to score until Strempel pulled off a great saving tackle to deny the Irishman. Two minutes later McCalliog kept his footing to fire in a dangerous cross, which John Richards crashed past Grapenthin to give Wolves an early lead and a precious away goal. Richards and Dougan were eagerly chasing every long-kick from Phil Parkes, generally creating panic amongst the German defenders. McCalliog's over-enthusiastic clash with Weise earned him a first-half booking. Earlier, the Austrian referee caused Wolves' hearts to rise to their throats when in the 20th minute he pointed emphatically to the penalty spot, only to relieve the tension when it became clear that he had actually given an offside decision. The temperature continued to fall, but the players warmed the atmosphere after the restart. First Dougan headed Dave Wagstaffe's cross just wide. Then it was Jena's turn, Parkes saving brilliantly when Scheilter threatened to score, following this with a great catch when Irmscher's cross looked dangerous. Stein was substituted in the 50th minute, Roland Ducke taking his place. The miss of the night came when Preusse somehow shot over from only 3 yards out. At the other end, John Richards had a couple of good chances to wrap it up. Under more stable conditions he would probably have scored with the first, but as things were he was unable to reach Jimmy Mac's centre. His second chance came when he met Wagstaffe's neat cross only to shoot weakly at goal. Time was running out for Jena. Realising this they pressed the Wolves defence hard. Unfortunately for them they came up against a resolute Frank Munro, ably supported by the dependable John McAlle and the magnificent Mike Bailey. Full-backs Bernard Shaw and Derek Parkin also won their personal battles. Preusse's miss aside, Wolves seldom looked in real danger. Steve Daley came on for Waggy after 79 minutes as Wolves continued to pound the home goal. Grapenthin took the ball from Dougan's feet, then Parkes was called upon to keep out an effort from Scheilter. John McAlle tried to add to his UEFA Cup goal tally; he was so far up the pitch he might have needed oxygen as his tame shot went straight into the goalie's grateful arms. Then it was all over. Wolves had weathered a storm in more ways than one; they had won a great victory, although they probably should have scored three or four; hopefully one would be sufficient to do the job.

Wolves' team in East Germany: Parkes; Shaw, Parkin; Bailey, Munro, McAlle; McCalliog, Hibbitt, Richards, Dougan, Wagstaffe. Subs: Arnold, Taylor, Eastoe, Curran, Daley.
Carl Zeiss: Grapenthin; Rock, Preusse; Weise, Strempel, Kurbjuweit; Irmscher, Stein (R. Ducke), Schlutter, P. Ducke, Scheilter. Subs: Blochwitz, Klauss, R. Ducke, Hoppe.
Referee: Line Mayer (Austria)
Score: Wolves 1, Carl Zeiss Jena 0
Wolves' scorer: Richards.
Attendance: 9,764

Wolves 3 Carl Zeiss Jena 0
UEFA Cup, Round 3, 2nd leg, home

The return leg was played at Molineux on Wednesday 8 December 1971, a night that saw Wolves gain an emphatic victory over the East Germans, who obviously didn't travel well. The visitors showed almost no hint of the skill displayed at their own pitch; maybe they needed some ice? Wolves' Golden Army stormed in to the attack from the first whistle and scored in the 8th minute when Kenny Hibbitt smashed in a headed pass from the

Doog. The somewhat aptly-named 'Hans' Grapenthin kept the howling Wolves at bay to prevent our lads getting a second with a marvellous display of agility and positional play, but thankfully not for too long. On 35 minutes the Doog flashed in a great downward header to make it 2-0. Then again Dougan, this time on 59 minutes, sent in a smart shot that hit the goalie's legs on its way into Jena's net. Grapenthin's well-timed dive at Dougan's feet stopped the big Irishman from notching his second hat-trick of this UEFA campaign. The East Germans made a couple of changes, Hoppe for Stein at half-time and Klauss for Scheilter on 65 minutes; neither had much effect on the result. Young Alan Sunderland came on for Kenny Hibbitt, who had taken a knock, on 71 minutes. Once again Waggy was fantastic, producing a series of wonderful runs and accurate crosses. Mike Bailey was outstanding as per usual. So, Big Dekka Dougan scored a brace and Ken Hibbitt got the other to make it another satisfying night at the Golden Temple. Then it was back to the Gunmaker's Arms for a pint and a chat about the game – wonderful stuff!

> Wolves' team at Molineux: Parkes; Shaw, Parkin; Bailey, Munro, McAlle; McCalliog, Hibbitt (Sunderland), Richards, Dougan, Wagstaffe. Subs: Arnold, Taylor, Daley, Sunderland, Curran.
> Carl Zeiss: Grapenthin; Rock, Preusse; Weise, Strempel, Kurbjuweit; Irmscher, Stein (Hoppe), Schlutter, P. Ducke, Scheilter (Klauss). Subs: Blochwitz, Klauss, R. Ducke, Hoppe.
> Referee: Karlo Kruashvili (USSR)
> Score: Wolves 3, Carl Zeiss Jena 0 (Wolves won 4-0 on aggregate)
> Wolves' scorer: Dougan (2), Hibbitt
> Attendance: 24,811

So many rounds in this competition – it seemed never-ending. Not like the old days of European competition when the third round was usually the final. In the quarter-final Wolves were drawn against the current leaders of Serie A, Italian giants Juventus. Wolves had only played against Juventus once in their history prior to this game, when they lost the third-place play-off in a tournament in Brussels in May 1958.

Juventus 1 Wolves 1
UEFA Cup, Quarter-Final, 1st leg, away

Now Wolves were up against the big boys. The other quarter finalists were AC Milan (Italy), Ferencvaros (Hungary), Lierse (Belgium), U.T. ARAD (Rumania), Zeleznicar Sarajevo (Yugoslavia) and Tottenham Hotspur. The first leg of this quarter-final was played in Turin's National Stadium on Wednesday 7 March 1972. The Italian big-hitters proved to be difficult to beat, their resolute defence and technically gifted attack giving Wolves their hardest game of the competition so far. Star-studded Juventus moved the ball around quite beautifully and eventually took the lead in the 37th minute through Pietro Anastasi. Then, much to the home side's chagrin, Jimmy McCalliog equalised for Wolves in the 65th minute. Juve changed goalkeepers after 20 minutes when Piloni damaged his arm, Carmignani replacing him. Frank Munro was majestic, like a Field-Marshall, pushing, pointing, and plugging gaps as usual. Phil Parkes was also outstanding, saving first from goal-ace Anastasi, and again on 71 minutes, this one a point-blank close-range effort from Franco Causio. Wolves' only real shot of the first period came from left-back Gerry Taylor.

Wolves were under siege and unable to break out with any real conviction. The secondhalf was different; Bill McGarry sent his boys out with a new vigour. The referee blew up for a foul when Jimmy Mac was obstructed inside the Juve half. Waggy ran over the ball and Mac squared it for Taylor to centre. At first it seemed like this attack would flounder like all that had gone before, as Furino headed the ball clear, but the ball dropped to Jimmy Mac, whose first time 20-yard volley found the Italians' net to bring Wolves level. Gerry Taylor was injured, the versatile Alan Sunderland taking his place at left-back, while Antonello Cuccureddu replaced Furino for the home team. In a bizarre incident, Bill McGarry was sent off for coaching from the touchline shortly after the Doog had been booked for dissent. The 1-1 result was equitable. Wolves had produced an assured performance full of confidence and dash, particularly in the second half, which they undoubtedly had the better of. The generous Juve supporters applauded Wolves loudly as they left the field. For this match the great John Charles sat on the Wolves bench helping out with translations; a pity he wasn't playing for us. The now-famous Italian manager Fabio Capello was in the Juventus team.

> Wolves' team in Italy: Parkes; Shaw, Taylor; Hegan, Munro, McAlle; McCalliog, Hibbitt, Richards, Dougan, Wagstaffe. Subs: Arnold, Daley, Sunderland, Curran, Eastoe.
> Juventus: Piloni (Carmignani); Spinosi, Marchetti; Furino (Cuccureddu); Morini, Salvdore; Causio, Haller, Anastasi, Capello, Novellini.
> Referee: M. Loraux (Belgium)
> Score: Wolves 1, Juventus 1
> Wolves' scorer: McCalliog
> Attendance: 45,000

Fans read in the newspaper that five of Juve's stars would be unavailable for selection in the return leg – like we worried? We were chuffed!

Wolves 2 Juventus 1
UEFA Cup, Quarter-Final, 2nd leg, home

Back at Molineux on Wednesday 22 March 1972, the Italians again proved a difficult nut to crack, in the process demonstrating the unpleasant side of petulant Italian football. Again their attack included Helmut Haller, scorer of West Germany's opening goal in the 1966 World Cup Final. We just had to beat them didn't we? The talented Haller showed his class with some lovely football, but also gave his usual theatrical performance, diving all over the place to win free-kick after free-kick. Like the first leg this was another tight game, but Wolves fought tenaciously to come out on top, 2-1 on the night and 3-2 on aggregate. Apparently the missing Juve stars weren't injured. They were rested so as to be fresh for their forthcoming Serie A match against Torino, scheduled for the following Sunday – a game which might decide the Italian championship. The under-strength Italians were first-class. I guess this was a tribute to the squad system, which at that time was a bit of an alien concept for us Brits to get our heads round. In-form Danny Hegan had a great game, scoring for Wolves on 34 minutes with a superb 30-yard chip. Nineteen minutes later, Derek Dougan netted his 9th goal in 8 matches in this competition with a

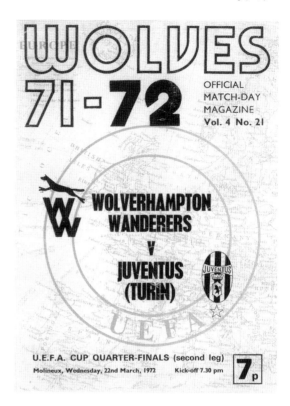

Front cover of the programme for the UEFA Cup quarter-final between Wolves and Juventus.

deftly-flicked header from Waggy's corner. Only the Doog could caress the ball into the net this way. Late in the game, blond superstar Helmut Haller pulled one back for Juve from the penalty spot after Frank Munro had handled, giving us the jitters for the final few nail-biting minutes. McAlle and Wagstaffe were booked for Wolves, Longobucco for Juve; Derek Parkin got cramp and Gerry Taylor took over his left-back spot. Were we relieved to hear the final whistle! You could almost hear a giant sigh of relief at the end from every Wolves fan – it had been tense, but the lads had done it. And so, on to the semi-finals. That night the Bonkses mild in the Gunmaker's tasted like nectar; mind you, it always did!

> Wolves' team at Molineux: Parkes; Shaw, Parkin (Taylor); Hegan, Munro, McAlle; McCalliog, Hibbitt, Richards, Dougan, Wagstaffe. Subs: Arnold, Taylor, Daley, Sunderland, Eastoe.
> Juventus: Piloni; Spinosi, Longobucco; Marchetti, Roveta, Salvdore; Cuccureddu, Haller, Novellini, Savoldi, Viola.
> Referee: Michel Kitabdjian (France)
> Score: Wolves 2, Juventus 1 (Wolves won 3-2 on aggregate)
> Wolves' scorers: Dougan, Hegan
> Attendance: 40,421

Next was a trip to Budapest to face Hungarian aces Ferencvaros. Wolves hadn't visited the city since 1963, when they played a friendly against old rivals Honved. Tottenham were drawn to play AC Milan in the other semi-final.

Ferencvaros 2 Wolves 2
UEFA Cup, Semi-Final, 1st leg, away

The first leg of Wolves' second European semi-final was played on a beautiful sunny afternoon in the vast Nep Stadium in Budapest on Wednesday 5 April 1972, kick-off 5.30 p.m. Wolves managed to maintain their excellent away form in a hard-fought game, forcing a 2-2 draw, showing a determined attitude after John Richards had put Wolves one-up on 19 minutes. Derek Dougan cleverly took the defenders away before back-heeling the ball to Richards, who didn't miss. Ferencvaros came back strongly, scoring 2 in 8 minutes. Istvan Szoke got the first on the half-hour from the penalty spot, then the Magyars took the lead. The great Hungarian centre-forward Florian Albert netted from open play, shooting past Parkes following Szoke's tempting cross – 2-1 at half-time. So far not too bad, apart from a booking for Shaw, and a birthday yellow card for Waggy. Sandwiched in between the Hungarian goals, Richards had a great chance to equalise for Wolves, but the striker hit his shot straight at the keeper. After 74 minutes, Wolves' hearts sank as the home team were awarded another penalty. Again it was Bernard Shaw who handled. This time Parkes magnificently saved Szoke's shot with his left foot. Next it was the turn of Ferencvaros to go close as Ku headed just over. Wolves recovered, and boosted by the penalty save they won a corner. Dave Wagstaffe swung the ball in, and Frank Munro was perfectly placed to nod the equaliser. Kenny Hibbitt and Jimmy Mac smacked in powerful shots that unfortunately didn't result in goals. In fact, Wolves had almost three times the number of efforts on goal the home team had. The referee whistled for time and Wolves had drawn a tough away fixture – what a night!

> Wolves' team in Hungary: Parkes; Shaw, Taylor; Hegan, Munro, McAlle; McCalliog, Hibbitt, Richards, Dougan, Wagstaffe. Subs: Arnold, Parkin, Daley, Sunderland, Eastoe.
> Ferencvaros: Voros; Novak, Pancsics; Megyesi, Vepi, Balint; Szoke, Brankovics, Albert, Ku, Mucha (Rakoski). Subs: Rakosi, Fusi, Horvath, Geczi.
> Score: Wolves 2, Ferencvaros 2
> Wolves' scorers: Munro, Richards
> Scorers for Ferencvaros: Szoke, Albert
> Attendance: 44,763

Wolves 2 Ferencvaros 1
UEFA Cup, Semi-Final, 2nd leg, home

The second leg was played at Molineux on Wednesday 19 April 1972, in front of a disappointingly small crowd of just over 28,000. I couldn't understand why there was such a low turnout for a European semi-final. Wolves had no intention of losing this important game in which history repeated itself, and in which Phil Parkes was once again outstanding. Alan Sunderland came in at right-back for the suspended Bernard Shaw, and making his European debut on the left wing in place of the also-suspended Dave Wagstaffe was 18-year-old Steve Daley. It was 'new boy' Daley who put the home side ahead in the first minute. From the kick-off, Munro's raking long pass was only cleared as far as Sunderland, who sent in a high floating cross which goalkeeper Voros missed, the ball

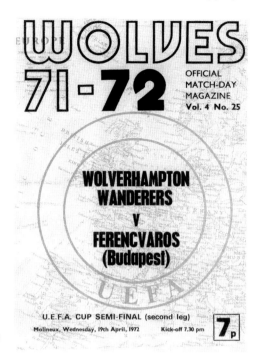

Front cover of the programme for the UEFA Cup semi-final between Wolves and Ferencvaros.

falling to Daley. His scrambled effort went through a forest of legs and into the net. Just before half-time, up popped Frank Munro as he had in the away leg to put Wolves 2-0 up. Phil Parkes again saved a penalty from Szoke with his leg. This time it was Alan Sunderland who handled, after Lajos Ku had pulled a goal back for Ferencvaros 2 minutes after the interval. It was a fabulously entertaining game, in which Daley and Hibbitt went close, Dougan hit the bar and Sunderland sent in a 30-yard screamer before Taylor cleared a Jozsef Mucha effort off the line. Balint and Munro were booked, but it wasn't a dirty game. Wolves won the game 2-1, 4-3 on aggregate, but boy it was close! Three penalties against Wolves in the 2 legs, Parkes saving 2 of them; what a semi-final. At the final whistle we cheered and clapped for all we were worth. It was just like the old days again. Gunmaker's, here we come!

> Wolves' team at Molineux: Parkes; Sunderland, Taylor; Hegan, Munro, McAlle; McCalliog, Hibbitt, Richards, Dougan, Daley. Subs: Arnold, Eastoe, Curran, Stephens, Rutter.
> Ferencvaros: Voros; Horvath (Novak), Pancsics; Vepi, Juhasz, Balint; Szoke (Fusi), Ku, Brankovics, Albert, Mucha. Subs: Rakosi, Novak, Fusi, Geczi.
> Referee: Christoe Michas (Greece).
> Score: Wolves 2, Ferencvaros 1 (Wolves won 4-3 on aggregate)
> Wolves' scorers: Daley, Munro
> Attendance: 28,662

Sixty-four clubs had originally set out to contest this competition, and so it was a marvellous testimony to English football that two First Division clubs reached the final. Unfortunately for Wolves it was one of our cup bogey teams.

Wolves 1 Tottenham Hotspur 2
UEFA Cup, Final, 1st leg, home

Now Wolves were in the big one – a European final at last. The first leg was played at Molineux on Wednesday 3 May 1972; a more satisfying crowd of 38,000 turned out for this one. In the previous rounds Spurs had knocked out Keflavic 15-1, FC Nantes 1-0, Rapid Bucharest 5-0, UT Arad 3-1 and AC Milan 3-1. Would it be our turn to triumph this time? There is absolutely no doubt that Wolves should not have lost this first leg of their first European final. They certainly had enough of the play and chances to win comfortably. Sadly Wolves came up against in-form Martin Chivers. The England centre-forward got both Spurs' goals, a stunning right-foot shot and a header. On 21 minutes Pat Jennings cleared upfield, the ball eventually ending up near the centre-spot at the feet of Danny Hegan. Seeing the big Irish goalkeeper still out of his goal, Danny hit a high, looping shot, à la Pele, which the scrambling Jennings somehow managed to tip over his crossbar – it was a breathtaking moment. Of course, as we all know, a number of years later a young man by the name of Beckham actually went one better than Pele and Hegan when he scored that stunning goal against Wimbledon. But back to Danny's effort – what a goal it would have been. As it was, the crowd went wild with the thrill of witnessing this marvellous piece of vision and skill; Hegan possessed both in abundance. Remember, it had only been in November that McGarry had said he'd listen to offers for this great player – we all thought McGarry had been nuts – maybe it was a shrewd piece of psychological management – I guess we'll never know for sure. As I've already mentioned, Martin Chivers had an outstanding game, also hitting the top of a post in the 5th minute with a crashing free-kick. In the 59th minute, Mike England swung in a free-kick, Chivers rose high above Frank Munro, and with Phil Parkes stranded, powered his header into Wolves' net. It was a crippling blow. It took Wolves until the 72nd minute to fashion an equaliser. Another free-kick was this time quickly taken by Hegan; he squared to McCalliog and the Scot fired in a low rocket shot that hit Jennings on its way into the net – 1-1 – it was nothing short of what Wolves deserved. A draw might not be too bad, but a win would be better to take to White Hart Lane. Wolves attacked incessantly either side of the interval, corner after corner coming to nothing except to provide lots of goalmouth action. For some reason Richards and Dougan hadn't got their shooting boots on and Spurs recovered to threaten the home side's goal. Then came Chivers once again – 'Cometh the hour, cometh the man'. In the 88th minute he surprised everyone, Parkes in

Wolves' team at Molineux: Phil Parkes; Bernard Shaw, Gerry Taylor; Danny Hegan, Frank Munro, John McAlle; Jimmy McCalliog, Kenny Hibbitt, John Richards, Derek Dougan, Dave Wagstaffe. Subs: Rod Arnold, Derek Parkin, Hughie Curran, Steve Daley, Peter Eastoe.
Tottenham: Phil Jennings; Joe Kinnear, Cyril Knowles; Alan Mullery, Mike England, Phil Beal; Alan Gilzean, Steve Perryman, Martin Chivers, Martin Peters, Ralph Coates (John Pratt). Subs: Ray Evans, Terry Naylor, John Pratt, Jimmy Pearce, Barry Daines.
Referee: Tofik Bakhramov (USSR). (This was the referee that allowed Geoff Hurst's goal to stand in the 1966 World Cup Final at Wembley.)
Score: Wolves 1, Tottenham Hotspur 2
Wolves' scorer: McCalliog
Scorer for Tottenham: Chivers (2)
Attendance: 38,362

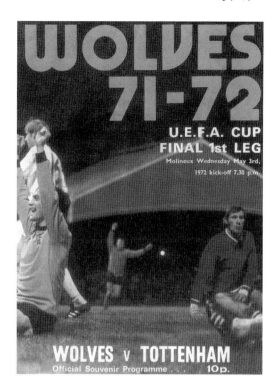

Front cover of the programme for the UEFA
Cup Final between Wolves and Tottenham.

particular, with a blistering shot from 25 yards out. Big Phil dived valiantly, but as he subsequently picked the ball out of his net could only reflect upon what might have been. A marvellous show by Martin Chivers won it for Tottenham; he was really the difference between the two sides. There were bookings for Bernard Shaw and Joe Kinnear. I'll tell you what, the beer in the Gunmaker's tasted a bit watery that night.

Could Wolves win at Tottenham? Could we hold Martin Chivers in check? We'd soon know the answer to these questions, and hopefully to a number of others. The 'word on the streets' was that McGarry was about to leave Wolves to manage Coventry City. Just the kind of distraction needed before playing such an important match. It must have had a disrupting effect. The team was scheduled to leave the following weekend for a close-season tour of USA, New Zealand and Australia – would 'everyone' be going?

Tottenham Hotspur 1 Wolves 1
UEFA Cup, Final, 2nd leg, away

The damage had been done in the first leg at Molineux. Now on Wednesday 17 May 1972, Wolves faced a daunting prospect at White Hart Lane. It was a proper uphill task to say the very least; Spurs had always been one of Wolves' cup bogey teams. A big crowd turned out to see the match, but prior to the kick-off they witnessed a first – legendary goalkeeper Pat Jennings presenting our very own Phil Parkes with the trophy for Wolves' 'Player of the Year', as voted by Wolves Supporters Club. The good news was that both

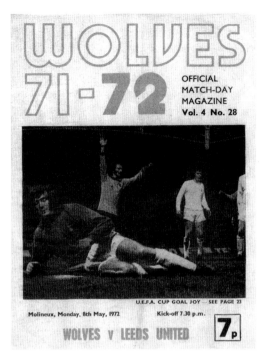

Front cover of the programme for Wolves v. Leeds United.

Mike Bailey and Derek Parkin were fit again; the bad news was that neither was going to start the game. The referee was Laurens van Ravens. He was the guy that had sent off Danny Hegan and booked Bernard Shaw in Coimbra in the first round. Wolves started well and tried their hardest, but couldn't get the early breakthrough that their domination deserved. The pattern of the game was a lot like the first leg, and there's little doubt that Wolves should have won both legs, especially this one; it was a near thing at that. Pat Jennings once again demonstrated his own unique brand of goalkeeping to keep the rampant Wolves at bay, particularly in the first half-hour of the game, when he made a string of quality saves, in the process staking another claim to be talked of as the best in the world at his trade. Then tragedy struck, just as it had at Molineux, only this time it wasn't Chivers. On 30 minutes Alan Mullery, playing in what was to be his last game for Spurs before his transfer to Fulham, ran in on the blind-side of Phil Parkes who was about to catch the ball, to power a great close-range header past the big keeper, giving Spurs an undeserved lead. Wolves renewed their incessant waves of pressure, culminating in the move that finally brought a break. On 41 minutes Dave Wagstaffe smashed in one of the goals of all time, one that had 'goal of the season' written all over it. His fiercely-struck shot skimmed in off Jennings' far upright to set up a frantic battle – Wolves attacking, Spurs defending. Incidentally, a similar Wagstaffe screamer in the 5-1 Molineux thrashing of Arsenal on November 20th 1971 had won BBC's 'Goal of the month' competition. Jennings was playing out of his skin, and on 61 minutes kept out a ferocious header from Frank Munro. Then he got down smartly to stop Jimmy Mac's dangerous 70th-minute cut-back which might have produced a goal. McGarry sent on Mike Bailey for Kenny Hibbitt and Wolves again drove forward. We thought Wolves had equalised when John Richards skilfully guided Waggy's free-kick to the Doog, who got the ball

Memorabilia from the UEFA Cup Final against
Spurs on display in Wolves' trophy cabinet.

into the Spurs net, but the euphoria was only momentary as the ref ruled it out for offside. Phil Parkes wasn't about to be out-shone, and he too had his moments. The pick of them were his saves from excellent headers by Gilzean and Chivers. Dougan took a knock after 83 minutes and had to leave the field, his place being taken by Hugh Curran. The Dutch ref whistled for time and it was all over. Wolves had battled bravely all through this cup final, but couldn't find that extra piece of luck that would have beaten this star-studded Spurs team. One-apiece was certainly not a fair reflection of the game; neither was the 3-2 aggregate score over the two-legs. Wolves should have won their first European trophy, but as they say where I come from, 'It's them what guz in uz counts!' Personally, I think that Chivers' spectacular late goal in the first leg at Molineux was what cost Wolves this final. It came at a decisive moment, just when Wolves believed they had done enough to at least get a draw.

Wolves' team at White Hart Lane: Phil Parkes; Bernard Shaw, Gerry Taylor; Danny Hegan, Frank Munro, John McAlle; Jimmy McCalliog, Kenny Hibbitt (Mike Bailey), John Richards, Derek Dougan (Hugh Curran), Dave Wagstaffe. Subs: Rod Arnold, Derek Parkin, Mike Bailey, Hughie Curran, Steve Daley.
Tottenham: Phil Jennings, Joe Kinnear, Cyril Knowles, Alan Mullery, Mike England, Phil Beal, Alan Gilzean, Steve Perryman, Martin Chivers, Martin Peters, Ralph Coates. Subs: Ray Evans, Terry Naylor, John Pratt, Jimmy Pearce, Barry Daines.
Referee: Laurens Van Ravens (Holland).
Score: Wolves 1, Tottenham Hotspur 1 (Wolves lost 3-2 on aggregate)
Wolves' scorer: Wagstaffe
Scorer for Tottenham: Mullery
Attendance: 54,303

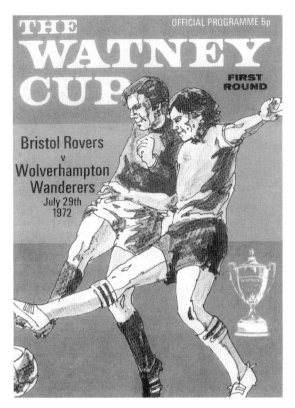

Front cover of the programme for
Bristol Rovers v. Wolves.

In what was their last match of the 1971/72 season, Wolves had lost their first cup final in a European competition, although the fact that their opponents were Tottenham made it somehow not seem like a European final. Wolves had finished the league season in 9th place, only 11 points behind champions Derby, who took the title courtesy of Wolves. On the night of Monday 8 May, in a highly controversial game, Wolves beat Cup and League double favourites Leeds 2-1 amid allegations of attempted match-fixing. A never to be beaten official gate of 53,394 was listed by Wolves, but from where I was standing on the South Bank the crowd looked to be a lot larger than that. Leeds had to settle for second place in the League behind Derby after winning the FA Cup two days earlier.

In the summer of 1972 Wolves entered the Watney Cup, Britain's first commercially sponsored tournament, which was open to the two highest scoring teams in each Division of the Football League in the previous season. Only clubs not involved in European competitions were allowed to enter. On 29 July 1972, Wolves lost their only game in this competition 2-0 away to Third Division Bristol Rovers.

Wolves returned to the Texaco Cup in the season that followed, attempting to win back the trophy they had won two years earlier.

1972/73

Wolves 5 Kilmarnock 1
Texaco Cup, Round 1, 1st leg, home

Wolves started the first leg of the 1972/73 Texaco Cup with a tremendous 5-1 victory at Molineux on Tuesday 12 September 1972 against Kilmarnock. Once again the fans hoped that the old Molineux feeling was back. Well, those of us who bothered to turn up did, as one of Molineux's smallest-ever crowds were treated to a smashing Wolves win, five goals being booted in during a magical 20-minute spell. For a time we thought it was going to be business as usual, i.e. another poor Molineux performance, as disaster struck on 19 minutes with Bailey putting the ball into his own net to give the visitors the lead. The Scots now defended by putting ten men, plus the goalie, behind the ball. It was a tactic, though not pretty, that worked on every level, frustrating the hell out of Wolves; we went in one-down. At the start of the second half Wolves had clearly found a new lease of life and were brimful of attacking ideas. On 49 minutes Gerry Taylor's centre found the head of Dougan and it was 1-1. Not quite 60 seconds later, John Richards latched on to the ball to beat Hunter with a well-placed shot. A Kenny Hibbitt piledriver cannoned off the stumps before Dougan added a third – Gosh, what a difference! Two minutes later Wolves won a penalty after the Doog had put Richards through only for Hunter to pull him down in the box; flamboyant referee Roger Kirkpatrick pointed to the spot without hesitation. Jimmy McCalliog scored, using his own stylised run-up to make it 4-1, followed on 68 minutes by Richards getting his second of the night after a neat build-up. It was a fantastic second-half performance, one of the best ever seen from Wolves at Molineux.

Wolves' team at Molineux: Parkes; Shaw, Taylor; Bailey, Owen, McAlle; McCalliog, Hibbitt, Richards, Dougan, Kindon. Sub: Charlton, Hegan.
Kilmarnock: Hunter; Dickson, Cairns; Gilmour, Rodman, Lee; McSherry, Maxwell, Morrison, Smith, Cook. Subs: Whyte.
Referee: Roger Kirkpatrick (Leicester).
Score: Wolves 5, Kilmarnock 1
Wolves' scorers: Dougan (2), Richards (2), McCalliog
Attendance: 8,734

FIRST ROUND FIRST LEG TUESDAY 12 SEPTEMBER 1972

WOLVERHAMPTON WANDERERS
v. **KILMARNOCK**
Kick off 7.30p.m.

OFFICIAL PROGRAMME 7p

Front cover of the programme for Wolves v. Kilmarnock in the Texaco Cup.

Kilmarnock o Wolves o
Texaco Cup, Round 1, 2ⁿᵈ leg, away

All Wolves needed was to avoid a big defeat, and that's exactly what they did. The 0-0 draw in Scotland was perfect. Predictably, even less people attended the game than at Molineux. The away leg was played at Rugby Park on Tuesday 26 September 1972. Bill McGarry didn't even go to the match, preferring to watch two other games to see if he could spot some talent with which to strengthen his first-team squad. He reportedly needed a pair of full-backs, as Bernard Shaw's suspension and Derek Parkin's illness meant they would both be sidelined, Parkin for some time. McGarry had already said that he was interested in signing Derek Jefferson from Ipswich. Wolves travelled to Scotland in Albion's new luxury team coach, which they had borrowed for the occasion. This was a strange game – almost on the half-hour an electrical fault blacked-out the stadium for 20 minutes. The club appealed for an electrician over the loud speaker and two fans answered their SOS call – it's a pity they fixed the fault because this turned out to be an abysmal game played by

Wolves' team in Kilmarnock: Parkes; Shaw, Taylor; Bailey, Munro, McAlle; Hegan, Hibbitt, Richards, Dougan, Kindon. Subs: Charlton, Wagstaffe.
Kilmarnock: Stewart; Whyte, Robertson; Gilmour, Rodman; Maxwell; Stevenson, McCulloch, Morrison, McSherry, Smith. Sub: Cairns.
Referee: R. Davidson
Score: Wolves 0, Kilmarnock 0 (Wolves won 5-1 on aggregate)
Attendance: 4,500

two teams who knew that Wolves had already won the tie; many people left long before the end – they should have had their money refunded. Only three incidents are worth noting. Wolves might have scored on 15 minutes when Hegan and McAlle produced an excellent interchange before sending Kindon away, but the barrel-chested striker's hard cross evaded everyone. On 70 minutes Shaw centred for Richards to head on, and there was Danny Hegan, an almost cert to score – but he didn't; he skied the ball over the crossbar. Near full-time Taylor made a rare up-field forage without oxygen, but his fierce long-range shot was clawed away by Stewart.

1972 Ipswich Town 2 Wolves 1
Texaco Cup, Round 2, 1st leg, away

Injury-hit Wolves were forced to field a very young forward line, including Eastoe and Sunderland; both were only 19 years old. Out were Taylor, Wagstaffe, Hegan, Dougan and Hibbitt; new buy Jefferson was suspended. They put up a fighting performance in a close game, but unfortunately it wasn't quite good enough on the night. Maybe our youthful attack proved to be too much of a handicap, or maybe Bobby Robson's Ipswich were just too good for us? Whatever it was, they narrowly beat us 2-1 at Portman Road on Tuesday night, 24 October 1972. John Richards scored for Wolves in the 37th minute, heading in Alan Sunderland's corner. Wolves defended resolutely until the 68th minute when Rod Belfitt headed the Ipswich equaliser from Mick Lambert's cross. Thirteen unlucky minutes later Lambert himself hit a powerful shot that went in off a post. Phil Parkes did well to save a header from Trevor Whymark, and Steve Kindon had a late chance to bring the score level following a good run, but he lifted his shot over the Ipswich bar. Losing this game 2-1 wasn't the end of the world; we could still do it.

> Wolves' team at Portman Road: Parkes; Shaw, McAlle; Bailey, Munro, Owen; McCalliog, Sunderland, Eastoe, Richards, Kindon. Subs: Charlton, Daley.
> Ipswich: Best; Mills, Harper; Morris, Hunter, Beattie; Hamilton, Viljoen, Belfitt, Whymark, Lambert.
> Referee: G. Kew (Amersham).
> Score: Wolves 1, Ipswich 2
> Wolves' scorer: Richards
> Attendance: 14,245

Wolves 0 Ipswich Town 1
Texaco Cup, Round 2, 2nd leg, home

Wolves were out! At Molineux on a sad Tuesday night, 7 November 1971, Ipswich gave us a lesson in football; the Texaco Cup would have to wait for another time. Maybe it was playing an English team in this competition for the first time that failed to ignite the spark to light Wolves' flame; maybe we just weren't good enough? Either way, Wolves had no excuse this time as they fielded an almost full-strength team. Wolves were now simply losing far too many floodlit matches at home; the long gone proud record of never having been beaten under the Molineux floodlights now seemed a million years ago. Yes folks, it was another dismal showing at Molineux – I guess we should have been used to this by now! Once again we wouldn't be going through to a semi-final. Wolves certainly – and I repeat – once again had enough chances to win the game, but the boys couldn't find the net. Unlucky for some, number 13 reared its head again, that was the number of minutes before Ipswich scored to increase our woes, making it doubly difficult for us to get back into this tie. Now we needed 4 to win, not 1! It was Lambert who did the damage, just as he had at Portman Road. His excellent cross reached Hamilton and the winger headed Ipswich into a 3-1 aggregate lead. Wolves might have been forgiven for chucking in the towel, but being Wolves of course they didn't. They stormed back at the visitors, John McAlle's 26th-minute centre finding the head of Jimmy Mac. He headed the ball down to Richards, but with only David Best to beat, the young striker hit a tame shot straight at the Ipswich keeper. Dougan came on for Hibbitt after 70 minutes and immediately added more dash to Wanderers attacks, but still they couldn't score. In the dying minutes Parkes was lucky that Johnson's shot hit his legs. Unfortunately the fat lady *had* already sung – and another quest was over.

> Wolves' team at Molineux: Parkes; Shaw, McAlle; Bailey, Munro, Jefferson; McCalliog, Hibbitt, Richards, Kindon, Wagstaffe. Subs: Charlton, Dougan.
> Ipswich: Best; Mills, Harper; Morris, Hunter, Beattie; Hamilton, Viljoen, Johnson, Whymark (Woods), Lambert. Subs: Sivell, Woods.
> Referee: Gordon Hill (Leicester).
> Score: Wolves 0, Ipswich 1 (Wolves lost 3-1 on aggregate)
> Attendance: 12,029

The Texaco Cup went on to be called the Anglo-Scottish Cup, a watered-down competition for teams in lower leagues, in which Wolves competed unsuccessfully in seasons 1992/93 and 1993/94.

1972/73 was 'almost' one of the greatest ever seasons for Wolves; a season of 'almosts'. In the League Wolves finished in a creditable 5th spot with 47 points, to earn a place in the 1973/74 UEFA Cup. A disappointing 6-match run-in cost Wolves dearly as they dropped 7 points out of 12 to miss out on any chance of 3rd or 4th place. Another unfortunate 'almost' saw Wolves knocked out of the FA Cup in the semi-final at Maine Road, going down 1-0 to Leeds. Billy Bremner scored the only goal of the game; the only goal Wolves conceded in the entire five rounds of the competition. Those that were there or who saw the highlights on TV will never forget John Richards' great shot rebound agonisingly from the inside of the post into Harvey's hands – Oh what might have been! That year's cup final was the one in which Jim Montgomery made that fantastic double-save to thwart Leeds and win the cup for Sunderland. On 18 August 1973, Wolves won the FA Cup third-place play-off from the previous season, beating Arsenal 3-1 at Highbury. The third 'almost' that season was when Wolves lost the League Cup semi-final to cup bogey team Tottenham Hotspur, just as they had done in the 1971/72 UEFA Cup Final. Again Wolves went down 2-1 at home, but this time they won 2-1 at White Hart Lane. So the score was locked at an aggregate 3-3. Now Spurs had the advantage of playing 30 minutes of extra-time in front of their own fans, and of course, they scored to win the tie 4-3 on aggregate. John Richards finished the season as second-top Division 1 goalscorer with 27. He had played in every game: League, FA Cup, League Cup, Texaco Cup and Watney Cup, as had goalkeeper Phil Parkes, a great testimony to their fitness. Still, it was a great season, even if we had to face a lot of disappointments – a lot of 'almosts'!

Remember January 1973? I bet you don't? That was the fateful month Great Britain joined that exclusive club – the Common Market! Then in April, VAT was introduced – funny how everything seemed to cost a lot more after these two monumental events! Never mind, Wolverhampton's finest, no not Wolves this time – Slade – were top of the pops with 'Cum on Feel the Noize'.

Leeds' celebrations following Billy Bremner's goal that ended Wolves' FA Cup run.

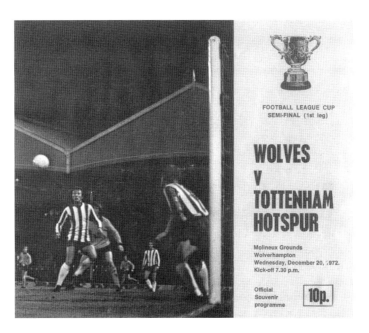

Front cover of the programme for the League Cup semi-final between Wolves and Tottenham Hotspur.

1973/74

Next season, 1973/74, the official *Molinews* programme was changed to a 'new look' and a new size. All was explained in Volume 6 No. 1; we had to comply with continental-size paper, the result being an economical saving, which was passed on to the fans (when I was a Sales Manager, this phrase was known as an 'inverse benefit'!) The 7-pence programme went up by 1 penny to 8p, which in my book is an increase of over 14% (where was this saving that was being passed on?) Still, I guess it couldn't be helped! Wolves were back in the UEFA Cup, qualifying via their 4th-place finish in the league:

OS Beleneses 0 Wolves 2
UEFA Cup, Round 1, 1st leg, away

Again a monumental sixty-four teams started out to contest the 1973/74 UEFA Cup competition. Wolves kicked off their campaign in Lisbon, Portugal; this time they would be against OS Beleneses. Without wishing to give offence, in Lisbon, Beleneses are considered to be the third in status behind Benfica and Sporting Lisbon. Benfica play in the original 'Stadium of Light', which I once managed to visit for a league game against Elvas – talk about big!

If you wanted to travel to the Beleneses game with the official Wolverhampton Development Association, the two-day, one-night trip, Molineux to Lisbon and back, would have set you back £35, including all your travel arrangements (coach transfer, Molineux to and from Manchester Airport and all transfers in Portugal) and half-board hotel accommodation Mind you, you had to pay extra for your guaranteed match ticket, which would be supplied at cost. This tie was played on Wednesday 26 September 1973, with Wolves again inflicting defeat on Portuguese opponents. The Doog went into this campaign attempting to break his scoring record of 1971/72 when he notched a creditable 9 goals in this competition; he wanted to break into double-figures this time. Gary Pierce made his European debut in goal for Wolves and played well. It proved to be an emotional and memorable night for John Richards, who finally managed to score a goal after almost 13 hours of famine, before being uncharacteristically dismissed for retaliation.

Although I didn't get to this match, I did manage to see a game in Beleneses' picturesque Americo Thomaz Stadium a few years later. I dragged my wife along to the Belem area of Lisbon on a scorching day to watch Beleneses play a local derby against

Kate Shipley at Beleneses'
Americo Thomaz Stadium
in Lisbon, Portugal, 1991.

Setubal, the city on the other side of the River Tagus from Lisbon. I'd promised my wife a nice seat in the shady part of the Stadium, but unfortunately I was wearing a green tee-shirt – Setubal's colours. Try as I might I couldn't convince anyone that I wasn't a Setubal fan, and as the stands were not admissible to visiting supporters we had to sit in an area where there was no shade whatsoever. Temperatures reached into the high nineties, baking us like loaves in an oven. The football was played at such a slow pace that we left before full-time. I guess the players were struggling in the heat – I know we were. A glass or two of ice-cold beer soon fixed that.

Anyway, in the UEFA Cup match Wolves were just too good for the Portuguese, whatever the temperature. On 10 minutes Jimmy McCalliog put John Richards through and he finished with a fierce shot from around 20 yards to put Wolves 1-0 up – he must have been ecstatic, it was his first of the season. Then it all went sour for John. Twelve minutes from the end he clashed with defender Pietera and both players were shown a red card by the Spanish referee for fighting. The fact that Frank Munro had been booked in the 33rd minute for a somewhat robust tackle belied the fact that this was otherwise a clean game played in a good-natured spirit. A small disturbance in the crowd followed to sour an otherwise good night. On 14 minutes some good work by Mike Bailey presented Richards with a good chance, and the young striker could and should easily have increased his tally, but sadly got under the ball to strike his effort over the crossbar. Skipper Mike Bailey was injured after the restart, and was substituted for Danny Hegan. In the 35th minute Richards unselfishly squared the ball to Dougan, only for the Irishman to miscue when he really should have scored – he'd already got 6 goals in 8 league games. The Doog atoned for his miss in the 54th minute by heading Wolves into a 2-0 lead from Wagstaffe's

Wolves' team in Lisbon, Portugal: Pierce; Taylor, Parkin; Bailey (Hegan), Munro, McAlle; McCalliog, Hibbitt, Richards, Dougan, Wagstaffe. Subs: Sunderland, Hegan, Daley.
Beleneses: Mourinho; Murca, Calado; Freitas, Pietera, Quaresma; Quinto, Eliseu, Carros, Godinho, Gonzales.
Referee: Franco Martinez (Spain).
Score: Wolves 2, Beleneses 0
Wolves' scorers: Dougan, Richards
Attendance: 8,925

cross. That's how it stayed, but as the teams filed off the field the ungracious Portuguese crowd slow-handclapped and threw cushions and other missiles. Munro and McAlle were outstanding, with Hibbitt and Richards the pick of Wolves' forwards.

Wolves 2 OS Beleneses 1
UEFA Cup, Round 1, 2nd leg, home

Back at Molineux Wolves carried on where they had left off in Portugal, comfortably beating Beleneses 2-1 on Wednesday night, 3 October 1973. Mike Bailey hadn't recovered from the injury to his calf muscle, and his usual deputy Danny Hegan was suffering from a pulled muscle and was doubtful. If this wasn't bad enough, John Richards' automatic one-European-match ban meant that he would also be missing from Wolves line-up. Young Peter Eastoe made his European debut for Richards and Alan Sunderland came in for Bailey. Manager Alexjandro Scopelli must have worked hard to fire up his players because Beleneses came out fighting and stunned Wolves by grabbing a surprise goal, Murca smacking the ball home following a corner on the left to make the aggregate score 2-1. I'm pleased to say that the Portuguese now decided not to press for the equaliser, but to defend in numbers, and didn't they do well? They held Wolves at bay until the 20th minute, when Kenny Hibbitt's penetrating pass was pushed back to Peter Eastoe by the Doog. Eastoe was in the right place at the right time to steer the ball home and restore Wolves' two-goal cushion. The game now entered a bit of a boring phase and we had to wait some time for a bit more excitement. Mourinho saved well from Dave Wagstaffe, then in the 72nd minute, Derek Parkin's cross was headed on by Dougan, and there was Jimmy Mac racing in. With a display of exquisite technique, he leaped high to volley Wolves' second goal of the night to wrap it up for the home side. It was a strange game in many ways – highs of some lovely innovative play from Wolves and lows when nothing seemed to have a script of any kind. Wolves missed the prompting of Mike Bailey and the guile of Danny Hegan. Nevertheless, we won, that was the main thing.

Wolves' team at Molineux: Pierce; Taylor, Parkin; Sunderland, Munro, McAlle; McCalliog, Hibbitt, Eastoe, Dougan, Wagstaffe.
Beleneses: Beleneses: Mourinho; Murca, Calado; Freitas, Cardoso, Quaresma; Quinto (Toninho), Eliseu, Carros, Godinho, Gonzales.
Referee: Hans Joachim (Weyland, West Germany)
Score: Wolves 2, Beleneses 1 (Wolves won 4-1 on aggregate)
Wolves' scorers: Eastoe, McCalliog
Attendance: 16,010

Lokomotiv Leipzig 3 Wolves 0
UEFA Cup, Round 2, 1st leg, away

In the next round Wolves had to travel to East Germany once again, this time to Leipzig to play Locomotiv on Wednesday 24 October 1973. Phil Parkes returned in goal and Geoff

Palmer made his European debut at right-back. However, there was no Mike Bailey, no John Richards and no Dave Wagstaffe. No-one in the Wolves camp could quite believe the result, as our boys were beaten 3-0, their first-ever away defeat on their UEFA Cup travels. I suppose it had to happen one day! Except that this was another of those games when Wolves played much better than their opponents but had absolutely no luck with their finishing. Leipzig set out their stall from the off; they chose to defend and try to hit Wolves on the break, a strange kind of tactic for the 'gung-ho' type of fan to appreciate. It worked! Playing at centre-forward for the East Germans was Hans Matoul who according to newspaper reports was a goal machine famous for scoring sensational goals. He lived up to his reputation by putting Leipzig ahead in the 37th minute. Gunter Sekora floated in a free-kick, which Phil Parkes tried to punch; he missed, presenting Matoul with the easy task of dispatching the ball into Wolves' net. Half-time came and went, and Wolves returned to their all-out attacking style. Surely these constant waves of attack must bring a reward, but no, those damned pieces of wood once again got in the way. Steve Daley hit the post in the 47th minute and the Doog's well-flighted 54th-minute header smacked the crossbar. And so it continued, Wolves attacking, Leipzig defending and hitting the visitors on the break, generally dealt with efficiently by Munro and McAlle, the latter getting himself in the referee's book after a clumsy 64th-minute challenge. On 75 minutes Matoul got himself into a good position in Wolves' penalty area and went down in a heap following an innocuous challenge by Frank Munro. The ref pointed to the spot – a harsh decision against the big Scot. However, Parkes' record of saving penalties was first-rate, particularly in European games. This time Big Phil could do nothing as the ball sped past him to give Leipzig a totally undeserved two-goal lead. Two-nil wouldn't be the end of the world, but Wolves decided to keep going forward instead of maybe shutting up shop. With 8 minutes of the match remaining substitute Koeditz headed in a free-kick to make it a disastrous 3-0 to Leipzig. Not since Barcelona in 1960 had a side put three past Wolves in a competitive European game.

Wolves' team in Leipzig: Parkes; Palmer, Parkin; Hegan, Munro, McAlle; McCalliog, Hibbitt, Sunderland, Dougan, Daley. Subs: Eastoe.
Locomotiv: Friese; Sekora, Grobner; Giessner, Fritzche, Geisler; Moldt, Frenzel, Lisiewicz, Matoul, Lowe. Sub: Koeditz.
Referee: R. Innoy (Belgium).
Score: Wolves 0, Locomotiv 3
Attendance: 16,860

In the League Wolves had been turning in some quite mediocre performances. It was as if something was holding them back. The UEFA Cup aside, they had only won once in their previous twelve outings. So to pull back a three goal deficit they would have to get it all together, produce an outstanding display of attacking football and score some goals.

Wolves 4 Lokomotiv Leipzig 1
UEFA Cup, Round 2, 2nd leg, home

Before kick-off the disappointingly low turnout buzzed with excitement and anticipation, everyone prayed that Wolves would do it, although I'm not sure that even the most loyal

Wolf thought they could. Locomotiv Leipzig definitely didn't think so. So on Wednesday 7 November 1973, the stage was set for another marvellous night at Molineux. Again Wolves were without the driving force of Mike Bailey, and the craft of the suspended Jimmy Mac, and now they had also lost the goal-scoring feats of John Richards, who was also suspended, while Frank Munro had had flu all week. The good news was that Waggy was back. Barry Powell made his European debut in Mike Bailey's number 4 shirt. This was a match that those of us who bothered to go were privileged to witness, even though the aggregate result was enough to make even the hardest-hearted man cry. Wolves were absolutely fabulous. The shooting boots were on, the passing and interplay marvellous. The only thing missing was that little slice of luck that separates success from failure. Wolves most definitely didn't fail on this November night. They practically threw everything at the East Germans, all but the kitchen sink, with goals from Frank Munro and Big Steve Kindon, who bustled his way through the Leipzig defence all night. Wolves' third was scored by Derek Dougan, and finally Kenny Hibbitt got the fourth in the 83rd minute, but sadly it was not to be. Locomotiv got the all-important away goal, scored in the 72nd

Steve Kindon and Derek Dougan end up on the ground after a Wolves attack has been frustrated in the UEFA Cup-tie against Locomotiv Leipzig.

A Leipzig defender heads the ball away, watched by Kindon and Sunderland.

minute, sandwiched between Wolves' goals, by the most inappropriately-Christian-named Wolfran Lowe. So the tie finished 4-4 on aggregate, but sadly Wolves went out of the competition on the technicality of the away goals rule! The word I shouted at the final whistle is unprintable. The faithful were sick as parrots! But despite the despair, everyone was proud of the way our guys fought; they very nearly did it! One real mistake and a bad refereeing decision in Leipzig cost Wolves dear!

> Wolves' team at Molineux: Parkes; Palmer, Parkin; Powell, Munro, McAlle; Hibbitt, Sunderland, Kindon, Dougan, Wagstaffe. Subs: Pierce, Taylor, Daley.
> Locomotiv: Friese; Sekora, Grobner; Grebel, Fritzche, Geisler; Moldt, Frenzel, Lisiewicz, Matoul, Lowe. Subs: Koeditz, Hammer, Altmann, Niklasch.
> Score: Wolves 4, Locomotiv 1 (Aggregate score 4-4 – Wolves lost on the away goals rule)
> Wolves' scorers: Dougan, Hibbitt, Kindon, Frank Munro
> Attendance: 14,530

It wasn't to be an English club's year. Leeds only managed to get through one more round than Wolves. Ipswich made it as far as the quarter-final. Tottenham Hotspur did best, reaching the final, only to be beaten.

In 1973 Bill McGarry finally sold Danny Hegan, as he had threatened on many an occasion. I don't think they got on all that well. Regardless of that, I want to single Danny out for a little praise. Hegan was a particular favourite of mine, despite his relatively short Wolves career of 65 appearances, plus 5 as a sub, in which he netted eight times. Sunderland paid good money for him, but he was actually sacked for persistent infringement of Wolves club rules. Hegan was born in Coatbridge, Scotland, but was capped six times by Northern Ireland. He was a lovely passer of the ball, and had great vision; a real crowd pleaser, a fan's favourite.

In January 1974 the catastrophic national power crisis took on new status when Edward Heath's Conservative Government introduced the 3-day working week. Yes, Ted forced most people to only work 3 days a week. Restrictions on the use of electrical power meant that floodlit football became scarcer than rocking-horse droppings. The Prime Minister's emergency policy to combat the economic crisis and the shortage of electrical power as a consequence of the coal miners' strike, led to the allocation of energy to industry on a 3-days per week basis. The country was split into regions receiving power on an alternate basis, i.e. 3 days with power and 4 days without. Great for Ted Heath maybe, but not for me personally! I was a Field Sales Manager for the whole of the UK at the time, and thus had sales executives working the length and breadth of the country. Consequently I had to work an official 6-day week – without extra pay! Floodlit sport now became a non-event. The crisis grew worse, forcing the Government to call a General Election in February 1974, which they narrowly lost to Harold Wilson's Labour Party. Because of the power crisis Wolves had been forced to play their fourth-round League Cup-tie against Exeter City at Molineux on Tuesday afternoon, 20 November 1973. Naturally, the resultant gate was extremely low at 7,623 souls – I think that possibly around 7,000 others stayed away because it was only Exeter.

In March 1974 First Division Wolves sold Jimmy McCalliog to Second Division Manchester United – Oh how the world has changed! The fee of £60,000 was only £10,000 less than Wolves paid Sheffield Wednesday for his services in October 1969. Jimmy Mac helped United secure the Division 2 Championship in their first year after

Jimmy McCalliog.

being relegated. He then moved to Southampton where he won an FA Cup Winners medal against Man United to go with his loser's medal from the 1966 final, which his Sheffield Wednesday had lost 3-2 to Everton. At Wolves Jimmy played 204 games and was a substitute on six other occasions. In all he scored 48 goals, many of them from the penalty-spot, when his characteristic pausing run and dropping shoulder deceived many a goalkeeper. He won 5 full caps for Scotland, although only one came during his six-and-a-half years with Wolves.

Back in the League in 1973/74, Wolves finished in 12th place, with 41 points. Not too bad, we all thought. However, the best of that season came at Wembley on 2 March 1974, when Wolves won the League Cup for the first time. My father and I managed to get tickets for the final, unfortunately for different parts of the stadium, but never mind, we were going to be there. We set off very early, seven of us travelling in two cars, skidding on black ice in Dudley along the way. We arrived in Wembley without further mishap, managed to swap one ticket with a nice Wolves fan so that we could stand together, and after a great lunch of T-bone steak and chips with all the trimmings, settled down to watch the pre-match entertainment. The massed bands of the Corps of Royal Engineers were good, but didn't really rock! We cheered wildly as 'our' RAF police dog beat the 'Man City' RAF police dog in an obstacle race – a good omen? One month after becoming Wolves' first-choice in goal, and coincidentally on his 23rd birthday, Gary Pierce turned in a 'man of the match' performance to help our lads win the League Cup. Gary had a stormer, making save after save to keep out favourites Manchester City's fantastic attack of Mike Summerbee, Colin Bell, Francis Lee, Denis Law and Rodney Marsh. City didn't have it all their own way; Wolves too, had their moments. On 43 minutes the Old Gold and Black end went crackers. Sunderland and Palmer combined well on Wolves' right, the latter swinging in a dangerous cross, which Kenny Hibbitt volleyed past the City goalie Keith McCrae. With the game coming up to the three-quarter mark, Rodney Marsh conjured up a chance, and Colin Bell scored with a hard low shot. Chances followed at both ends. Barry Powell came on for Waggy, who'd pulled a muscle. Bell hit the bar while we were down to 10 men, and still the score stayed at 1-1. The sands of time were fast running out. But then, with my nails almost down to the quick, Alan Sunderland crossed a grub-hunter which came off the heel of Willie Donachie right into the path of John Richards, who scored to seal a fabulous 2-1 win against a star-packed City line-up. The City players sportingly applauded Bailey and his men all the way down the steps from the Royal Box. Oh boy! – Was it fantastic? – You bet it was!

Wolves' team at Wembley: Gary Pierce; Geoff Palmer, Derek Parkin; Mike Bailey, Frank Munro, John McAlle; Kenny Hibbitt, Alan Sunderland, John Richards, Derek Dougan, Dave Wagstaffe (Barry Powell). Sub: Barry Powell.
Manchester City: McCrae; Pardoe, Donachie; Doyle, Booth, Towers; Summerbee, Bell, Lee, Law, Marsh. Sub: Carrodus.
Referee: Mr E.D. Wallace (Crewe)
Score: Wolves 2 Manchester City 1
Wolves scorers: Hibbitt, Richards
Manchester City scorer: Bell

I'm looking through my match programme as I write this, and all the wonderful memories of that great day are flooding back.

Winning the League Cup, our first major trophy for 14 years meant that we would be back in the UEFA Cup again the following season. Sadly though, in March 1974, the

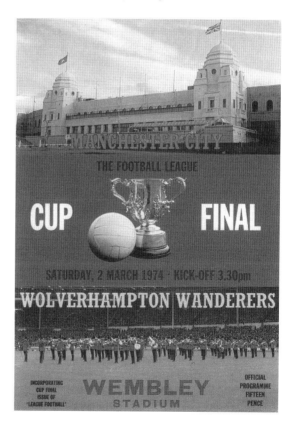

Front cover of the programme for the 1974 League Cup Final between Manchester City and Wolves.

Derek Dougan and Denis Law after the League Cup Final.

fabulous goalscoring partnership of Dougan and Richards seemed to have come to an end. After the League Cup Final, Richards didn't play again that season, while the ageing Doog now became restricted to appearances from the substitutes bench.

It was in March 1967 that the Doog signed for Wolves from Leicester as replacement for Hughie McIlmoyle and Bob Hatton; he cost £50,000. Doog scored 9 in 11 of the closing games of 1966/67 in partnership with Ernie Hunt, followed by 17 in 38 games in 1967/68. The Dougan-Richards partnership really came together in the 1971/72 season, although they had played together in the 3-1 away tie against Fiorentina in the Anglo-Italian Cup on 16 May 1970, a game in which they both scored. They also played in the same Wolves team on a few occasions in 1970/71. In 1971/72, their first season together produced 40 League and UEFA Cup goals: 24 for the Doog and 16 for Richards. In 1972/73 they shared 53 goals in all competitions, Richards getting 36 and Dougan 17. The following season Doog got 15, with Richards scoring 17 despite missing the final 13 games through injury;, his last match of that season being the League Cup Final victory at Wembley. Dougan missed 1 game and was a substitute in 7 of the matches when Wolves were without Richards. The duo scored a total of 125 goals in the 127 games of their partnership in two-and-a-half seasons. Derek Dougan signed off at Molineux on Saturday, 26 April 1975, coming on as a 78th-minute substitute in a 1-1 draw with Leeds. Dougan played his last 6 full games for Wolves in 1974/75, plus he was a substitute three times. Two of the six were in the UEFA Cup, which is where we go now:

1974/75

FC Porto 4 Wolves 1
UEFA Cup, Round 1, 1st leg, away

In round 1 Wolves were again off to Portugal – this time to Oporto, where their opponents were FC Porto, a team packed with world stars. Flavio had played for Brazil in the 1966 World Cup. Teofilio Cubillas had been the golden boy of the Peruvian national side. The first leg of this tie was played in the Etadio Das Antas, on Wednesday, 18 September 1974. The bad news for Wolves was that John Richards' hamstring would keep him out of this game. Nor would Dave Wagstaffe play, young John Farley coming in on the left wing, with Alan Sunderland playing in place of Richards. In a repeat of the tie in Leipzig almost a year earlier Wolves were once again left bemoaning their lack of good fortune, particularly in front of goal. With the temperature in the high seventies, both teams started brightly. Porto already looked pretty good without the goal start that John McAlle gave them in the 3rd minute. His totally unnecessary 30-yard back-pass soared way over the head of the stranded Phil Parkes and bounced into the net. Wolves shook themselves and came back strongly at the home team with a number of promising attacks, but were unable to keep up the frenetic pace in the heat of the 50,000-capacity stadium. Cubillas was at the heart of most Porto attacks, skilfully prompting his strikers with a string of innovative passes that more often than not produced an attempt on goal. In the 28th minute Brazilian star Flavio missed a sitter, following some superb inter-passing by the Portuguese team. Cubillas then broke Wolves' hearts on 37 minutes when he crashed in number two. Four minutes later, they were on the receiving end of a piece of breathtaking skill that produced a devastating move for Porto's third goal. Flavio sent a precision pass to Manuel Gomez and the 17-year-old scored with a strong shot. Wolves were 3-0 down at half-time, and reeling from the battering they were taking. McGarry knew he had to change something and brought Steve Kindon on for the strangely subdued Dougan, but although this added much needed pep to Wolves' attacks, still no goal-joy came our way, despite the supreme efforts of the indefatigable Mike Bailey. Finally in the 63rd minute, Wolves produced a moment of magic. Alan Sunderland's penetrating run was uncompromisingly halted inside the box – penalty! No! The myopic referee pointed to a spot just outside the area – he must have been blind, it was a clear penalty. The wall lined up, and Kenny Hibbitt sized up the chance. He surprised the Porto players by laying the ball square to Derek Parkin. Luckily, his shot rebounded to Bailey, who made no mistake from a tight angle to claw one back for Wolves. This unfortunately stung the Portuguese back into action, and eventually their clever play resulted in young Gomez racing onto another excellent pass from the wonderfully skilful Flavio to slot the ball home, making it a humiliating scoreline of 4-1 to Porto. Still Bailey wouldn't give in. With the game approaching the dying minutes, Wolves' skipper might have scored with two fine efforts, before injury forced him to leave the field, Steve Daley substituting. The French referee's whistle drew to a close Wolves' latest European disappointment. Losing by three clear goals was horrible!

> Wolves' team in Porto: Parkes; Palmer, Parkin; Bailey (Daley), Munro, McAlle; Hibbitt, Powell, Sunderland, Dougan (Kindon), Farley. Subs: Daley, Kindon.
> FC Porto: Tibi; Murca, Teixeira, Rolando (Aurelio); Simoes, Rodolfo, Nunes; Cubillas, Abel (Lemos), Flavio, Gomez. Subs: Aurelio, Lemos.
> Referee: P. Helies (France).
> Score: Wolves 1, FC Porto 4
> Wolves' scorer: Bailey
> Attendance: 39,529

Wolves now had the daunting task of trying to reverse a 4-1 deficit; this kind of thing was getting to be a joke.

Wolves 3 FC Porto 1
UEFA Cup, Round 1, 2nd leg, home

Trying to turn round a 3-goal deficit seemed impossible given Wolves' recent performances in this competition, hence the extremely low turnout. My guess was that most half-hearted fans probably felt that it wasn't worth paying out good money to witness the implausible. They were most definitely wrong, because on Wednesday 2 October 1974, the true Molineux faithful were treated to another cracking night of committed football. The atmosphere was once again electric: the brightness of the floodlights, the chanting and cheering; there seemed many more people inside our famous stadium than was reported. The question on everyone's lips was, could Wolves actually pull off a miracle and win this tie? At least the Brazilian genius of the first leg, Flavio, wouldn't be playing this time. In the end it was a couple of pieces of wood that would have the final say in determining the result. In the 3rd minute Frank Munro sent over a delicious free-kick which Derek Dougan met perfectly, but unfortunately his header crashed against the bar. Miraculously the ball came back to the big Irishman, but he put his follow-up header straight into the goalie's hands – 'rats!' Seconds later we all jumped as high as the Doog when Mike Bailey popped up to turn in a John Richards shot that was otherwise going nowhere – 1-0 on the night, 4-2 on aggregate and plenty of time left. On to the 16th minute and piece of wood No. 2. Sunderland whipped the ball over and Richards' shot smacked against the foot of an upright. With a bit of luck, by now Wolves would have been back on level terms. A match rescue mission straight out of *Boys Own* was looking good until the 37th minute. That was when Cubillas burst our balloon with a miscued cross-cum-shot that hit Phil Parkes arm as he advanced from goal and deflected into our net! Did the ball actually touch any part of Geoff Palmer on its way into Wolves' goal, specifically his chest, as has been reported in a number of other

Frank Munro jumps to head the ball in the second leg of the tie against Porto.

publications? – anyway, 'double rats!' Incidentally, one day when I was with Graham Hughes at Wolves, I asked Geoff Palmer about this alleged own-goal. Geoff told me that he didn't remember scoring this own-goal, and that I could quote him on this – so there you are! Either way, the goal was a real body-blow for Wolves. On any other day the ball would have rebounded to safety or gone harmlessly out of play. Actually all it did was cancel-out Wolves away goal. The score remained 1-1 at the interval. Three cups of blood, plus a good gnaw on a couple of bones and Wolves emerged for the second-half looking like a bunch of snarling animals. It only took them a minute to get one back. Sunderland crossed the ball, Dougan rose high to head it on, and there was Steve Daley to nod it home – fantastic! In the 79th minute Wolves won a free-kick, which Derek Parkin floated into the danger area. Dougan met the ball cleanly, and it was 3-1 on the night to us – only one goal behind now. What followed was a display of powerful all-out attacking from Wolves. The Portuguese tried everything they could think of to waste time and slow the game down, reverting to the kind of Oscar-winning histrionics that in those days only the continentals could perform. Going down as if poleaxed when not even touched, feigning injury, disputing everything. The referee made little allowance for Porto's disgraceful behaviour, and in fact only played just over one-minute of time-allowed, thus failing spectacularly to punish the Portuguese for their spoiling tactics. Wolves couldn't quite do it, losing the tie by the odd goal. We fans were convinced that this ref was never going to give us anything, he sure came up with one or two bizarre decisions, and believe me that's not sour grapes. The Doog scored what proved to be his last-ever goal for Wolves on the following Saturday against Middlesborough in a 2-1 away defeat.

Wolves' team at Molineux: Parkes; Palmer, Parkin; Bailey, Munro, McAlle; Hibbitt, Daley, Richards, Dougan, Sunderland.
FC Porto: Tibi; Murca, Rolando; Gabriel, Leopoldo, Simoes; Rodolfo, Laurindo (Oliviera), Gomez (Lemos), Cubillas, Nunes. Subs: Oliviera, Lemos.
Referee: Adolf Prokop (East Germany).
Score: Wolves 3, FC Porto 1 (Wolves lost 5-4 on aggregate)
Wolves' scorers: Bailey, Daley, Dougan
Attendance: 15,924

None of the other English teams fared very well in that year's UEFA Cup either. Ipswich and Stoke went out in round 1, and Derby were knocked out in round 3.

That season, 1974/75, Wolves again claimed 12th place in the League, and were knocked out of both domestic cups in the first match; it just wasn't our year!

Belfast born-Derek Dougan, known to most people as 'the Doog', decided to retire after an illustrious and often controversial career spanning 20 years. He had begun his football journey with Distillery, originally at centre-half, before joining Portsmouth in 1957 as a centre-forward. After only 33 games he left Fratton Park for First Division Blackburn Rovers, where he scored 25 goals in 59 appearances. The Doog made headlines when on the eve of Blackburn's 1960 Cup Final with Wolves, he put in a transfer request; of course as we know, Wolves won 3-0. Aston Villa bought him for £15,000 in time for the start of the 1961/62 season. This time it was his various styles of haircut that made the news; I seem to remember a Huron Indian cut, before he shaved his head completely. In 1963 Villa transferred him to Peterborough United for £21,000, then in May 1965 he left 'The Posh' for Leicester. In March 1967, Wolves manager Ronnie Allen brought him to Molineux for a reported fee of £50,000, in what the Doog always called his 'best move'. Dougan was an instant hit with Wolves fans', scoring a hat-trick against Hull on his home debut and netting 9 times in 11 games to help Wolves win promotion to Division 1. A charismatic man, a thrilling player and one of the best headers of the ball I have ever seen

Opposite: Daley after scoring against Porto. *Right*: Derek Dougan.

– nobody slept when the Doog was playing. He held the office of PFA Chairman, and was a successful TV pundit with ITV. He forged great striking partnerships with Ernie Hunt (albeit short-lived), Peter Knowles, Frank Wignall, Hughie Curran and Bobby Gould, then in 1971/72 with John Richards. In his 9-year Wolves playing career Derek Dougan made 323 appearances, including 16 as substitute, scoring 123 goals including 5 hat-tricks. On the international stage he won 43 caps for Northern Ireland. After hanging up his boots he tried football management with Kettering Town. The Doog returned to Molineux as Saviour, Chairman and Chief Executive in 1982, heading up the Allied Properties (Bhatti brothers) successful bid.

In October 1974 two IRA bombs exploded in Guildford, followed by two more in Birmingham. I will never forget the horrendous scenes in England's second city the day after The Tavern in the Town was blasted.

THE YEARS 1975–79

Wolves, 'too good to go down', everybody agreed, now embarked on a run to obscurity. They started badly in 1975/76 and stayed that way, finishing 20th in Division 1, resulting in relegation to Division 2. What would we do? This time we had no Doog to get promotion for us.

In early 1976 Wolves' fabulous speedy left-winger Dave Wagstaffe was transferred to Blackburn Rovers. In his 12 years at Molineux, Dave scored 31 goals, including a couple of screamers, in 404 appearances. In May 1976 Bill McGarry got the sack, and was replaced by his assistant Sammy Chung. The Wolves war cry now became, 'Sammy Chung and his Golden Wanderers!' Contrary to expectations 1976/77 was a wonderful year in the Second Division – we walloped most teams, scoring 84 goals and losing only 7 games on our way to the title: Champions of the Second Division – Wolves were back! And in our Centenary year. In May 1977, First Division runners-up Manchester City came to Molineux in a game to mark Wolves' Centenary; 14,729 turned out to watch the game and pay their own respects. We lost 2-1, Dennis Tueart and Paul Power getting the goals for City, Kenny Todd scoring for Wolves.

Then, in the summer of 1977, Wolves' own Captain Courageous Mike Bailey left the club, transferring to North American Soccer League club Minnesota Kicks for a reported fee of £15,000. He made 432 appearances for Wolves, plus 4 as a substitute, scoring 25 goals. His two full England caps came during his time at Charlton Athletic, prior to joining Wolves.

In August 1977 the whole world was shocked by the news of the death of the King of Rock and Roll, Elvis Presley. Wolves' fans were equally shocked in December 1977 when the club allowed Frank Munro to join Celtic after turning out 371 times for Wolves, scoring 19 goals.

Unfortunately, the euphoria of Wolves Division 2 Championship season wasn't substantiated by sufficient consistency on the pitch. After reaching 15th spot in 1977/78, Wolves slumped to 18th in 1978/79, and after losing ten of the first 12 games Sammy Chung was sacked in November 1978. The new manager was John Barnwell.

Big Phil Parkes left the club not long after his testimonial, returning to Canada to play for Vancouver White Caps, for whom he'd played a number of games previously. Phil's last of 382 Wolves appearances was in the 2-1 victory over West Ham United at Molineux on 11 March 1978.

In the 1978/79 European Cup Final Nottingham Forest beat Malmo 1-0 to make Brian Clough's dream a reality.

Dave Wagstaffe in action.

Left: Mike Bailey holding the League Cup trophy. *Right*: Phil Parkes in action.

MOLINEUX: UPDATE

Continuing our earlier history of the Molineux Stadium, the year 1975 was to have serious consequences for our beloved home. The government introduced 'The 1975 Safety of Sports Grounds Act'. Molineux had remained virtually unchanged since 1939, apart from the Molineux Street Stand, which had been made all-seater. This act was now to force the first big change to the stadium. The distinctive seven-gabled Molineux Street Stand was deemed unfit to meet the act's safety regulations and therefore had to be replaced. Architects Mather & Rutter were commissioned to design a completely new stand rather than simply replace the old stand with its unique shape. The club finally managed to purchase the remaining late Victorian terraced houses in Molineux Street and North Street, and in all 71 houses were demolished to clear the space on which the new £2 million stand would be built at the rear of the old stand. The 'new' stand, with its 9,348 seats and 42 executive boxes, was officially opened on 25 August 1979, the opening fixture against Liverpool having been postponed as the stand wasn't ready in time.

The 'new' construction certainly attracted controversy, firstly, when Chairman Harry Marshall strangely allowed the installation of red plastic seats – at least they weren't blue and white! I have never met anyone who can tell me why the seats weren't arranged in a pattern of old gold and black! Secondly, the pitch was not moved, it remained where it had sat for years. Consequently after the debris of the old Molineux Street Stand was cleared away the front row of seats of the new stand were almost 100ft from the pitch. From the back row, the game was so far away it was a rumour! Almost a threepenny bus ride! The other joke was, responding to a piece of bad play, a fan seated on the back row shouted 'Oh God!' and a big voice replied, 'Yes, my son?' Seriously though, it *was* a long way from the pitch and naturally difficult to see without 20:20 vision, particularly when the play was on the Waterloo Road side. Thirdly, throughout this period, the team definitely needed strengthening. In time-honoured fashion, the majority of fans wanted money to be spent on the team, not on a stand of such huge proportions. The inevitable happened; the building of the Marshall's Mausoleum, sorry – new stand, went hand in hand with relegation at the end of the 1981/82 season. However, before reaching that tragic point, we need to look at the last of the European floodlit games.

1979/80

Back to 1979. Under new boss John Barnwell Wolves witnessed an Indian summer. This followed a truly dismal start. Of the first 19 games, 14 had been lost, 1 drawn and a measly 4 won – absolute rubbish! Then came the turnaround. After beating Birmingham at Molineux on Boxing Day, Wolves lost only 7 more games in the rest of the season. This performance got us up to 18th place, and safety. Barnwell and his assistant Ritchie Barker also steered Wolves to an FA Cup semi-final against Arsenal at Villa Park. None of us who were there could believe what we saw; Wolves just didn't play that day, allowing Arsenal to roll us over 2-0. Shortly after this Cup exit the Wolves manager fractured his skull in a serious car accident, spending the remainder of the season in hospital. He had to follow Wolves' battle for First Division survival from his hospital bed. Fortunately John Barnwell was out of hospital and back at work in time for the start of the 1979/80 season.

Before the season kicked-off Barnwell produced a stroke of genius by signing Emlyn Hughes from Liverpool for £90,000, to be his captain. Then in September he sold Steve Daley to Man City for close to £1.5 million, and three days later signed Andy Gray from Aston Villa for a similar amount. Gray scored on his debut and went on to get another eleven League goals, finishing one behind Richards in that season's scoring stakes.

Versatile Yorkshireman Steve Daley played in 218 senior games for Wolves, plus 26 as a substitute, scoring a total of 43 goals before Malcolm Allison took him to City. He later moved to Burnley and Walsall, having also played in the NASL with Seattle Sounders and San Diego Sockers, before ending his career at non-league Lye Town.

With his with his 'Big Red Book' tucked safely under his arm, Eamonn Andrews ambushed Emlyn Hughes after Wolves' 1-0 win over Liverpool at Molineux on Tuesday 26 February 1980. This episode of *This is Your Life* was recorded at the Wolves Social Club.

Andy Gray scored again on 15 March 1980 to ensure Wolves lifted the League Cup for the second time, beating Cloughie's Nottingham Forest 1-0 to qualify for the UEFA Cup – a fantastic achievement considering that European Cup-holders Forest had won this trophy on the two previous occasions. Sadly, I couldn't make it to Wembley for Wolves' 1979/80 League Cup triumph, but I did manage to see the highlights. Nottingham Forest were smooth and powerful, but maybe a touch over-confident. Mind you, they were pretty good. Centre-half Larry Lloyd wasn't available, David Needham playing in his place. Forest might have taken an early lead when Gary Birtles latched on to the ball, but thankfully he shot straight at Paul Bradshaw in Wolves' goal. After seeing off a string of Forest attacks, Wolves regrouped and took the game to the favourites. John Richards and Willie Carr combined well and managed to bundle the ball over the line, but were adjudged to have

Programmes for (left) Swindon v. Wolves in the League Cup semi-final and (right) Nottingham Forest v. Wolves in the final.

fouled Shilton. On 65 minutes Peter Daniel thumped a hopeful long high ball towards the Forest area. Shilton and Needham got in a bit of a tangle. The young centre-back chested the ball back to his goalie who he expected to be in his goal, but who had in fact come out to gather Daniel's cross. The ball ran free, and there was Andy Gray following up to smack it home from the 6-yard line. Later on, George Berry hit the woodwork, but it didn't matter, we'd won the League Cup for the second time. Emlyn Hughes proudly lifted the only domestic trophy that had hitherto eluded him in his long and distinguished career – it was a lovely sight to see. Cloughie got over his Wembley woes when Forest beat Hamburg 1-0 to retain the European Cup. And Wolves finished the season in a creditable 6th place.

Wolves' team at Wembley: Paul Bradshaw; Geoff Palmer, Derek Parkin; Peter Daniel, Emlyn Hughes, George Berry; Kenny Hibbitt, Willie Carr, Andy Gray, John Richards, Mel Eves. Sub: Colin Brazier.
Forest: Peter Shilton; Viv Anderson, Frank Gray; John McGovern, David Needham, Kenny Burns; Martin O'Neil, Ian Bowyer, Garry Birtles, Trevor Francis, John Robertson. Sub: John O'Hare.

The following season, 1980/81, Wolves were beaten in the semi-final of the FA Cup by guess who? Yep, Tottenham Hotspur again. The first game at Hillsborough finished all square at 2-2, but unfortunately we lost the replay 3-0 at Highbury! Why, who and how Wolves' management ever agreed to the replay at Highbury I will never be able to imagine. Gosh! It's right next door to Spurs' home ground White Hart Lane! – I guess that everyone in the country was as puzzled as myself Oh, and we slipped to 18th place in the League.

Left: Programme for the FA Cup semi-final between Tottenham and Wolves. *Right*: Emlyn Hughes in action for Wolves.

John Barnwell was certainly a believer in going for the best, if the newspapers were to be believed. According to press speculation, Michel Platini was set to join Wolves in the 1980/81 season, but a broken ankle scuppered the deal. At almost the same time, the Polish star Ziggy Boniek was also said to be on his was to Molineux, but nothing came of this, and in the end we got Uruguayan Rafael Villazan.

So, now we move on to Wolves' final European adventure. At least, it is as I write this.

1980/81

PSV Eindhoven 3 Wolves 1
UEFA Cup, Round 1, 1st leg, away

Back in Europe for our fourth go in this competition, and sadly this European adventure was to be as short-lived as the previous one; we didn't even make it to round 2. Dutch masters PSV Eindhoven pretty much put an end to our UEFA Cup dreams on Wednesday 17 September 1980 by beating Wolves 3-1 in Holland. Surprise, surprise. Wolves' want-away winger Dave Thomas played despite reports that he wouldn't. Actually he played well. Anyway, this was one of those games when you would have loved to throttle the officials or at least smash their spectacles. (Yes I did say spectacles – they must have needed them despite not wearing them on this night!) Wolves got off to a cracking start, Carr and Thomas prompting a number of dangerous-looking attacks. However, as in previous games Wolves just couldn't score when in control. Just past the half-hour mark, PSV's impressive trio of Ks: Kerkof, Koster and Kraay, combined well to tee-up the ball for Ernie Brandts. He walloped in a 25-yard cannonball that flew past Bradshaw, and we were one-down. The three Ks plus their mate Van der Kuylen and the rest of their gang now took charge; things didn't look promising. A super display from Paul Bradshaw in Wolves' goal together with some backs-to-the-wall defending kept the score to 1-0 at the break. Colin Brazier replaced Parkin at half-time, and a minute after the restart Wolves got a goal; George Berry sent in a looping cross that Andy Gray met cleanly to score with a great header. Then everything went pear-shaped. PSV now certainly moved up a gear; the speed of their attacks was at times breathtaking. Dutch international Adri Koster switched wings, creating many problems for Wolves. It was he that fastened onto another of Van der Kerkof's defence-splitting passes before beating Brazier to fire in a fabulous ball that Kraay put into Wolves net. The Gold-Black Army thundered on to the attack when a more cautious approach might have provided a better return. After the game Manager John Barnwell was fuming, labelling the East German match official a cheat for judging that Rafael Villazan had deliberately fouled Adri Koster. This match-turning incident happened in the 76th minute. Another of Koster's mazy runs was foiled by a strong but seemingly legitimate tackle by Rafael Villazan. The Uruguayan couldn't believe it when the referee pointed to the spot. The subsequent penalty was converted by Willie Van der Kuylen to give PSV a 3-1 advantage. Barnwell sent on Wayne Clarke for Richards in an attempt to salvage something, but it was too late. Subsequent examination on ATV's highlights programme revealed that the referee was probably correct in his decision. Gary Newbon and even ATV's Head of Sport, non other than the illustrious Billy Wright, thought it was! This game contained many bizarre incidents, but none dafter than when Andy Gray was booked for dissent as he shouted to his team mates to mark-up at a free-kick – crackers! It's true that at times Wolves were a bit slack at the back, and that PSV made certain that they punished this at every opportunity, but the ref and his accomplices should not have made so many appalling home-team-favouring decisions. Wolves had legitimate claims for complaint on at least five diabolical offside decisions that went against them, not counting the corners that weren't given, or the ignoring of far too many indiscretions by the home team. Funny isn't it? – the old saying is still true – you'll never beat the referee! Also a bit odd was the allegation that the match officials were wined and dined in the PSV boardroom until the early hours of the morning. Additionally, according to reports, they got big presents. Still, we'd overcome a 2-goal deficit before, hadn't we? And the officials for the home leg would be different!

Wolves' team in Holland: Bradshaw; Palmer, Parkin (Brazier); Villazan, Hughes, Berry; Thomas, Carr, Gray, Richards (Clarke), Eves. Subs used: Brazier, Clarke.
PSV: Doesburg; Wildschut, Postuma, Brandt, Stevens, Van der Kerkhoff, Kraay, Valke, Van der Kuylen, Poortvliet, Koster.
Referee: Siegfried Kirschen (East Germany).
Score: Wolves 1, PSV 3
Wolves' scorer: Gray
Attendance: 28,890

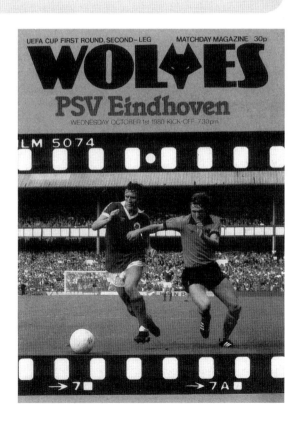

Front cover of the programme for Wolves v. PSV Eindhoven.

Wolves 1 PSV Eindhoven 0
UEFA Cup, Round 1, 2nd leg, home

At Molineux on Wednesday 1 October 1980, Wolves won 1-0 in what was always going to be a daunting task to reverse the 3-1 result in Eindhoven. Unless of course we got a friendly ref, which we didn't. Despite being faced with a mountain to climb, valiant Wolves started well, the forwards running intelligently into good positions, intent on capitalising on any space that became available. Richards and Gray tried everything they knew to get the ball in the net, in spite of the fouls constantly inflicted upon them. In goal for PSV, Pim Doesburg stopped everything that came his way. Aside from that, things were looking good, like Wolves would come out on top, when all of a sudden in the 38th minute the lights went out! No, I hadn't been hit on the head with a bottle or something, the stadium and the majority of Wolverhampton's town centre were plunged into darkness by a power-cut. And there we stood for around 25 minutes – in the dark – nothing new for a football fan! The game eventually restarted, but we had to wait until the second half for a Wolves goal. It came following a 50th-minute goalmouth melee, with Darlaston-born Mel Eves the scorer of what was destined to be the last Wolves' goal scored in a

Celebrations after Eves's goal against PSV Eindhoven.

Eves and Gray salute the Molineux crowd.

European competition. It was a bit of a strange match all round. I don't know if this match referee had heard about manager Barnwell's outburst after the first leg, but he definitely wasn't about to give Wolves anything. He denied Wolves two cast-iron penalties when Brandt brought down Andy Gray two minutes after Mel Eves' goal, and then legged-up John Richards. Both offences were clearly in the penalty area, but the Austrian ref waved play on. Urged on by Emlyn Hughes, Wolves threw everything into attack without another breakthrough coming. Colin Brazier got another taste of European competition, coming on for Hibbitt, and young Hughie Atkinson replaced Willie Carr. But once again the dream was over. The lads had done their best, every one of them a star. Another sight-challenged referee had broken our hearts. It's fair to say that the Dutch did have Wolves on the back foot a couple of times, Van der Kuylen and substitute Jung Mo Huh both being foiled by the excellent Paul Bradshaw. I'm sure that like me and the rest of Wolves' fans, no one envisaged the catastrophes that were looming up on the horizon. Nor that this would turn out to be our last European adventure for a very long time.

Wolves' team at Molineux: Bradshaw, Palmer, Parkin; Daniel, Hughes, Villazan; Hibbitt (Brazier), Carr (Atkinson), Gray, Richards, Eves. Subs used: Brazier, Atkinson.
PSV: Doesburg; Wildschut, Postuma, Brandt, Stevens, Van der Kerkhoff, Kraay, Valke, Van der Kuylen (Jung Mo Huh), Poortvliet, Koster. Sub used: Jung Mo Huh.
Referee: Franz Wohrer (Austria).
Score: Wolves 1, PSV 0 (Wolves lost 3-2 on aggregate)
Wolves' scorer: Eves
Attendance: 19,558

Manchester United also went out in round 1. However, Bobby Robson's Ipswich Town went all the way to the final and won it.

John McAlle moved on to Sheffield United for £10,000 in August 1981. John had joined Wolves as an apprentice in 1965 aged 15, making his first-team debut in 1968. In all, he played 496 times for Wolves, scoring 3 goals, oddly enough all in cup ties in September 1971.

That great Wolves servant Joe Gardiner also left the club in 1981. Joe played 139 times for Wolves in the 1930s, and was trainer all through the glory days of the 1940s and 50s, subsequently becoming Wolves' scout.

The summer of 1981 saw Wolves made a transfer signing that was to have disastrous consequences for the club. Alan Birch, older brother of Paul, who later played for Wolves, was purchased from Chesterfield Town for a fee of £180,000. It was seemingly not one of Barnwell's best signings, as Birch was subsequently sold to Barnsley after playing only 16 games: 13 in the league (plus 2 appearances as a substitute), 1 in the FA Cup and 2 in the League Cup. In September 1981 Emlyn Hughes' short stay came to an end after 75 games, in which he scored 2 goals. Oh, and by the way, Dave Thomas finally left the club after 16 appearances in 2 years. Barnwell also brought in Joe Gallagher from Birmingham to replace Hughes; the price £350,000. Also in 1981 Emlyn Hughes and Jack Taylor JP were awarded the OBE for their services to sport.

1981/82

In 1981/82 Wolves were again relegated. It was a season that saw Molineux witness pitch invasions by protesting fans, action groups, and a bag-load of bad publicity as the crowds stayed away. This sad chapter culminated in Barnwell's resignation in January 1982, which he tendered after taking legal advice. Wolves' board apparently approached Alex Ferguson, the then manager of Aberdeen, but he turned down their invitation. Coach Ian Ross took temporary charge of the team until Ian Greaves, the then Oxford Town manager was appointed in February 1982. Sadly, he failed to halt the slide, heralding the departure of a number of Wolves' favourites.

Wolves' record breaking left-back Derek Parkin was transferred to Stoke City in March 1982, where he played for one final season before hanging up his boots. His fabulous total of 609 appearances is a testimony to a truly marvellous player. 'Squeak' as he was famously nicknamed, scored 10 goals for Wolves in his 15 seasons with the club. It's amazing that such a cultured and consistent player was never rewarded with an England call-up; he had to content himself with 5 caps for the Under-23s.

Welsh international centre-half George Berry joined Stoke City on a free-transfer in the summer of 1982; he had played 160 times for Wolves first-team, scoring 6 goals. Midfielder Willie Carr also left the club for Millwall after making 289 appearances, including 7 as substitute, in the process scoring 26 goals. Willie won 6 full caps for Scotland prior to joining Wolves from Coventry in 1975.

The club found itself in tremendous financial trouble, with debts reported to be in excess of £2.5 million. Early in June 1982 Chesterfield Town issued a writ against Wolves for the non-payment of an outstanding instalment of a transfer fee – Alan Birch? In the wake of the disclosure of this crisis Harry Marshall resigned his position as Chairman in mid-June, and Doug Ellis took over, claiming that the club had been saved with just over 24 hours to spare. A few days later Ellis stoked the fires of anger in all Wolves' supporters by recommending that the club should go into liquidation, despite previously announcing that the club's assets would more than cover the outstanding debts. The official receiver was finally called in on 2 July 1982, along with the Football League, who set deadlines for rescue attempts from the five separate consortiums that were battling for control of the club. Wolves were minutes from going out of business despite ex-Wolves' goalkeeper Malcolm Finlayson's attempted rescue. At the eleventh-hour, a successful bid of around £2.3 million was accepted from a consortium fronted by Derek Dougan and property developer Doug Hope. They beat off the bookies favourites, a consortium led by Walsall Chairman Ken Wheldon and Doug Ellis, plus another involving Jack Hayward.

Behind the winning bid were backers Allied Properties – the Bhatti brothers. New Chief Executive Dougan dismissed manager Ian Greaves and appointed Wolves old boy Graham Hawkins to the hot-seat. Loyal Wolves servant Phil Shaw also left after 14 years as Secretary, as did Commercial Manager, ex-World Cup referee Jack Taylor. I remember Phil Shaw's many contributions to Wolves match-day programme with great fondness.

The club's first sponsorship deal was struck, Telford electronics company Tatung having this honour. The 'new stand' was renamed 'The John Ireland Stand' in honour of Wolves reinstated President, and the fans prayed for the Doog to work a second miracle and get the club back to where it should be – at the top. Remember, this would only be the third season that Wolves had been out of the First Division in 50 years, i.e. since 1932.

The John Ireland Stand, now remaned the Steve Bull Stand, view from the south. The building of this stand caused the decline of Wolves.

1982/83

In his first season as manager, 1982/83, Hawkins steered Wolves into 2nd place behind QPR – a great result; Wolves were back in Division 1! Mel Eves scored 18 of Wolves' 68 League goals, with Wayne Clarke getting 12 and Andy Gray 10.

Sadly, in August 1983, Wolves' record goalscoring striker John Richards moved on to Portuguese league club Maritimo of Funchal, Madeira, after a long-running dispute with Hawkins and Dougan that had seen him go on loan to Derby County for a short time. John Richards was a true Wolves legend, a player who would have graced any of Wolves' Championship-winning teams. He was also a gentleman in the Billy Wright mould. Born in Warrington on 9 November 1950, John signed for Wolves in July 1967, turning professional 2 years later. He made his first-team debut at The Hawthorns in the 3-3 draw with the Albion on 28 February 1970, and went on to score the magnificent total of 194 goals in 486 senior appearances, including 25 as a substitute. This goalscoring record stood for ten years until a young Black Country lad named Stephen George Bull took over his crown. He won 1 full England cap, plus 3 England 'B' caps, 6 for the Under-23s and 2 for the Under-21s, also being selected for the Football League on one occasion. Why he wasn't capped more than once remains a mystery to Wolves fans. As we know, John Richards later returned to Wolves to take on the role of Managing Director, sadly departing in the early part of the 2001/02 season.

John Richards in action.

THE YEARS 1983–90

The 1983/84 season began with hope, the fans brimful of confidence. Unfortunately, by the turn of the year these euphoric feelings had been reversed. Wolves were at the bottom and seemingly capable of going in only one direction – down! In November, Andy Gray was sold at a huge loss, the fee reputedly somewhere between £180,000 and £250,000; he had played 162 games for Wolves, scoring 45 goals. To the fans this was daft business, but what did we know? In the time-honoured tradition of so many other ex-Wolves, Andy came back to haunt us, scoring in his new club Everton's 2-0 win over Wolves to help push us that bit further towards Division 2. By Easter the game was up and we were certain candidates for the drop. Hawkins was sacked and Wolves finished bottom of Division One. This relegation was to herald an unprecedented spiral towards near oblivion.

On 8 June 1984, Wolves hired self-proclaimed joker Tommy Docherty as manager, the man who, in his own words, 'had more clubs than Jack Nicklaus'. Docherty's 'expertise' took Wolves down again, as they finished bottom of Division Two. The manager claimed he had no money for new players, but still found a way to introduce 18 new players into the proceedings. A demoralised squad tried their best, but failed. Wolves had no 'ace' goalscorer to rescue them.

Wolves' 1980 League Cup-winning team, the one that had also finished sixth in Division One that season, and incidentally the best for years, had now all-but been broken up, the last of them leaving in 1984: after making 234 appearances in Wolves' goal Paul Bradshaw left the club to join Vancouver White Caps, subsequently joining West Brom amongst other clubs. Peter Daniel moved to Sunderland in May, after a short stint with Minnesota Kicks. Hard-tackling right-back Geoff Palmer was transferred to Burnley in November 1984, briefly returning to complete a total of 496 games for Wolves in his two spells at the club, in the process helping Wolves to win two League Cups in 1974 and 1980.

In August 1984, another of Wolves' all-time greats, Kenny Hibbitt left the club, moving to Coventry City after almost 16 years with Wolves, in which time he played 574 games, including 22 as substitute, scoring 114 goals, many of them absolute crackers. Kenny was surely one of football's great bargains when Ronnie Allen signed him from Bradford Park Avenue for only £5,000 in November 1968. Born in Bradford on 3 January 1951, Kenny made himself immortal when he scored Wolves' first goal in the 1974 League Cup victory over Manchester City; a wonderful creative midfield talent. One of the most memorable emotional moments in football that I can remember, was when Kenny returned to Molineux on 27 March 1989 with Bristol Rovers. The crowd rose to him, the returning hero; it was a truly touching experience, even though they beat Wolves 1-0.

Wolves players Geoff Palmer (left) and Ken Hibbitt.

Next to leave the Molineux fold was Mel Eves, who joined Sheffield United in December 1984. Mel was born on 10 September 1956, in The Dartmouth Arms in Darlaston (not Wednesbury as has been stated so often in the past), where his father was the publican. As a teenager Mel played twice for England schoolboys, and subsequently for Wolves' youth team and the reserves, but he didn't actually sign until July 1975, when he left Wolverhampton Grammar School at the age of 18, making his first-team debut in the 0-0 draw against Ipswich Town at Molineux on 26 November 1977. Then at Stamford Bridge on 22 April 1978 Mel scored his first senior Wolves goal in the one-all draw with Chelsea. A week later, against Manchester United, he got his first goal at Molineux as Wolves beat the Red Devils 2-1. Three days later Mel followed up with another goal at Molineux, this time against Aston Villa – three in three games. He went on to make 214 first-team appearances for Wolves, scoring 53 goals in his 9 years at Molineux, twice being the club's top goalscorer: jointly with Andy Gray in 1981/82, and solely in 1982/83. The club was in the midst of the calamitous upheaval that almost saw its disappearance, and Mel too was caught up in the problems. Cash flow problems appeared to be the overriding factor that caused in the clearout of star names mentioned above. An injury in the sixth game of the 1983/84 season limited Mel's appearances, culminating in a loan period with Huddersfield Town. Wolves were still having problems scoring, so when Jim Barron took over as caretaker-manager in April 1984, he recalled Mel to Molineux, selecting him at number 10 for the visit to Watford, but after only 12 minutes on the Vicarage Road pitch he ruptured his Achilles tendon; it was to be his last game for Wolves. Because the injury was going to take a long time to heal properly, the club offered a new contract at lower pay, which Mel declined to accept; he never wanted to leave his beloved Wolves. In those pre Bosman-rule days, if a pay-cut was imposed upon a player, that player had the right to move, on a free-transfer. Mel Eves exercised his right and moved unpaid to Manchester City to get himself fit, under manager Billy McNeil he played in three reserve games. Sheffield United's manager Ian Porterfield was the first to offer Mel a contract, and so he decided to move to the Blades, where he joined up with his former Wolves' roommate,

Wolves players Mel Eves (left) and Willie Carr.

United's goalkeeper John 'Budgie' Burridge. In August 1986, he transferred to Gillingham on a 2-year contract, then in 1988 spent a season at West Brom and Walsall, trying to regain full fitness. Sadly injury forced him to retire in the summer of 1989, although he did manage one last season as a semi-pro with Telford United. In his 12-year first-class playing career, (14 years as a professional), Mel Eves scored over 75 goals, including 1 for the England 'B' team, for whom he won 3 caps.

Dougan quit in January, following further disputes with the Bhatti brothers, and in February the team embarked on a run of seven league games without scoring, albeit only six goals were conceded in these matches. After this, in the remaining 10 games, Wolves' pathetic forward line only scored 7 goals. In fact, from the beginning of December 1984, in 26 league games Wolves only managed to find the net 11 times! The fans shouted abuse and jeered at the directors – those that turned up, that is; we never saw the Bhatti brothers). Gates were falling below 6,000. Our once-proud Wolves were in free-fall, resulting in Docherty's much overdue sacking in July 1985.

Earlier in 1985 the tragic fire at Bradford City's Valley Parade ground had stunned the football world. Following the introduction of new safety guidelines in the aftermath of the Bradford disaster the Local Authority were forced to close two of Wolves' stands because of the predominance of wood in both structures. The pitch couldn't be moved towards the John Ireland Stand because of the lack of cash to re-site the floodlight towers. Molineux now resembled a morgue, particular for night matches. One reporter wrote, 'A two-side Molineux was more cemetery than symmetry'. Wolves' ghost town home was the laughing stock of the Football League. Allied Properties (Bhatti brothers) were taken to court, where the judge ordered the club to be wound up. A ten-day stay of execution bought sufficient time for the crisis to be averted.

Against this backdrop of uncertainty, quite naturally the on-pitch activities continued to mirror the debacle surrounding the club's finances. In 1985/86, chief scout Sammy Chapman was given the job of saving Wolves. When he couldn't, a second-time-around Bill McGarry tried for 2 months, then quit. Chapman agreed to have a second go in the manager's hot-seat, with Brian Little being hired as coach. Together they tried to avert what seemed like the inevitable – they failed. Wolves finished bottom but one of Division 3. Three relegations in three seasons! Divisions One to Four in successive years! Definitely the wrong kind of record to hold!

Molineux Stadium had declined rapidly. There was no money for repairs, let alone improvements. The once-proud stadium's dilapidated and shabby appearance was a disgrace, mirroring the fate of the Molineux Hotel, once the stately home of the Molineux family. Around this time there was talk of Wolves leaving Molineux altogether to ground-share with Walsall and Birmingham. Then in July 1986 the official receiver was called in for the second time. There was even a rumour that Wolves were considering swapping names with non-league Enfield so that the Wolves name would live on.

Sammy Chapman's brief second spell ended in August 1986, Brian Little taking over as caretaker-manager from August, until he too was pushed out in October after only a couple of months. In the meantime, the club was saved in true dramatic last-gasp style by John Bird, leader of Wolverhampton Metropolitan Council, in conjunction with Gallagher Estates Limited, ASDA and a consortium including Dick Homden, Jack Harris and Wolverhampton multi-millionaire Sir Jack Hayward OBE. The Council purchased the football ground and the surrounding land for £1.12 million. Gallagher's and ASDA would pay off Wolves' debts, subject to receiving planning permission to build a new ASDA supermarket on land at the north end of the site. Thankfully, the planning application was successful, enabling Molineux, and with it Wolves' pride, to be rebuilt.

Graham Turner, late of Villa, was appointed manager in October 1986. Then in November, Wolves were humiliated by non-league Chorley, beaten 3-0 in the second replay, after two 1-1 draws in the 1st round of the FA Cup – that was the pits! Also in November 1986, Turner signed Steve Bull from the Albion, and his fantastic goalscoring ability fired us into 4th place and the 1986/87 play-offs. But we lost to Aldershot.

The following season, Bully got 34, and Mutchy 19 League goals, helping Wolves win the 1987/88 Fourth Division Championship, plus the Sherpa Van Trophy Final at

Part of Molineux with part of Asda supermarket site, view from the north east.

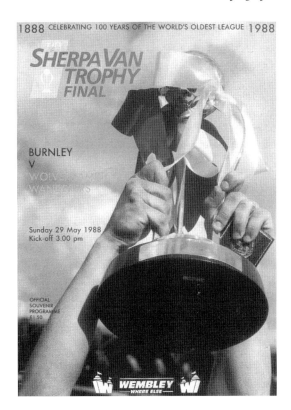

Front cover of the programme for the 1988 Sherpa Van Trophy Final between Burnley and Wolves.

Wembley, beating Burnley 2-0. It was a fantastic day out; I took my dad and my son – wonderful! It was like old times, even if it was at a lower level.

The next season, 1988/89, Bully got 37 goals in the league, and Andy Mutch scored 21 to fire Wolves to the Third Division title and back-to-back championships. Sadly, we uncharacteristically lost the Sherpa Van Trophy Final to Torquay United. This time it was a home and away 2-legged final. The aggregate score was 2-3.

Wolves celebrated their 100th year at Molineux with a game against Moscow Dynamo on Tuesday evening, 8 August 1989. In the Second Division in 1989/90, Wolves could only finish 10th, with Bully scoring 24, and Mutch netting only 11. The dream had been shattered. For a long time we all thought we could do it – all the way down and then all the way back in consecutive seasons not counting the extra one in Division 4, but it was not to be.

In 1990 Wolverhampton Council commissioned the Husband Design Group to carry out a feasibility study on the development of Molineux. Their report outlined options for the design and construction of three new stands, together with alternative methods of funding the cost. Step in Wolves' ace benefactor Sir Jack. He came up with the necessary money to bridge the gap between what was needed and what was available. Sir Jack subsequently purchased club and ground for around £2.1 million, and thus a new era had begun. With Sir Jack's backing the development received the go-ahead. McAlpine were awarded the building contract, with local architects the Alan Cotterell Partnership overseeing the project. Oh how different the previous 8 years might have been if Sir Jack's bid had been successful instead of the Bhattis'.

Three generations of Wolves fans – my father, Harry Shipley, flanked by my son John and yours truly – at Wembley for the 1988 Sherpa Van Trophy Final.

Molineux after the completion of the new stand. Note the position of the pitch

Right: Front cover of the programme for Wolves v. Moscow Dynamo.

Below: Molineux during redevelopment in 1991. The pitch has been dug up.

Molineux during redevelopment in 1991. The old North Bank Stand is being knocked down.

WOLVES 15-YEAR ROLLER-COASTER RIDE

1975/76   Relegated from Division 1.
1976/77   Champions of Division 2.
1977/78   15th in Division 1. (22 teams)
1978/79   18th in Division 1. (22 teams)
1979/80   6th in Division 1. (22 teams) A resurgence. Also won the League Cup.
1980/81   18th in Division 1. (22 teams)
1981/82   21st in Division 1. (22 teams) Relegated to Division 2.
1982/83   Runners-up in Division 2. (22 teams) Promoted to Division 1.
1983/84   Bottom (22nd) of Division 1. (22 teams) Relegated to Division 2.
1984/85   Bottom (22nd) of Division 2. (22 teams) Relegated to Division 3.
1985/86   Bottom but one (23rd of 24 teams) of Division 3. Relegated to Division 4.
1986/87   4th in Division 4. (24 teams). Lost play-off to Aldershot.
1987/88   Champions of Division 4. (24 teams). Promoted to Division 3.
1988/89   Champions of Division 3. (24 teams). Promoted to Division 2.
1989/90   10th in Division 2. (24 teams). Sadly, Wolves couldn't maintain the promotion momentum of the previous 2 seasons.

And now, a new entry for our list:

2002/03 Promoted to The Barclaycard Premier League as Nationwide First Division Play-off Winners. (26 teams).

NB: The Premier League was formed in season 1992/93, thus each Division of the football league improved its designated number by a factor of one; hence Division 2 became Division 1 and so forth.

MOLINEUX: FINAL UPDATE

Lord Justice Taylor's 1990 report following the Hillsborough disaster on 15 April 1989 meant that traditional terracing in the two highest divisions had to be phased out by August 1994, and in the two lower divisions by August 1999 or in the case of promotion to these divisions, within 3 years.

Work on phase 1, renamed the Stan Cullis Stand, started in October 1991. A new pitch followed in the summer of 1992, correctly positioned so that those seated in the John Ireland could see. Phase 2, the Billy Wright Stand alongside the Waterloo Road, was ready on 25 August 1993, with the final phase 3, the Jack Harris Stand opening in early December 1993.

To mark the official opening of this stand, and the 'new' completed Molineux, Hungarian side Kispest Honved were invited to play Wolves. On Tuesday 7 December 1993, a capacity crowd of 28,245 watched the visitors hold Wolves to 2-2 draw. For the first time in 9 years Molineux was once again a proper four-sided stadium. The John Ireland was refurbished in keeping with the three 'new' stands; all four had gold and/or black seats. Interestingly, just prior to the kick-off in this second match against Honved, 39 years after the first, there was a short delay because of problems with the floodlighting. Not a real problem compared to the roller-coaster ride of the previous 15 years. Anyway, it was certainly nothing to worry about, for as all Wolves fans know – 'OUT OF DARKNESS COMETH LIGHT'.

The Queen came to Molineux on 24 June 1994, 32 years after her first visit in 1962. She saw the magnificent stadium that Molineux has developed into. A stadium that every one of Wolves' supporters, players past and present, club officials and staff can be justifiably proud of. We all owe a huge debt of gratitude to the generosity of Wolves benefactor in chief, Sir Jack Hayward OBE, plus the many people who helped rebuild Molineux – The Golden Palace.

So, as they say – that's that! Well almost! The end, so far, of an epic 27-year journey under the Molineux floodlights 1953-1980 plus a few memories from subsequent years. In those 27-floodlit years Wolves played against many of the best teams in Europe, plus a few from further afield! – truly 'WOLVES AGAINST THE WORLD'.

Of course in recent years, Wolves' fans have enjoyed a few more highs and lows, such as beating 1-0 Leeds at Elland Road in the sixth round of the 1997/98 FA Cup, to reach another semi-final at Villa Park only to lose 1-0 to a star-studded Arsenal team destined to win the double that year; the game against Barcelona at Molineux on Saturday 1 August 1998; celebrating the Club's 125th anniversary; the tragedy of seeing the Albion steal

Above: The Billy Wright Stand, Waterloo Road, view from the south. This replaced the old Waterloo Street Stand.

Left: Front cover of the programme for Wolves v. Kispest Honved.

Wolves' benefactor Sir Jack Hayward at Molineux during the final phase of the reconstruction of Molineux. In the background the new Jack Harris Stand is being built. (Photograph supplied by Graham Hughes at Wolves)

second place in 2001/02; and our disappointment as Wolves lost to Norwich in the play-off semi-final. And more recently, thumping Leicester 4-1 at Molineux in the fourth round of the 2002/03 FA Cup, after a thrilling 3-2 victory over Newcastle in the third round. Then the ultimate and totally unashamed pleasure at the marvellous Millennium Stadium in Cardiff on Monday 26 May 2003, when the mighty Wolves reclaimed their rightful place among the elite of English football after 19 long and too often dreary years. Wolves are back, and this time it's the Premier League. Next season the faithful will once again be visiting places like Old Trafford, Highbury, Stamford Bridge, St James's Park, all places where our team Wolverhampton Wanderers have triumphed on numerous previous occasions.

In the year 2003, on 30 September Wolves will celebrate the 50th anniversary of their first-ever game played under floodlights at Molineux. How fitting that Wolves will once again be a member of the top division when this event is marked. Yes, there have been other more recent floodlit friendlies, but none that have recaptured or have gone any way towards evoking the wonderful atmosphere and excitement generated in those marvellous games in the 1950s, or those in the various European competitions in which Wolves competed. Well, not until now anyway.

For me, reliving those cherished memories in the process of compiling this celebration of Wolves' history under floodlights has been truly wonderful. The process evoked tearful bouts of nostalgia: thoughts of my mum and dad and the many people that I have had the privilege of accompanying to Wolves' games. It's been great to journey back to a time when in the eyes of most fans the game of football transcended the notion of big business and profits. A historic era when few people had heard about cash flow and balance sheets, let alone knew what they were.

Wolves' trophy cabinet
at Molineux.

Getting out my old programmes, souvenir editions and general Wolves memorabilia, and reading my notes about those magical Molineux nights and days has been a true labour of love. I have tried to capture the spirit of each occasion; the thrills and excitement that I have been privileged to experience in my sixty years as a supporter of Wolves.

Of course, football, like any other business, has to be concerned with the 'P' word – Profit – and how to generate more of the stuff. But to the fans, the game of football is all about a different 'P' word – PASSION. It's passion that puts bums on seats and keeps us coming back for more; passion that stimulates the very necessary sales in the club shop. Few clubs these days can truly say that they are underpinned by a solid financial foundation, so they need the passion of their fans and their officials to help carry them through. The collapse of ITV Digital has left an appalling fingerprint on far too many clubs, creating horrendous budgetary deficits, increasing debts and the cost of funding the borrowing that businesses need to run their day-to-day operation. Fans have to be realistic in their expectations; so do players in their wage demands – there is no such thing as a free lunch. Nor is success anything to do with divine right, it's about ability coupled with PASSION. Wolves' fans have passion. We, and Wolves, are also lucky, we have Sir Jack, a fantastic stadium, and a set of supporters that are the equal of any club, and now, after 19 years in the wilderness, we are a Premiership club, back in the top flight where we rightfully belong. If I may, on behalf of all Wolves' fans, I would like to shout a mepic thanks to Dave Jones and the players for realising our dream, and of course to Sir Jack, Jez, Rachael and everyone at Molineux for providing the perfect environment in which to do it. My ongoing message to Wolves fans everywhere is to continue to keep the faith, continue to have PASSION, and show it in the best way possible, by making sure we express our passionate support for our team as vocally as we can.

In the epic words of Kenneth Wolstenholme – 'they think it's all over – it is now.' However, that's only this book, for hopefully Wolverhampton Wanderers will live forever.

My sincere best wishes to all those involved with or are addicted to 'THE WOLVES'.

John Shipley

PS: Look out for my next book, *A Season to Remember: Wolverhampton Wanderers 1953/54*, the game-by-game story of Wolves' first-ever First Division Championship, to be published in 2004 by Tempus Publishing.